STORY THUS FAR

◎ Asahi is living a normal, sheltered life when she suddenly gets pulled into a pond and is transported to a strange new world. She gets sacrificed to a water dragon god, and he takes her voice from her. Because of her connection to the water dragon god's mysterious powers, Asahi is elevated to the position of priestess in her village. She is unable to find a way to return home, and time passes. As Asahi and the water dragon god spend time together, their relationship begins to change.

◎ A priestess of Naga informs the emperor of Asahi's and the water dragon god's existence, so he orders Asahi to lend him her power. When Kogahiko tries to kidnap Asahi a second time, the water dragon god and Asahi's friends rescue her. Tsukihiko, whose mother was in the same situation as Asahi before, attempts to trade his life for Asahi's freedom.

◎ Asahi decides to live with the emperor of Naga, and he asks for her hand in marriage. In order to protect Asahi, the water dragon god sends her back to her own world. Asahi is finally reunited with her family, but she can't seem to forget the water dragon god and the friends she's left behind. She's so troubled that she returns to the other world during a ceremony to call rain. She is overjoyed to be reunited with the water dragon god, but she barely has a moment with him before she gets snatched away into a deep darkness! The water dragon god snatches her back just in the nick of time, and he tells her to return to her own world.

◎ Meanwhile, a young man named Kurose in the modern-day world is plunged into darkness. The god of darkness, Tokoyami, places Kurose in another world where Kurose gets a measure of peace. Unfortunately, war with a neighboring country causes Kurose to lose the person he cares about...

The Water Dragon's Bride

9

CONTENTS

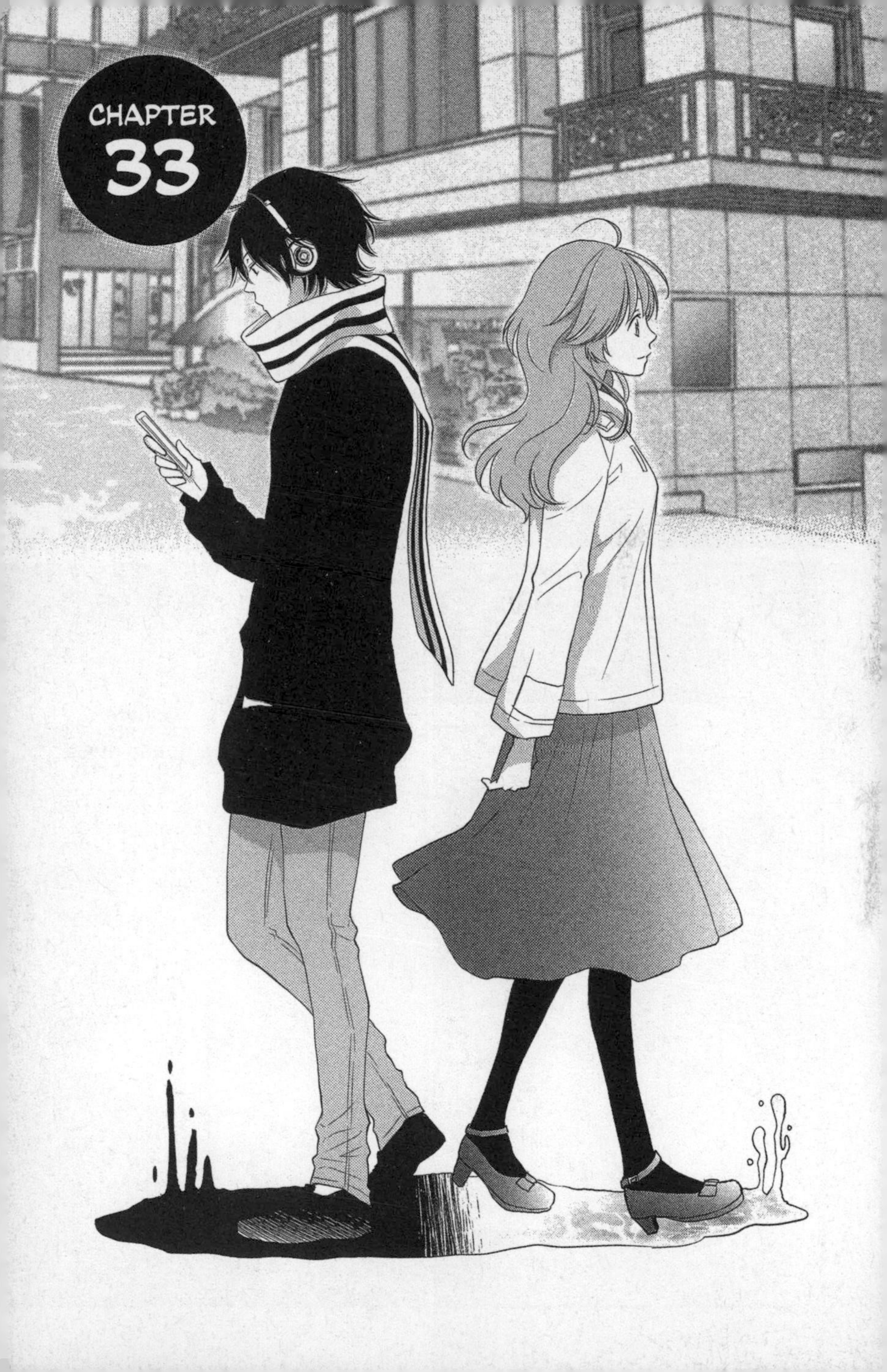
CHAPTER
33

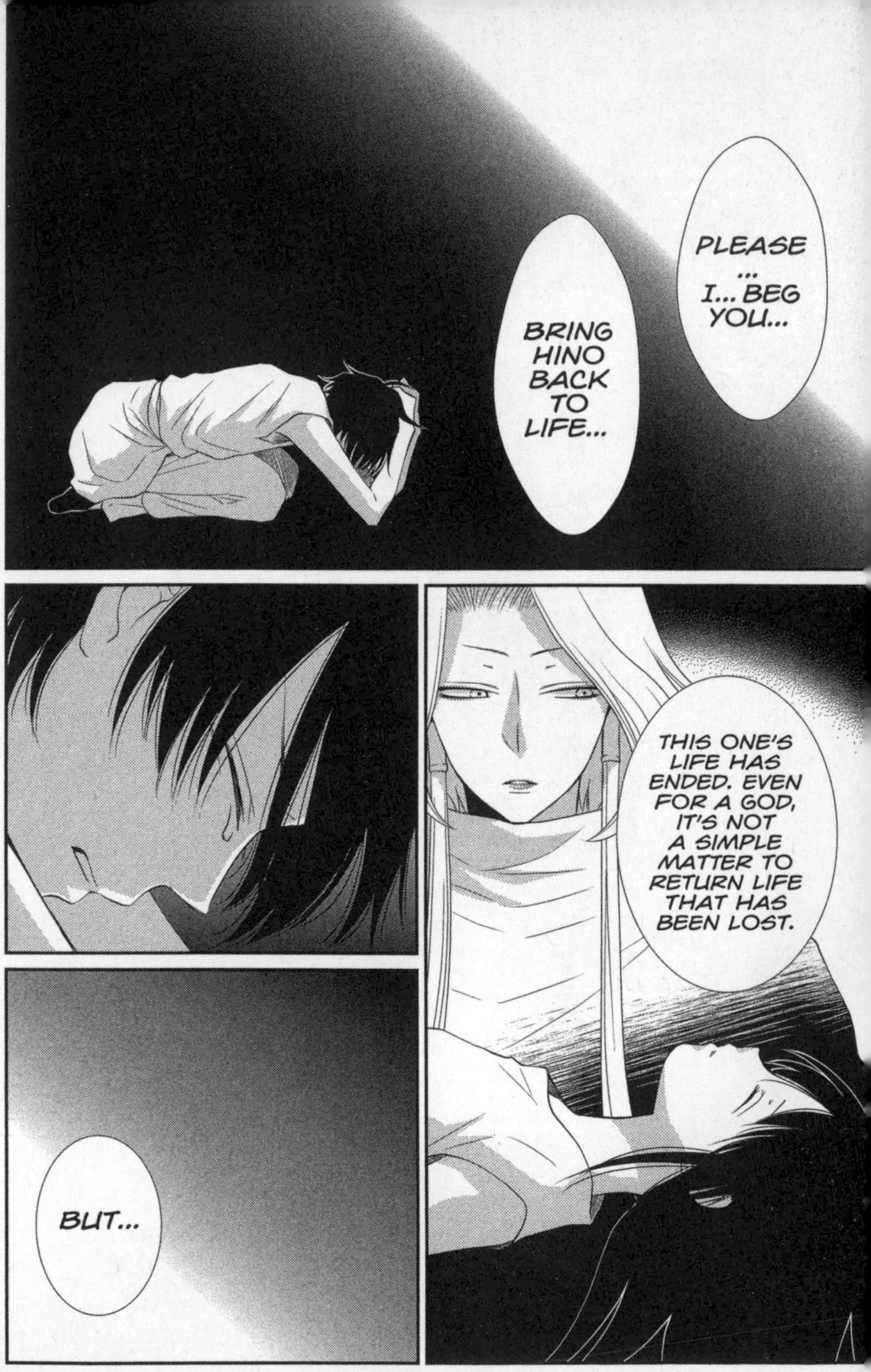
PLEASE ... I... BEG YOU...
BRING HINO BACK TO LIFE...
THIS ONE'S LIFE HAS ENDED. EVEN FOR A GOD, IT'S NOT A SIMPLE MATTER TO RETURN LIFE THAT HAS BEEN LOST.
BUT...

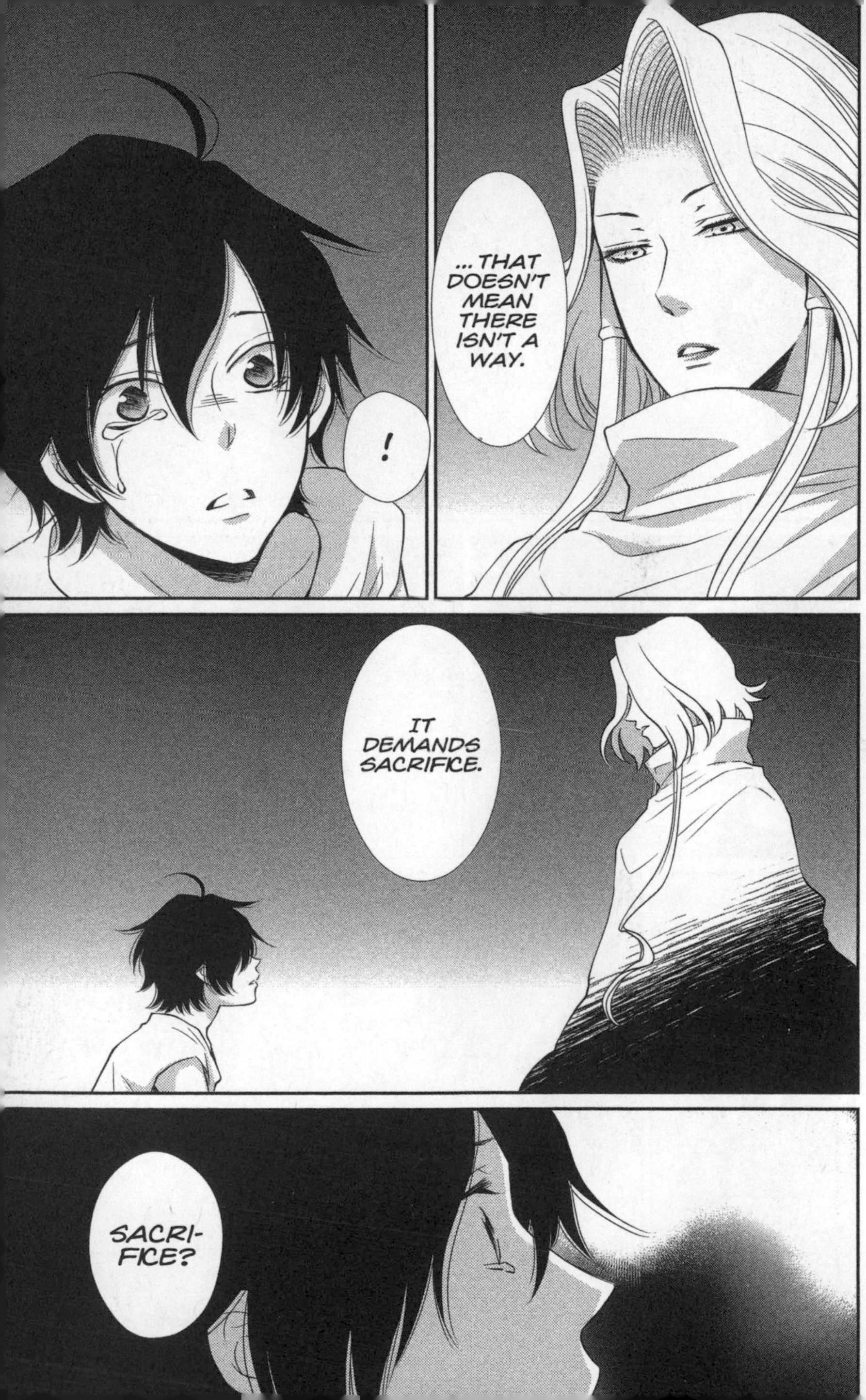
...THAT DOESN'T MEAN THERE ISN'T A WAY.
!
IT DEMANDS SACRIFICE.
SACRI-FICE?

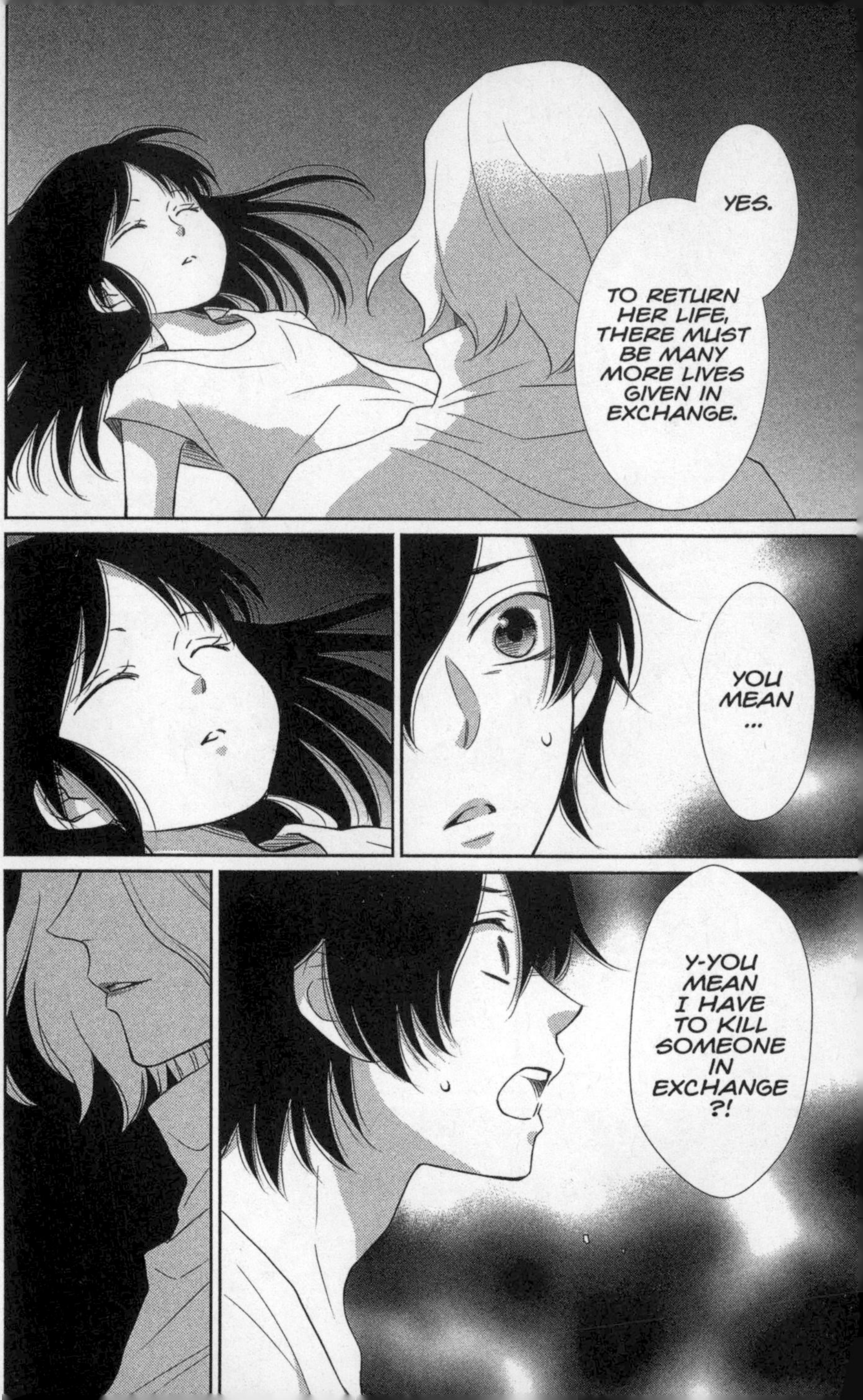
YES.
TO RETURN HER LIFE, THERE MUST BE MANY MORE LIVES GIVEN IN EXCHANGE.
YOU MEAN ...
Y-YOU MEAN I HAVE TO KILL SOMEONE IN EXCHANGE ?!

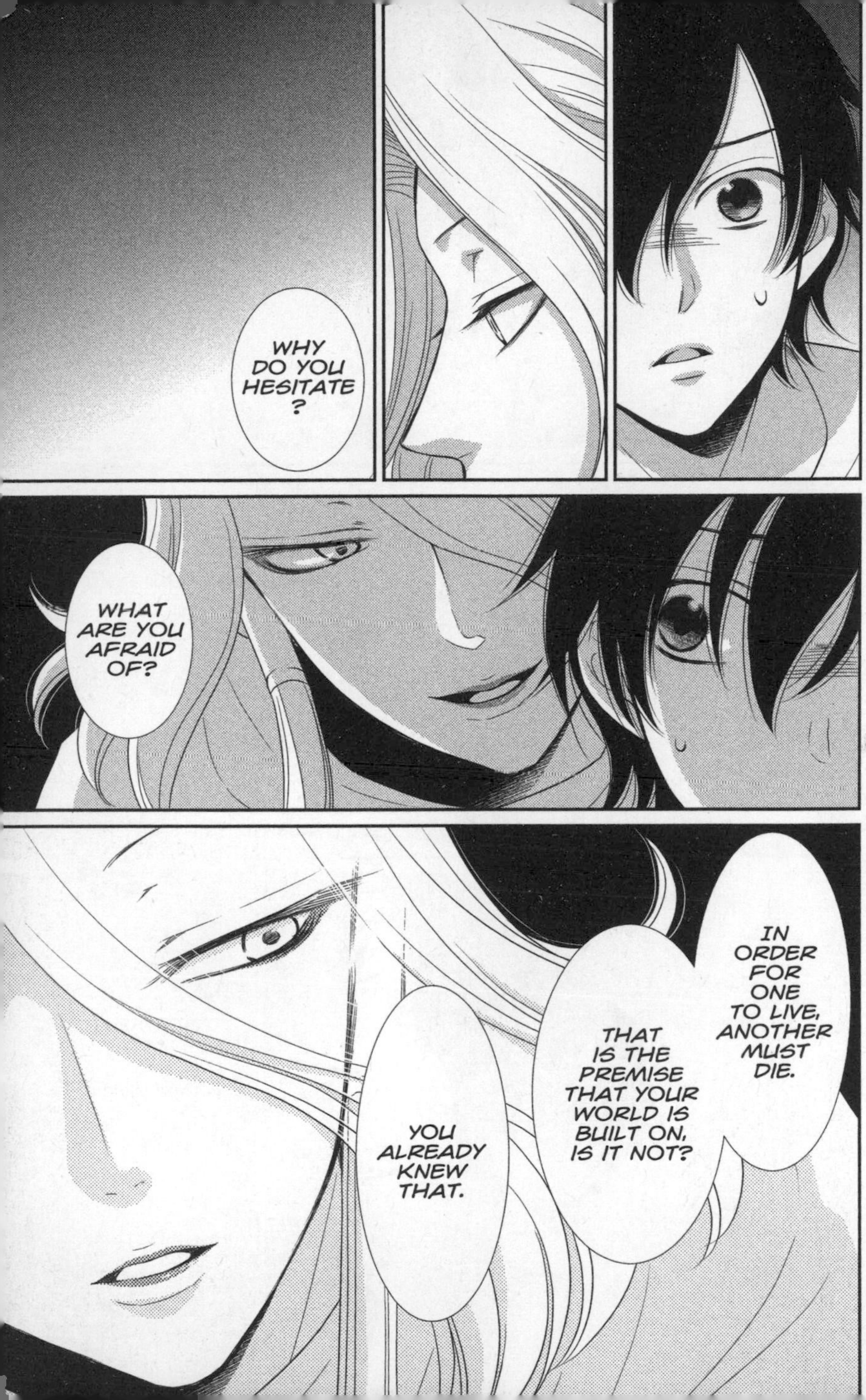
WHY DO YOU HESITATE?
WHAT ARE YOU AFRAID OF?
IN ORDER FOR ONE TO LIVE, ANOTHER MUST DIE.
THAT IS THE PREMISE THAT YOUR WORLD IS BUILT ON, IS IT NOT?
YOU ALREADY KNEW THAT.

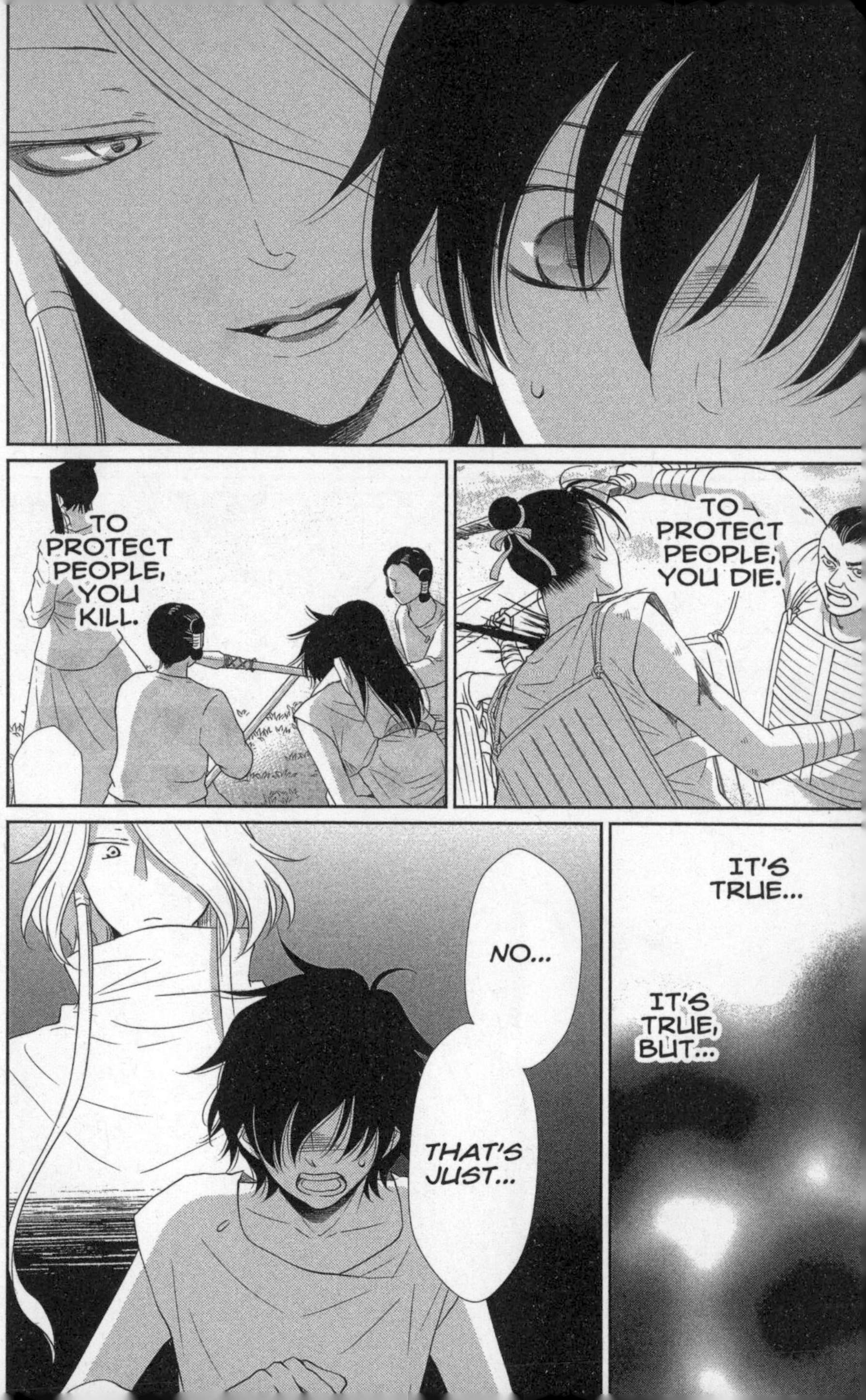
TO PROTECT PEOPLE, YOU DIE.
TO PROTECT PEOPLE, YOU KILL.
IT'S TRUE...
IT'S TRUE, BUT...
NO...
THAT'S JUST...

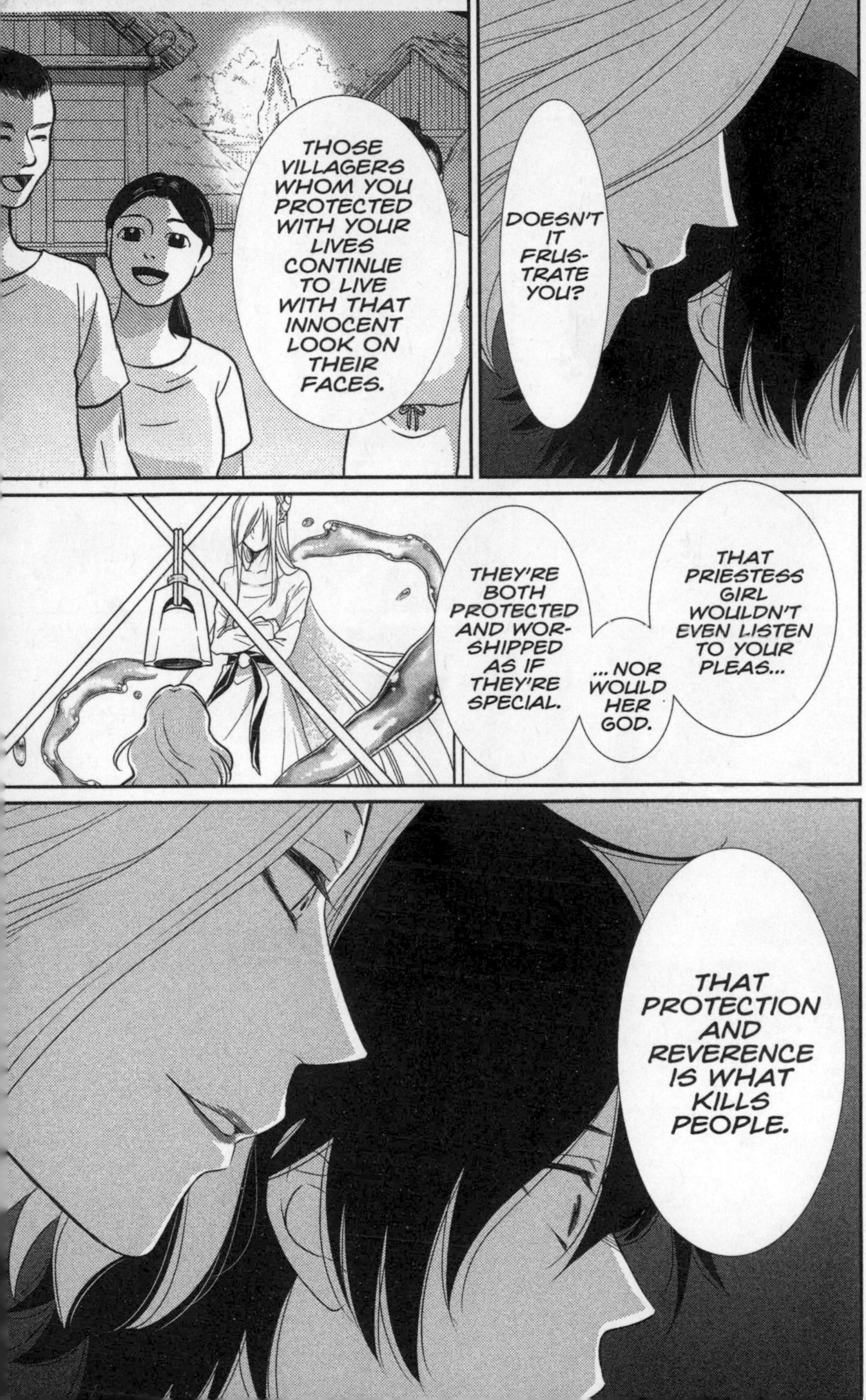

DOESN'T IT FRUS-TRATE YOU?
THOSE VILLAGERS WHOM YOU PROTECTED WITH YOUR LIVES CONTINUE TO LIVE WITH THAT INNOCENT LOOK ON THEIR FACES.
THAT PRIESTESS GIRL WOULDN'T EVEN LISTEN TO YOUR PLEAS...
...NOR WOULD HER GOD.
THEY'RE BOTH PROTECTED AND WOR-SHIPPED AS IF THEY'RE SPECIAL.
THAT PROTECTION AND REVERENCE IS WHAT KILLS PEOPLE.

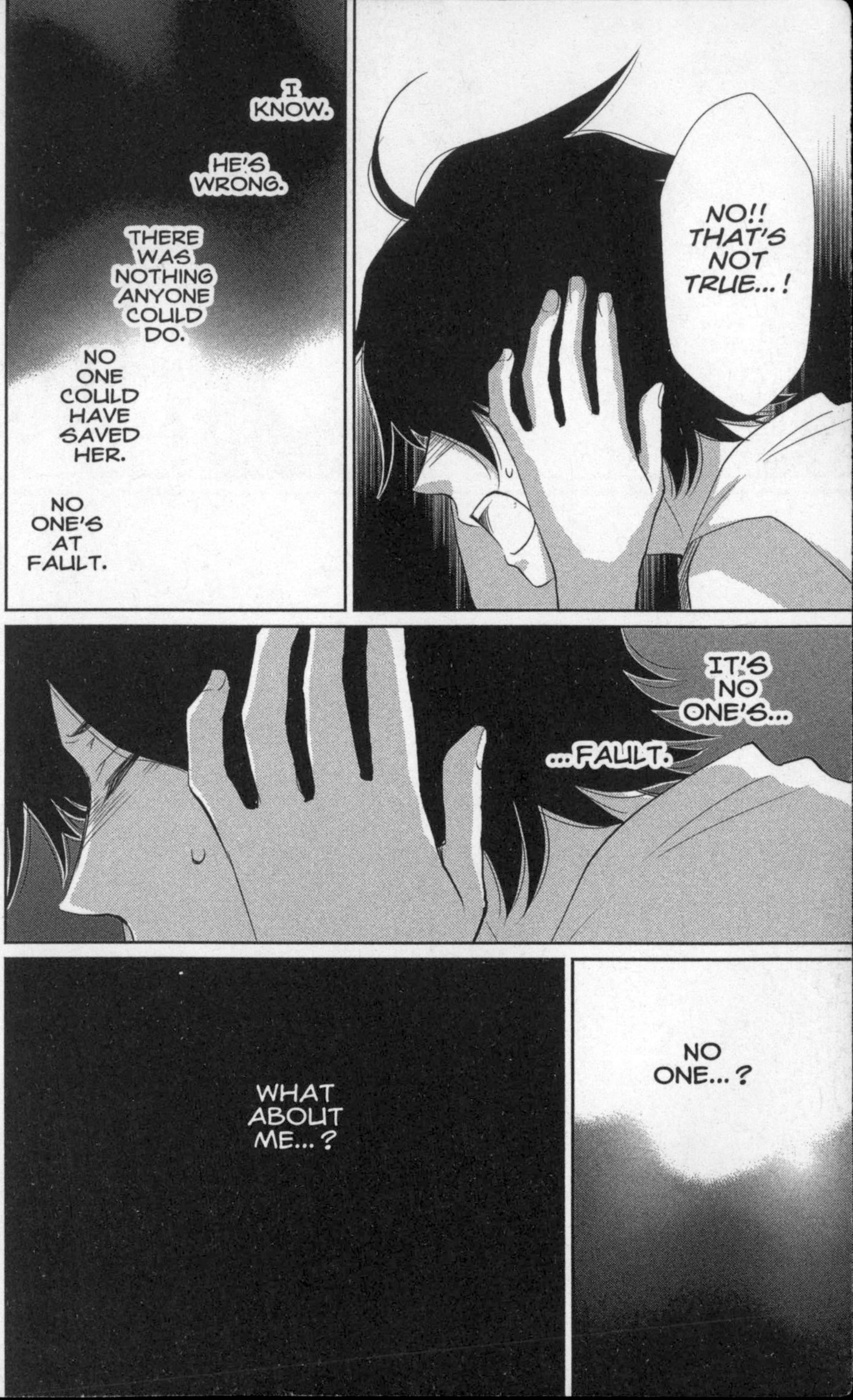
NO!! THAT'S NOT TRUE...!
I KNOW.
HE'S WRONG.
THERE WAS NOTHING ANYONE COULD DO.
NO ONE COULD HAVE SAVED HER.
NO ONE'S AT FAULT.
IT'S NO ONE'S...
...FAULT.
NO ONE...?
WHAT ABOUT ME...?

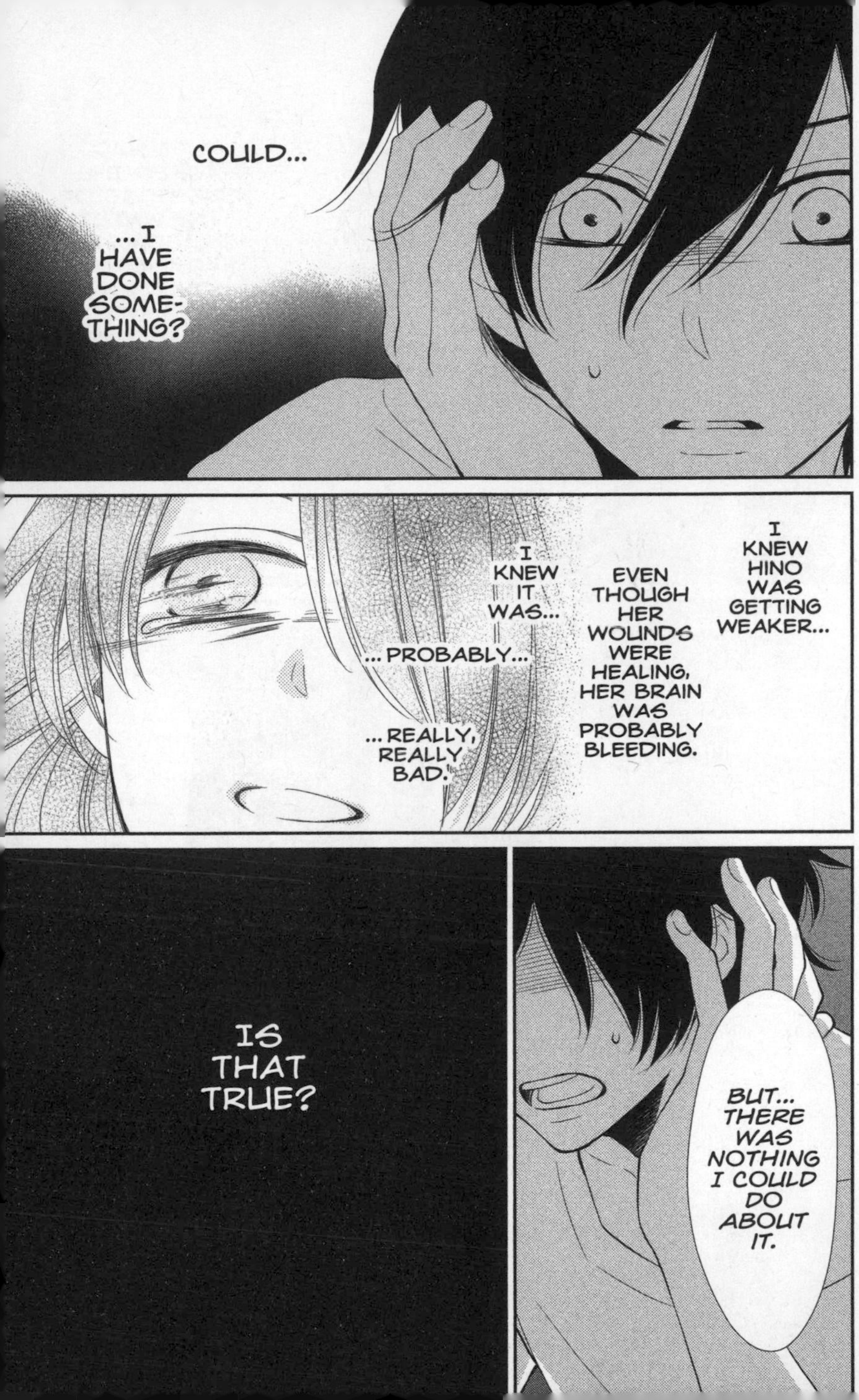
COULD...
...I HAVE DONE SOME-THING?
I KNEW HINO WAS GETTING WEAKER...
EVEN THOUGH HER WOUNDS WERE HEALING, HER BRAIN WAS PROBABLY BLEEDING.
I KNEW IT WAS...
...PROBABLY...
...REALLY, REALLY BAD.
BUT... THERE WAS NOTHING I COULD DO ABOUT IT.
IS THAT TRUE?

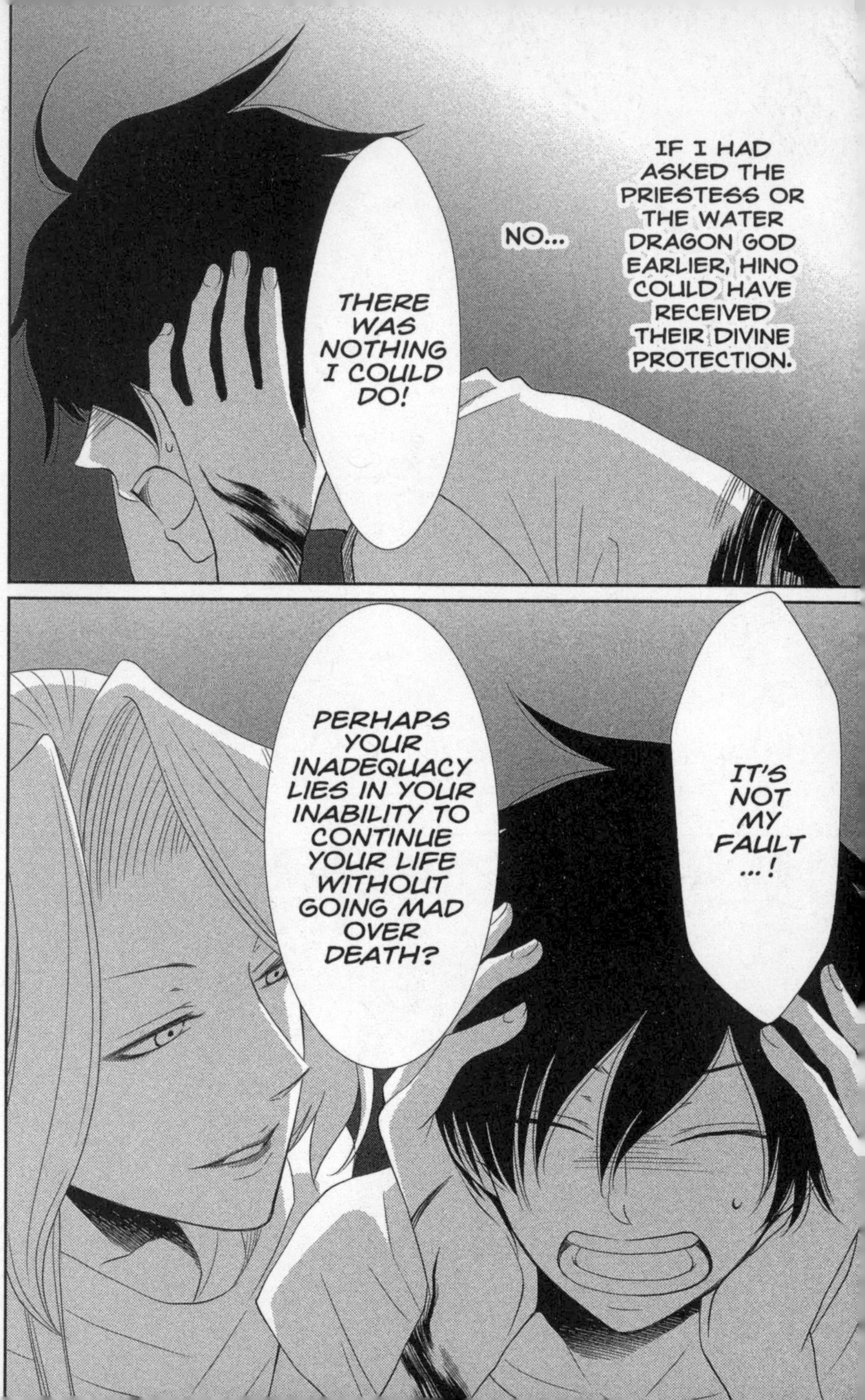
IF I HAD ASKED THE PRIESTESS OR THE WATER DRAGON GOD EARLIER, HINO COULD HAVE RECEIVED THEIR DIVINE PROTECTION.
NO...
THERE WAS NOTHING I COULD DO!
IT'S NOT MY FAULT ...!
PERHAPS YOUR INADEQUACY LIES IN YOUR INABILITY TO CONTINUE YOUR LIFE WITHOUT GOING MAD OVER DEATH?

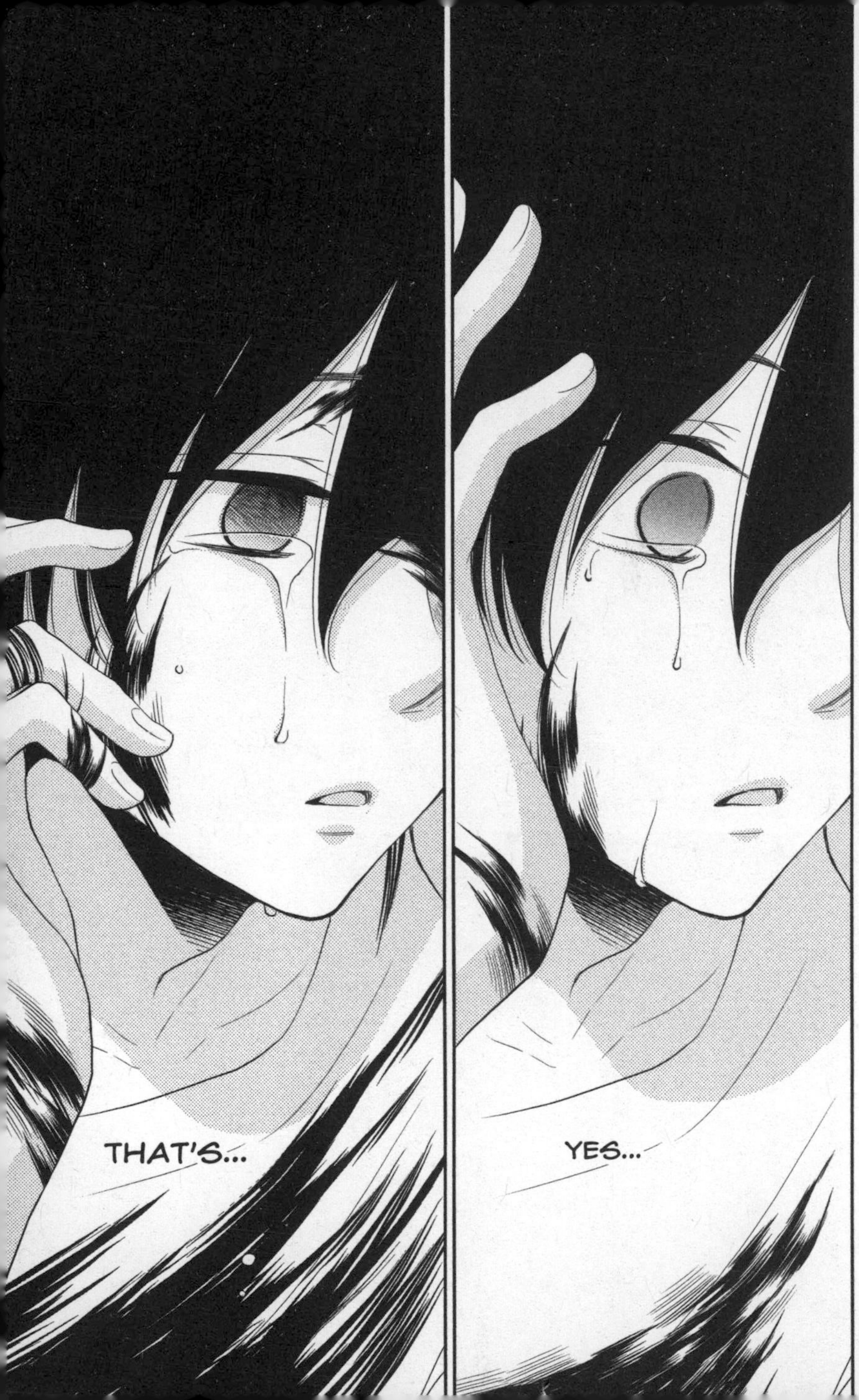
YES...
THAT'S...

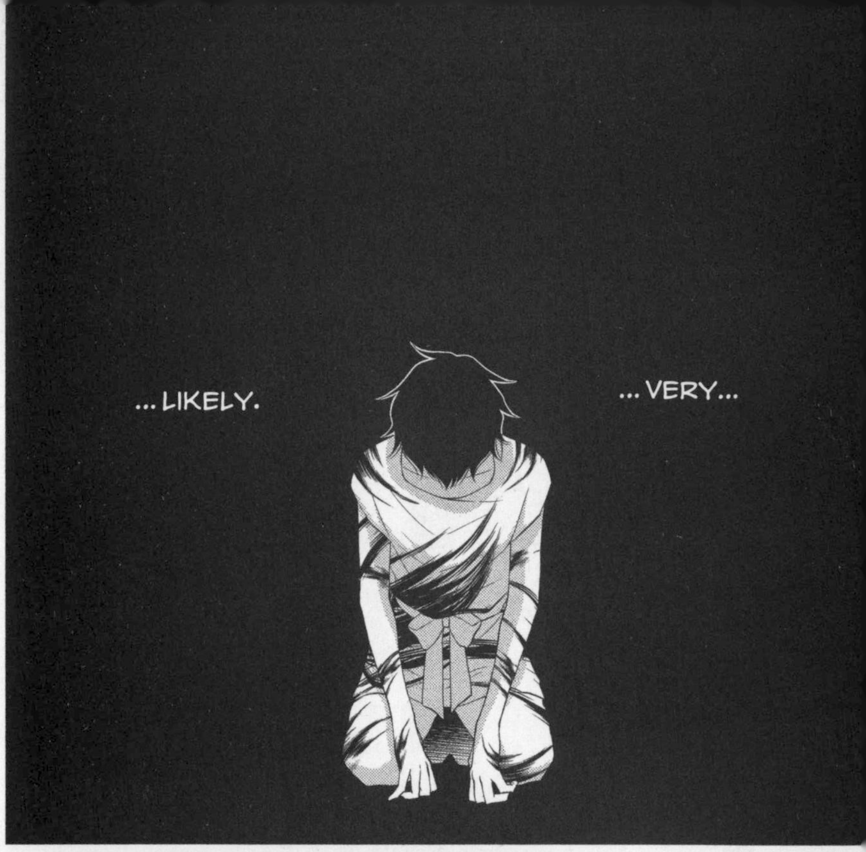
...VERY...
...LIKELY.
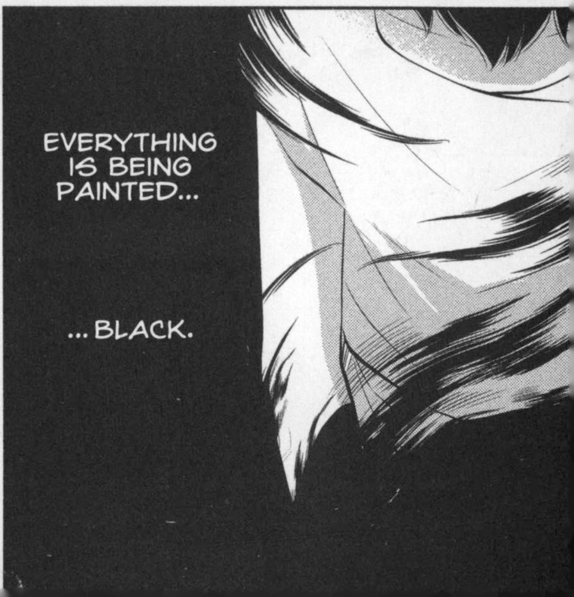
EVERYTHING IS BEING PAINTED...
...BLACK.
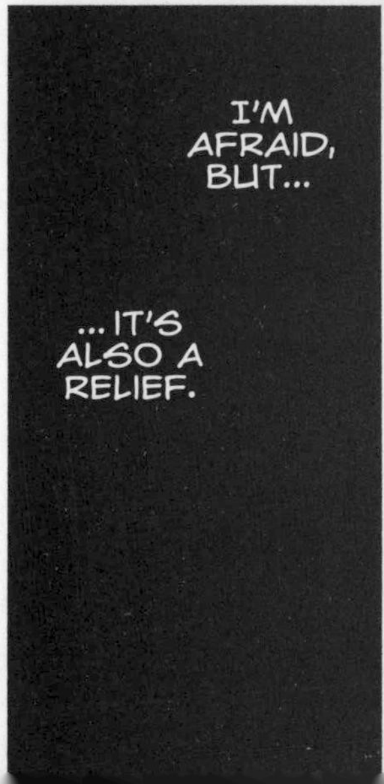
I'M AFRAID, BUT...
...IT'S ALSO A RELIEF.

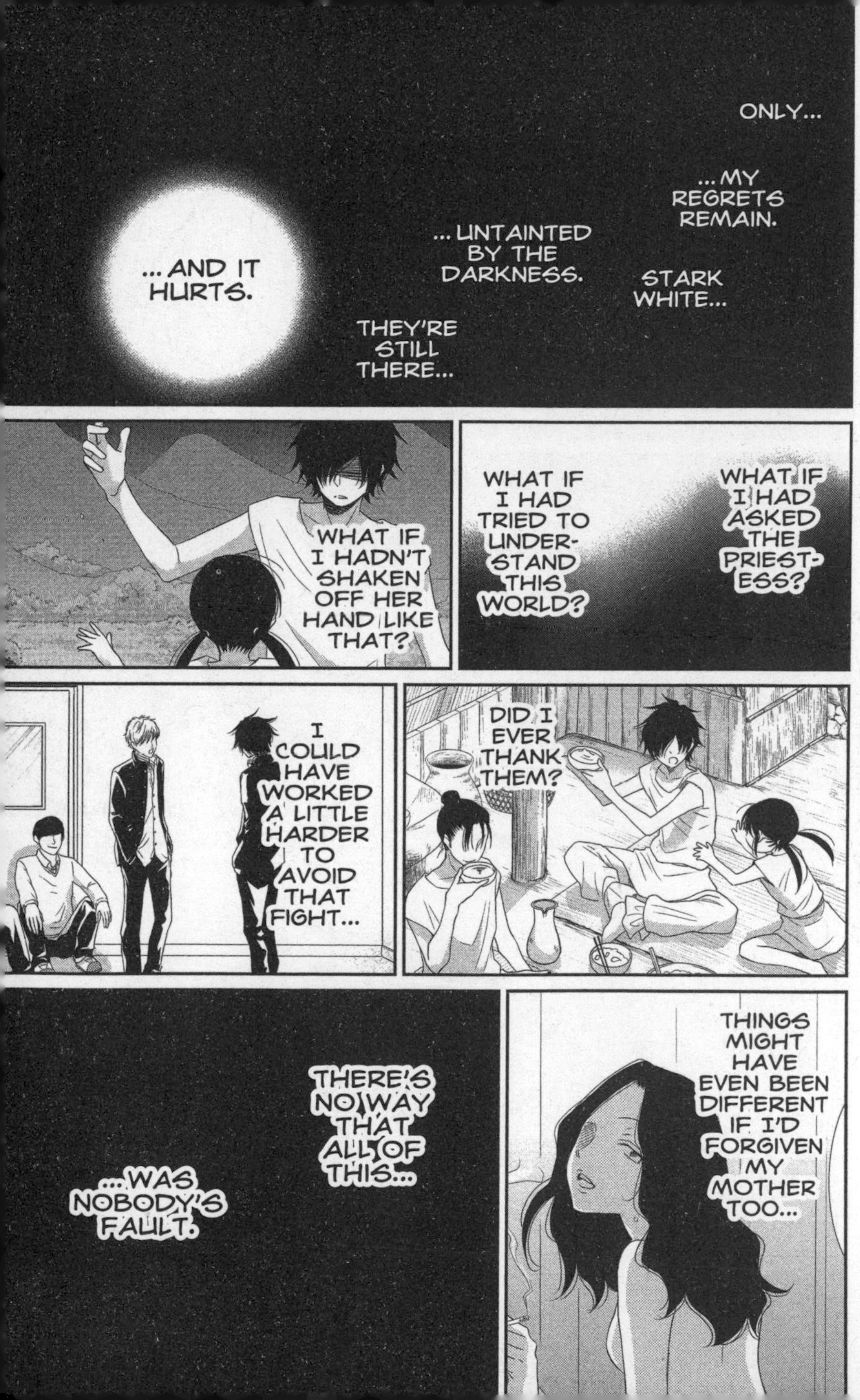
ONLY...
...MY REGRETS REMAIN.
STARK WHITE...
...UNTAINTED BY THE DARKNESS.
THEY'RE STILL THERE...
...AND IT HURTS.
WHAT IF I HAD ASKED THE PRIESTESS?
WHAT IF I HAD TRIED TO UNDERSTAND THIS WORLD?
WHAT IF I HADN'T SHAKEN OFF HER HAND LIKE THAT?
DID I EVER THANK THEM?
I COULD HAVE WORKED A LITTLE HARDER TO AVOID THAT FIGHT...
THINGS MIGHT HAVE EVEN BEEN DIFFERENT IF I'D FORGIVEN MY MOTHER TOO...
THERE'S NO WAY THAT ALL OF THIS...
...WAS NOBODY'S FAULT.

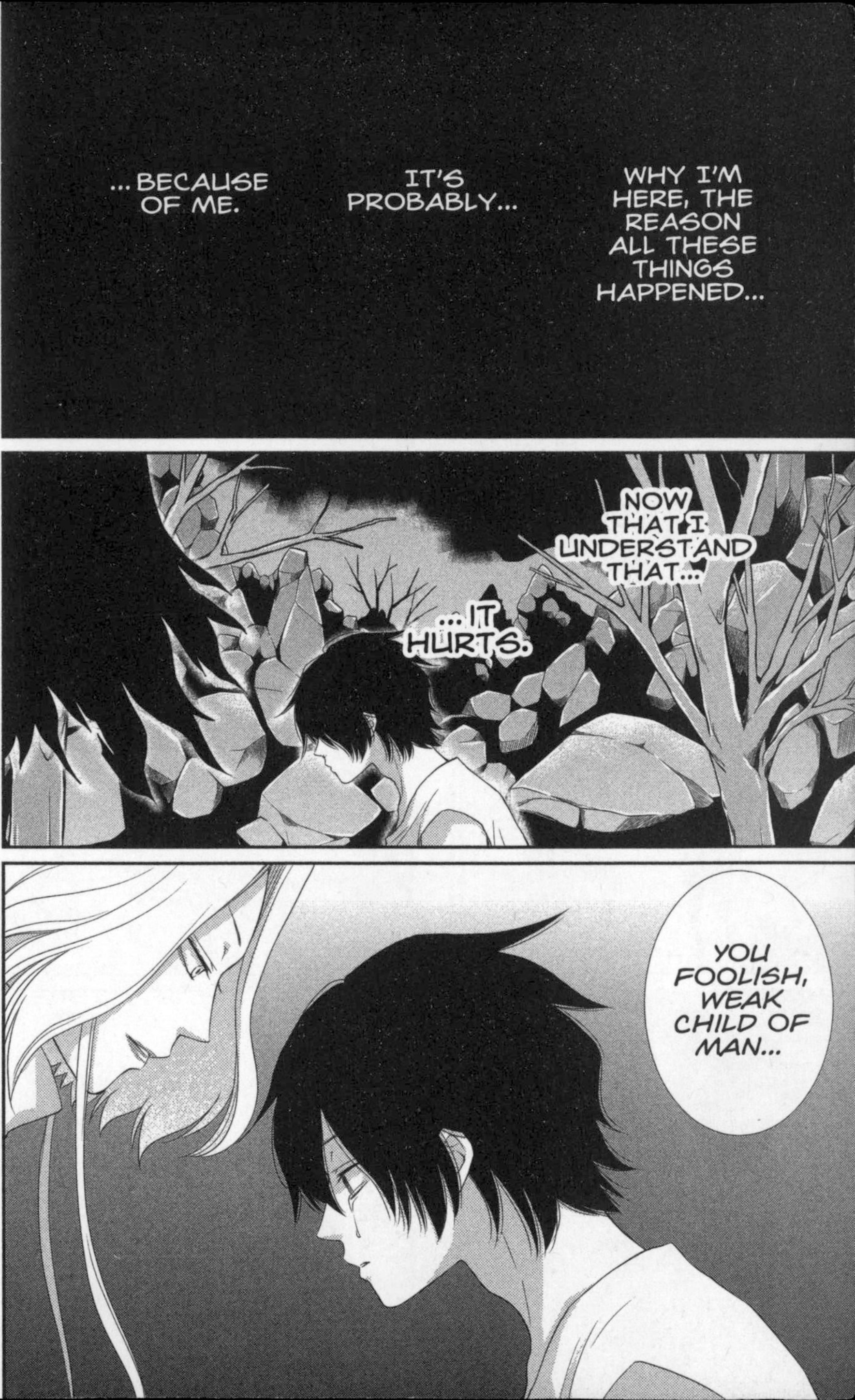
WHY I'M HERE, THE REASON ALL THESE THINGS HAPPENED...
IT'S PROBABLY...
...BECAUSE OF ME.
NOW THAT I UNDERSTAND THAT...
...IT HURTS.
YOU FOOLISH, WEAK CHILD OF MAN...

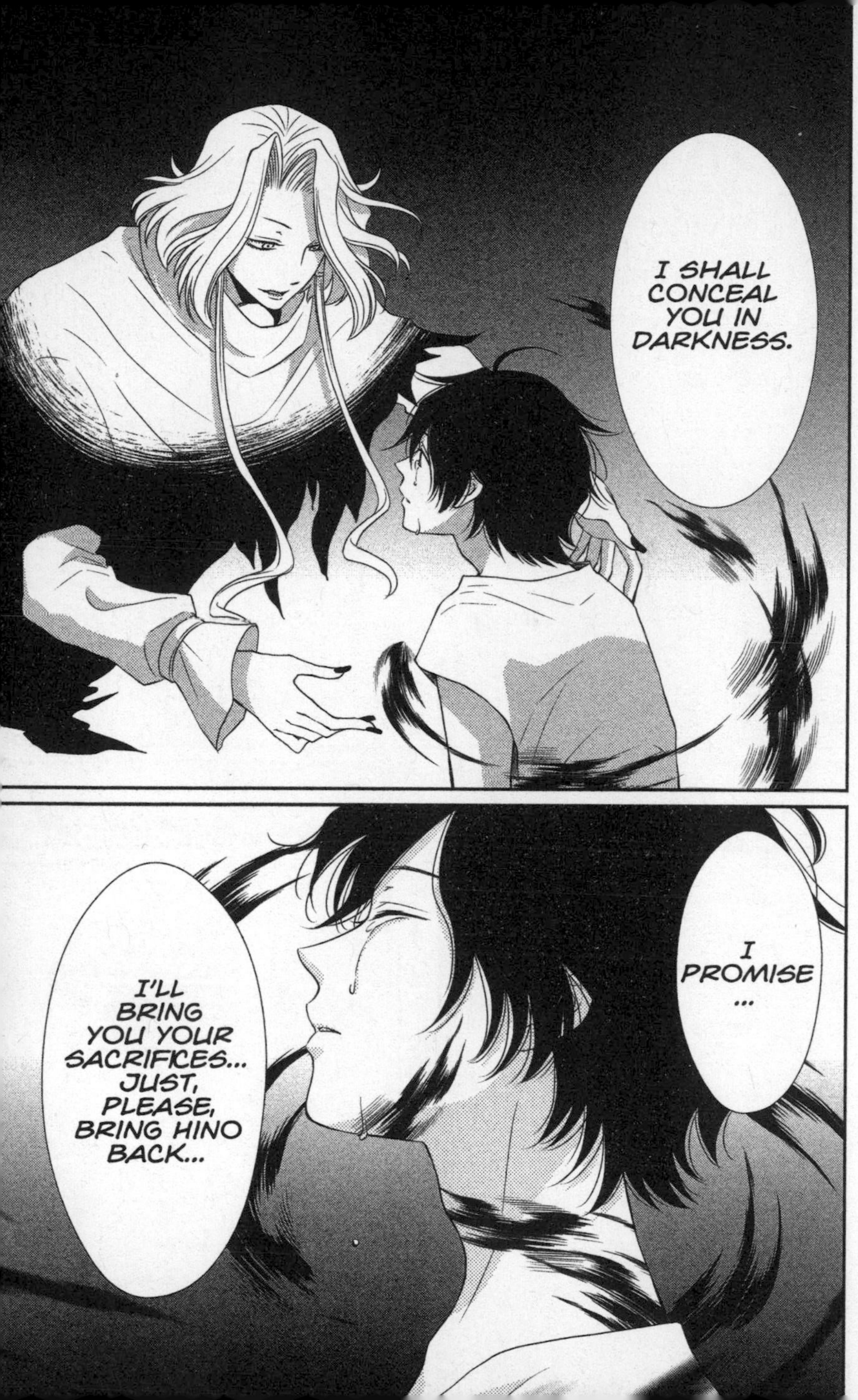
I SHALL CONCEAL YOU IN DARKNESS.
I PROMISE ...
I'LL BRING YOU YOUR SACRIFICES... JUST, PLEASE, BRING HINO BACK...

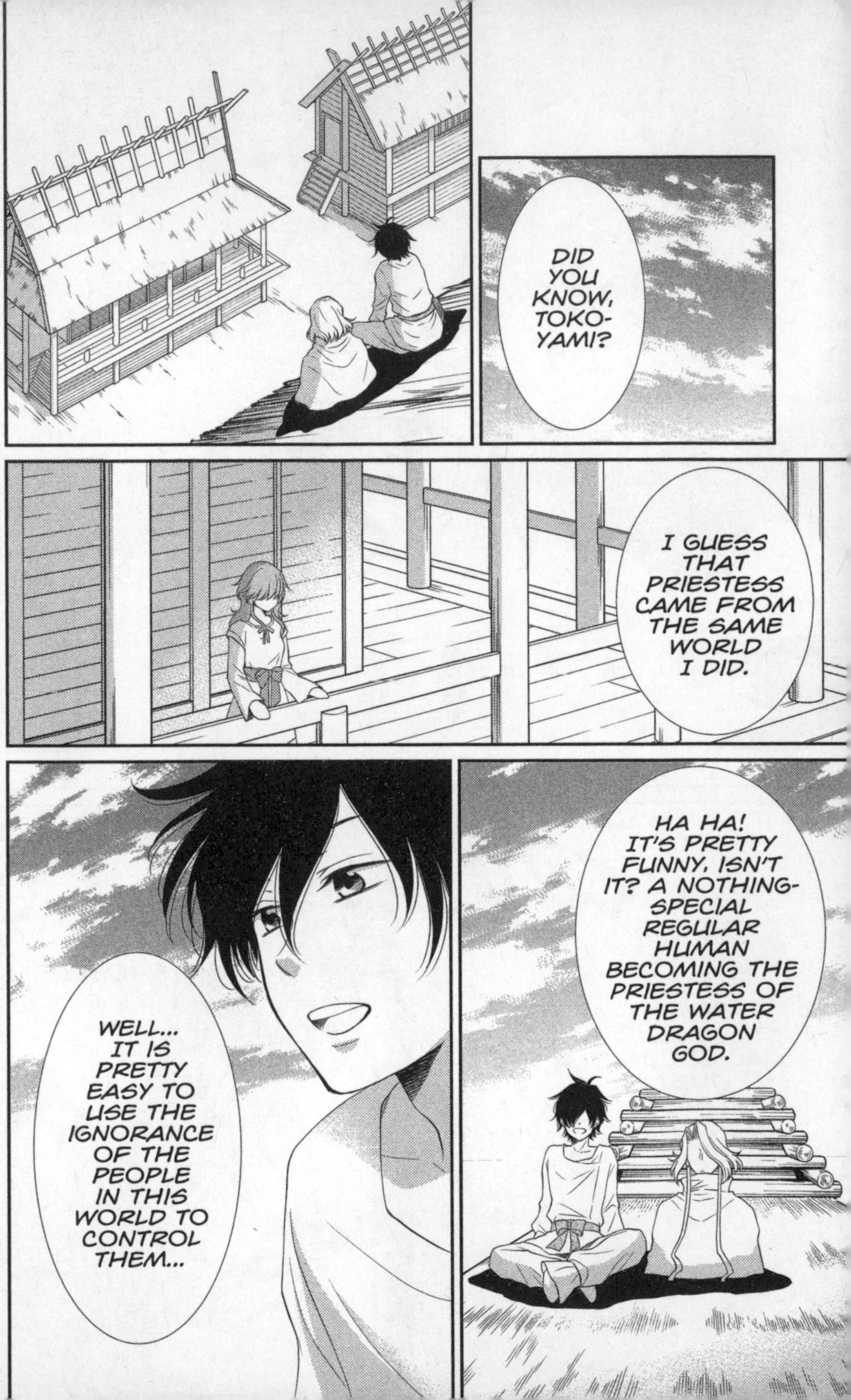
DID YOU KNOW, TOKO-YAMI?
I GUESS THAT PRIESTESS CAME FROM THE SAME WORLD I DID.
HA HA! IT'S PRETTY FUNNY, ISN'T IT? A NOTHING-SPECIAL REGULAR HUMAN BECOMING THE PRIESTESS OF THE WATER DRAGON GOD.
WELL... IT IS PRETTY EASY TO USE THE IGNORANCE OF THE PEOPLE IN THIS WORLD TO CONTROL THEM...

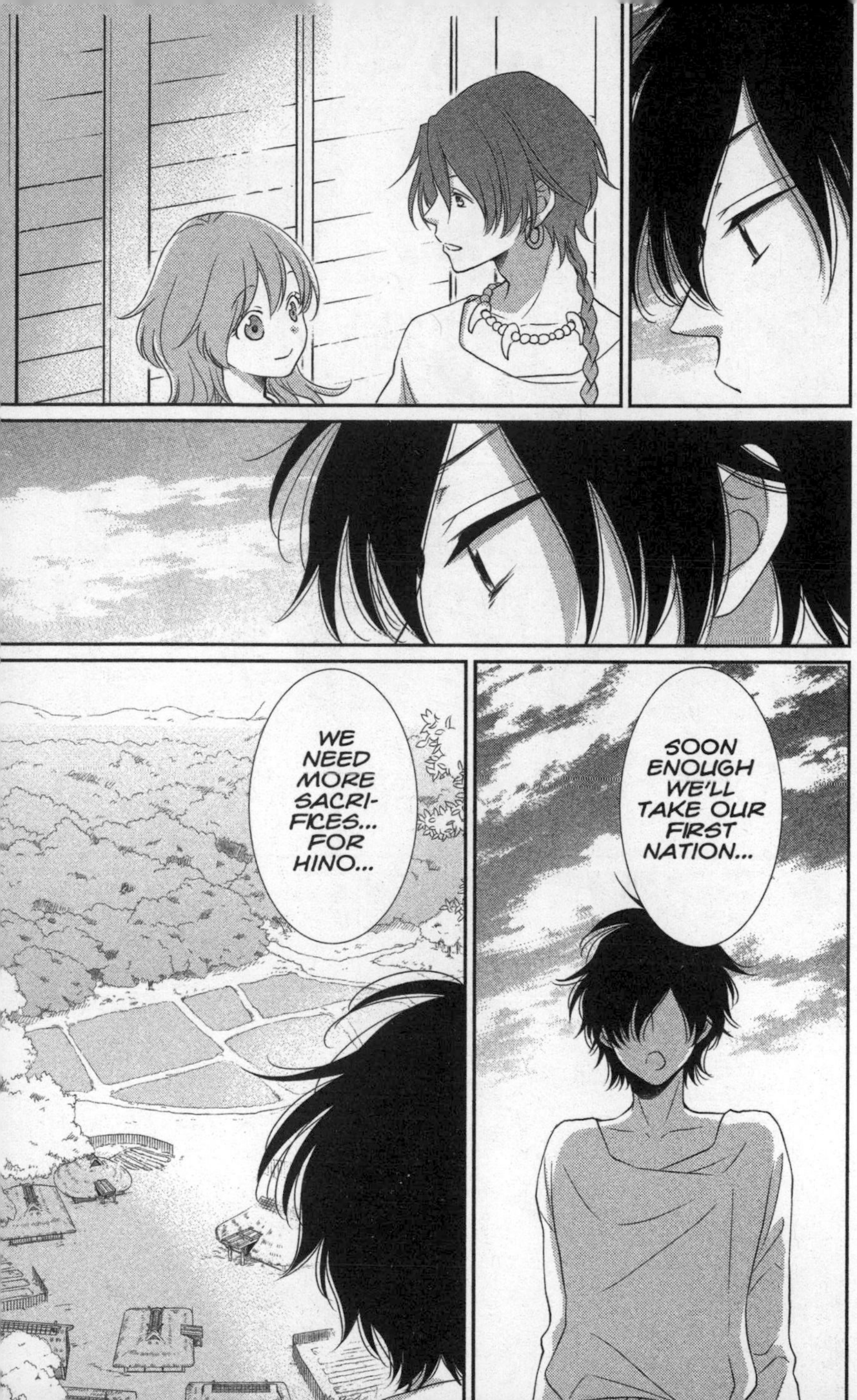
SOON ENOUGH WE'LL TAKE OUR FIRST NATION...
WE NEED MORE SACRI-FICES... FOR HINO...

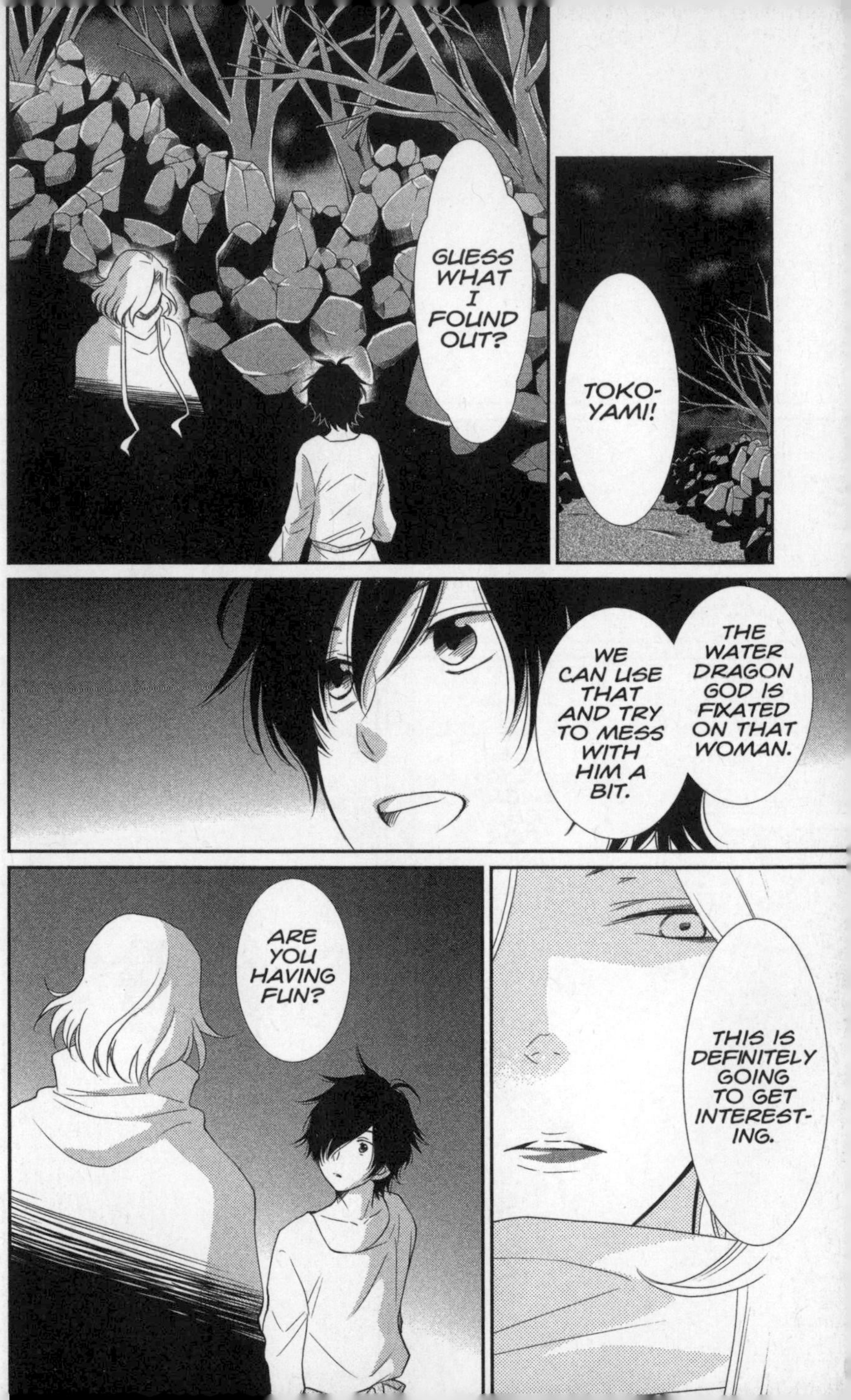
TOKO-YAMI!
GUESS WHAT I FOUND OUT?
THE WATER DRAGON GOD IS FIXATED ON THAT WOMAN.
WE CAN USE THAT AND TRY TO MESS WITH HIM A BIT.
THIS IS DEFINITELY GOING TO GET INTERESTING.
ARE YOU HAVING FUN?

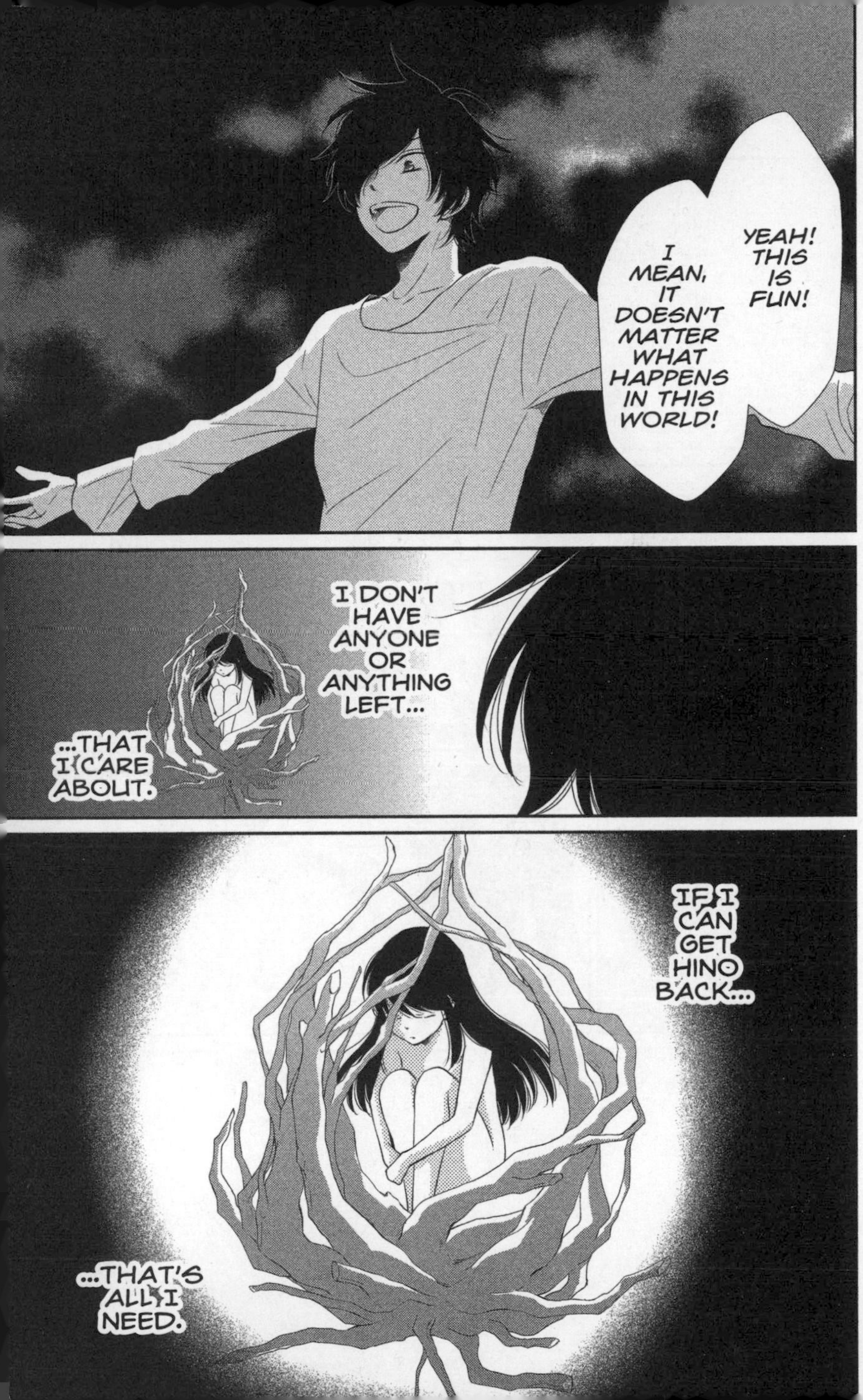
YEAH! THIS IS FUN!
I MEAN, IT DOESN'T MATTER WHAT HAPPENS IN THIS WORLD!
I DON'T HAVE ANYONE OR ANYTHING LEFT...
...THAT I CARE ABOUT.
IF I CAN GET HINO BACK...
...THAT'S ALL I NEED.

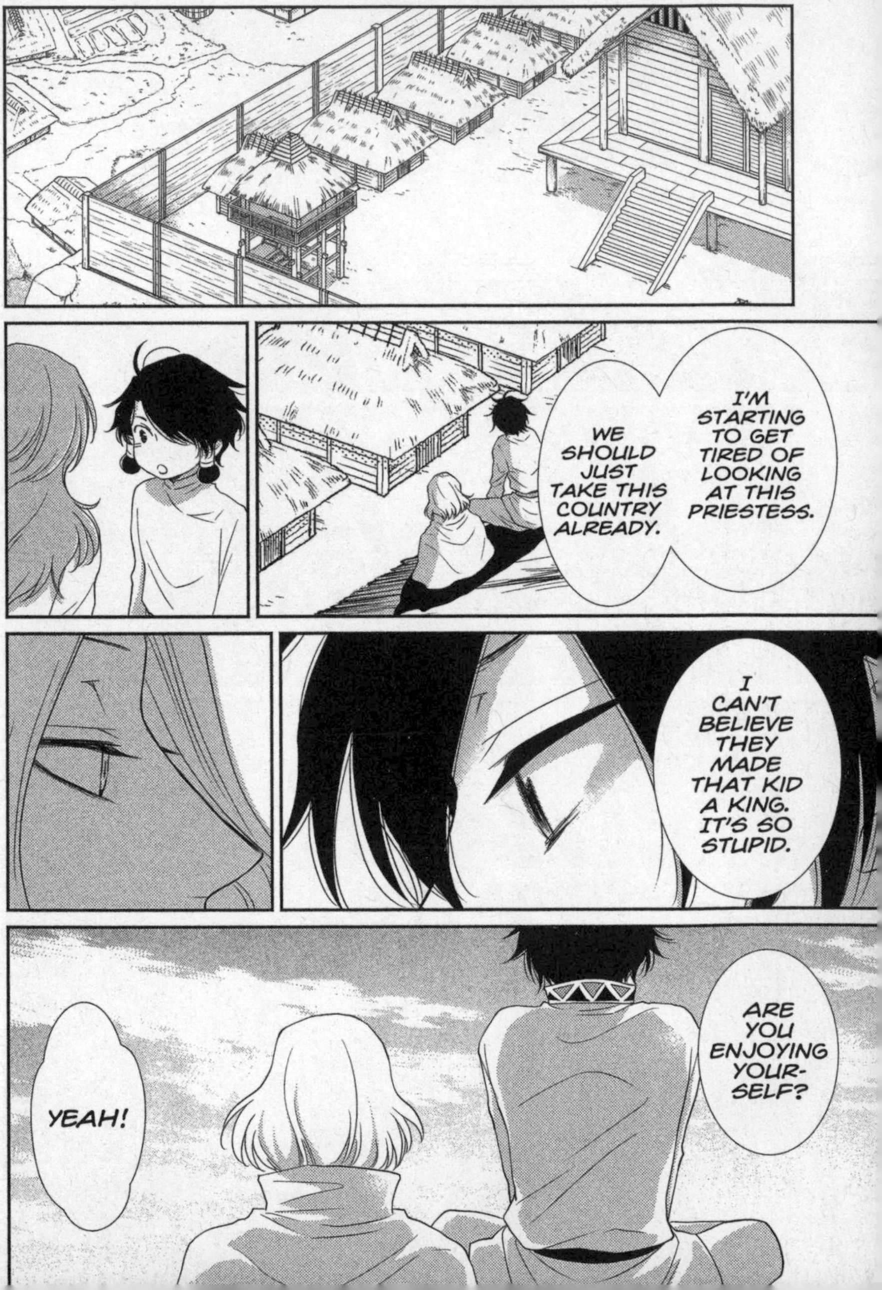
I'M STARTING TO GET TIRED OF LOOKING AT THIS PRIESTESS.
WE SHOULD JUST TAKE THIS COUNTRY ALREADY.
I CAN'T BELIEVE THEY MADE THAT KID A KING. IT'S SO STUPID.
ARE YOU ENJOYING YOUR-SELF?
YEAH!

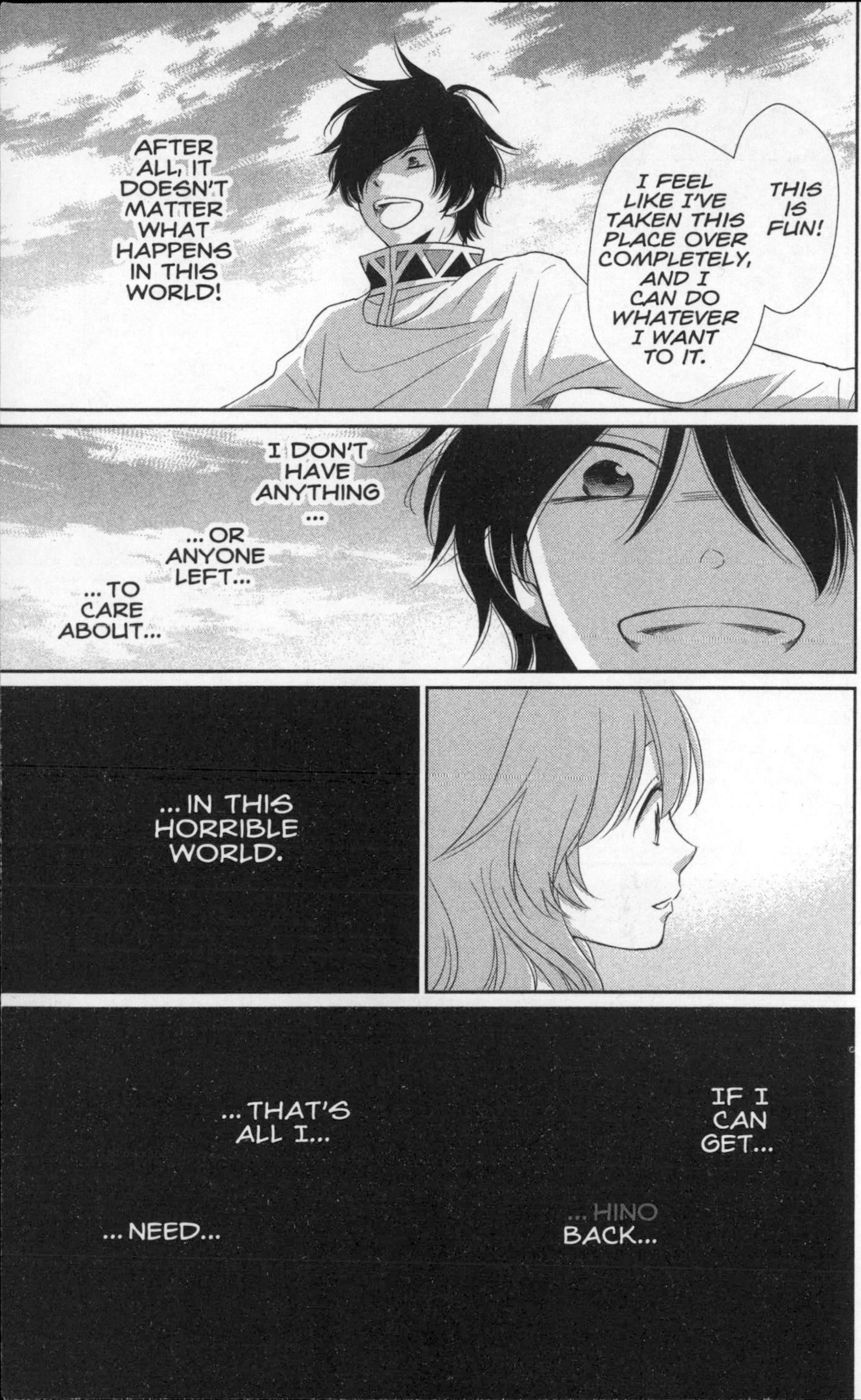
THIS IS FUN!
I FEEL LIKE I'VE TAKEN THIS PLACE OVER COMPLETELY, AND I CAN DO WHATEVER I WANT TO IT.
AFTER ALL, IT DOESN'T MATTER WHAT HAPPENS IN THIS WORLD!
I DON'T HAVE ANYTHING...
...OR ANYONE LEFT...
...TO CARE ABOUT...
...IN THIS HORRIBLE WORLD.
IF I CAN GET...
...HINO BACK...
...THAT'S ALL I...
...NEED...

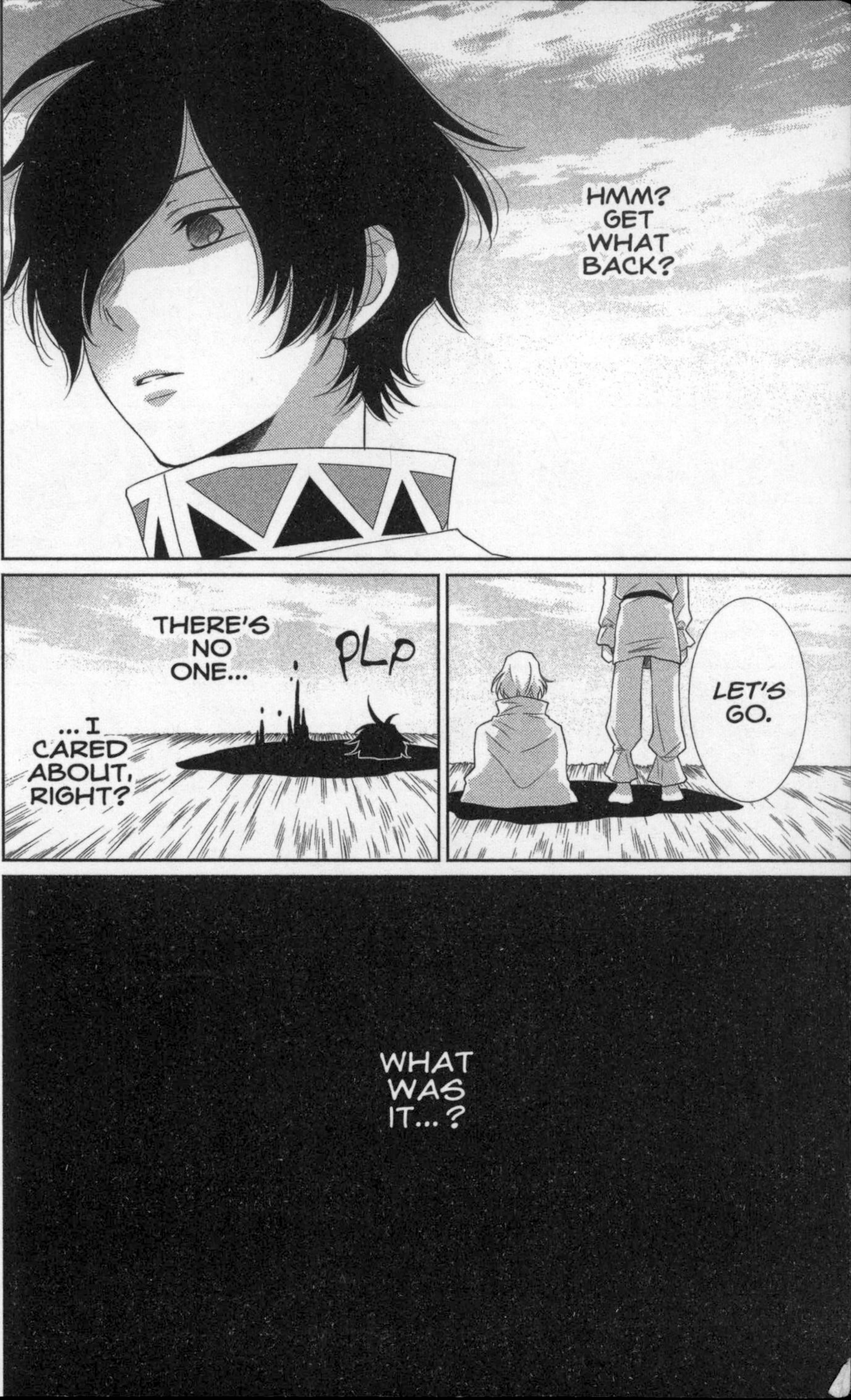
HMM? GET WHAT BACK?
LET'S GO.
THERE'S NO ONE...
PLP
...I CARED ABOUT, RIGHT?
WHAT WAS IT...?

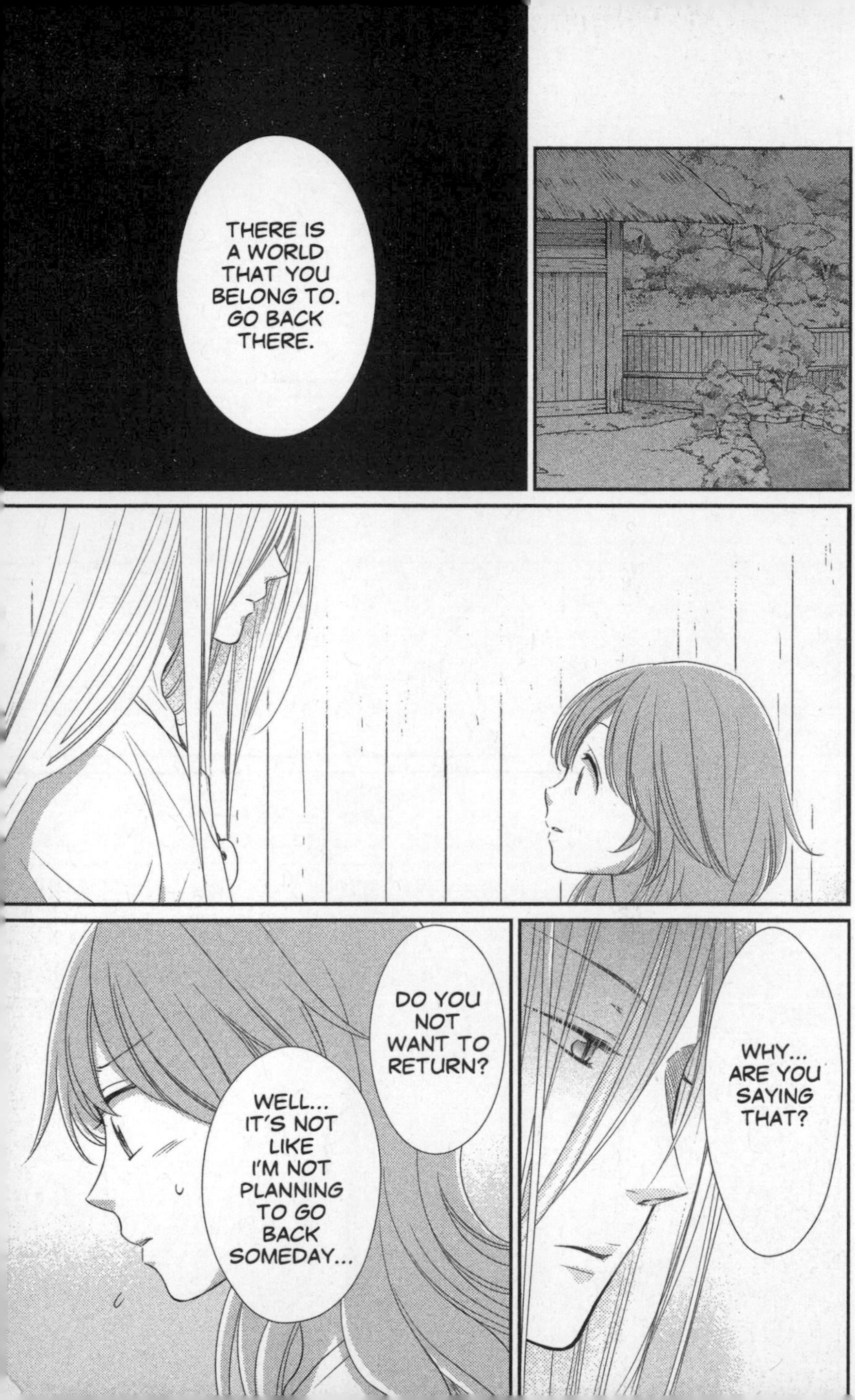
THERE IS A WORLD THAT YOU BELONG TO. GO BACK THERE.
WHY... ARE YOU SAYING THAT?
DO YOU NOT WANT TO RETURN?
WELL... IT'S NOT LIKE I'M NOT PLANNING TO GO BACK SOMEDAY...

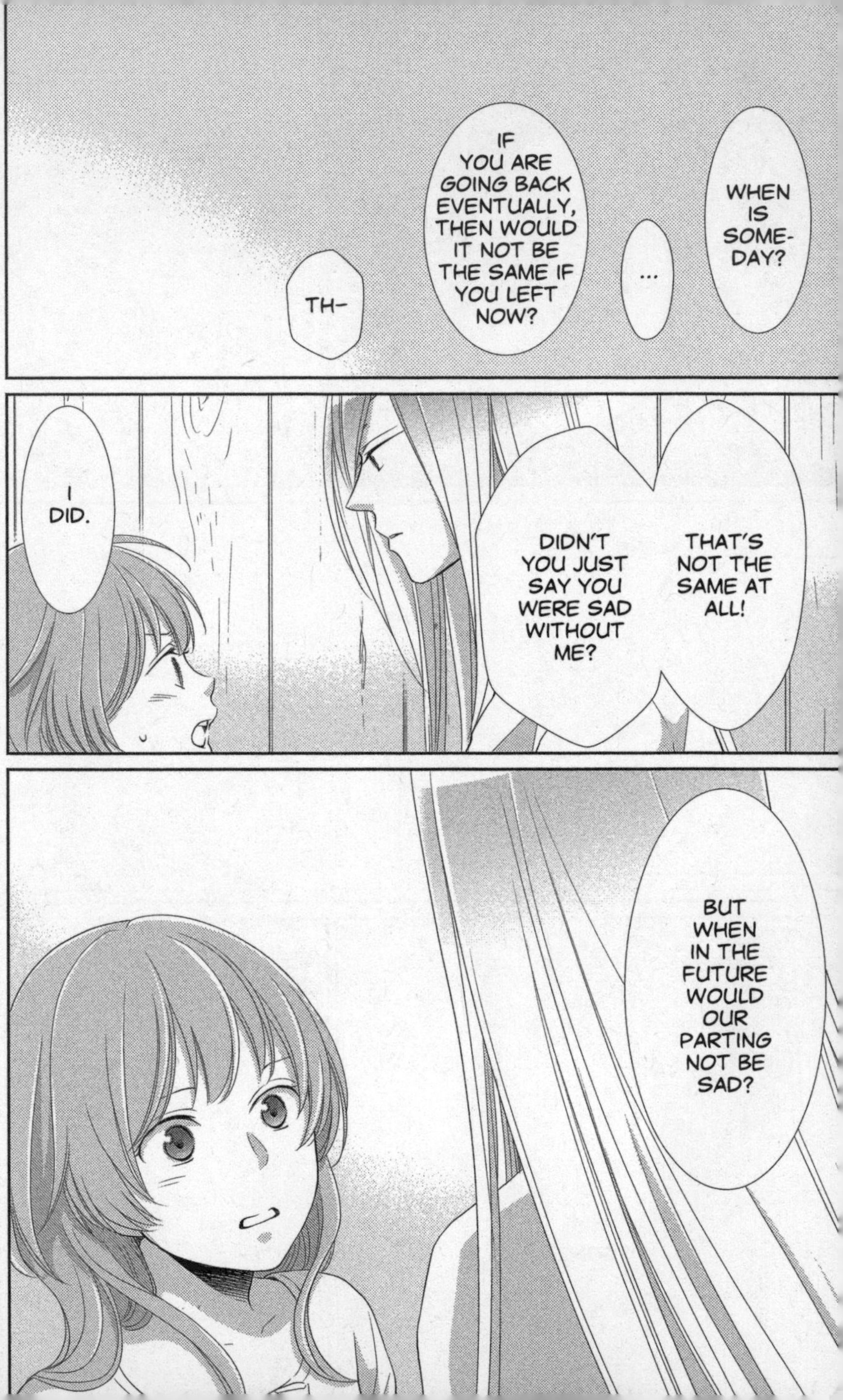
WHEN IS SOME-DAY?
...
IF YOU ARE GOING BACK EVENTUALLY, THEN WOULD IT NOT BE THE SAME IF YOU LEFT NOW?
TH-
THAT'S NOT THE SAME AT ALL!
DIDN'T YOU JUST SAY YOU WERE SAD WITHOUT ME?
I DID.
BUT WHEN IN THE FUTURE WOULD OUR PARTING NOT BE SAD?

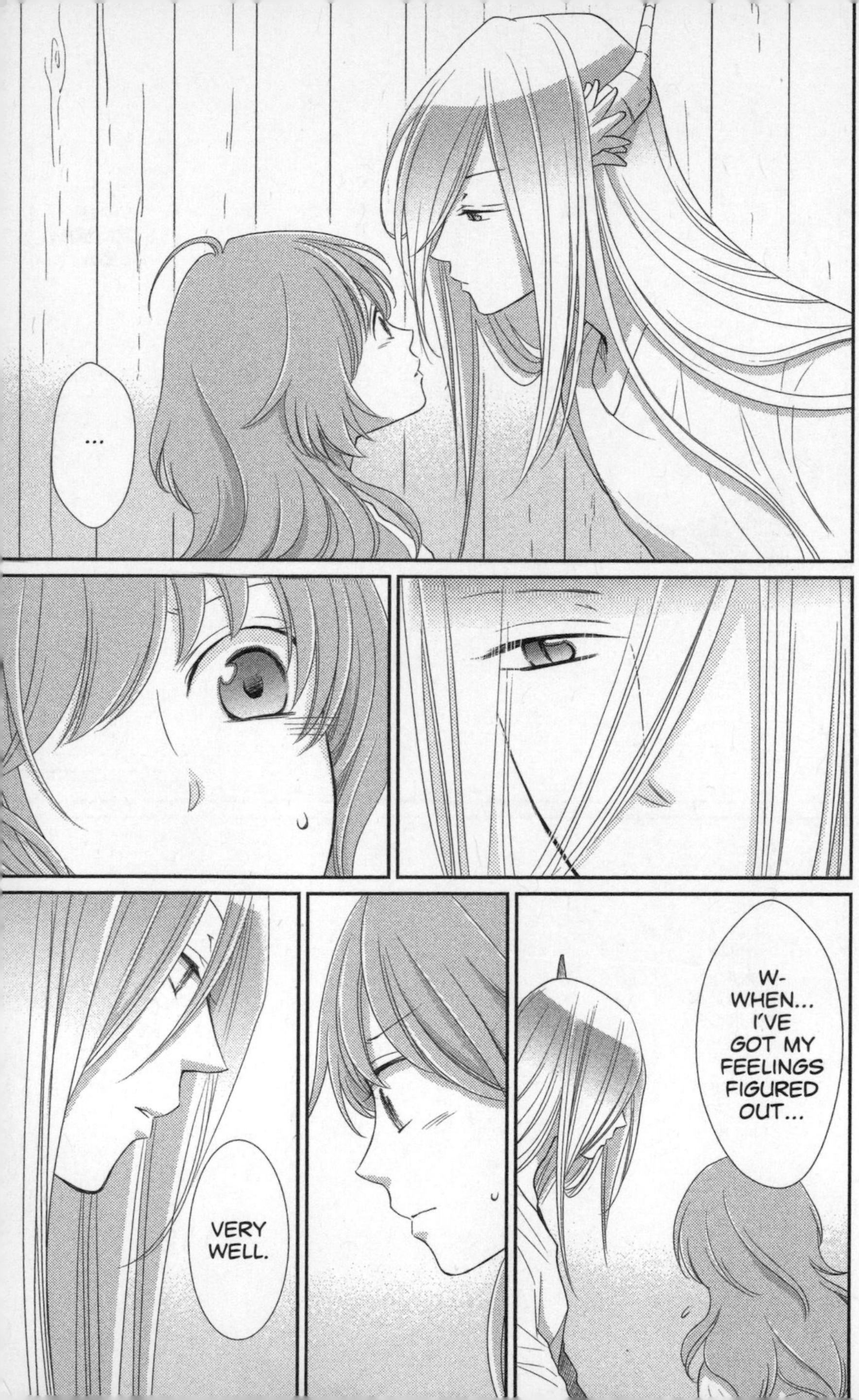
...
W-WHEN... I'VE GOT MY FEELINGS FIGURED OUT...
VERY WELL.

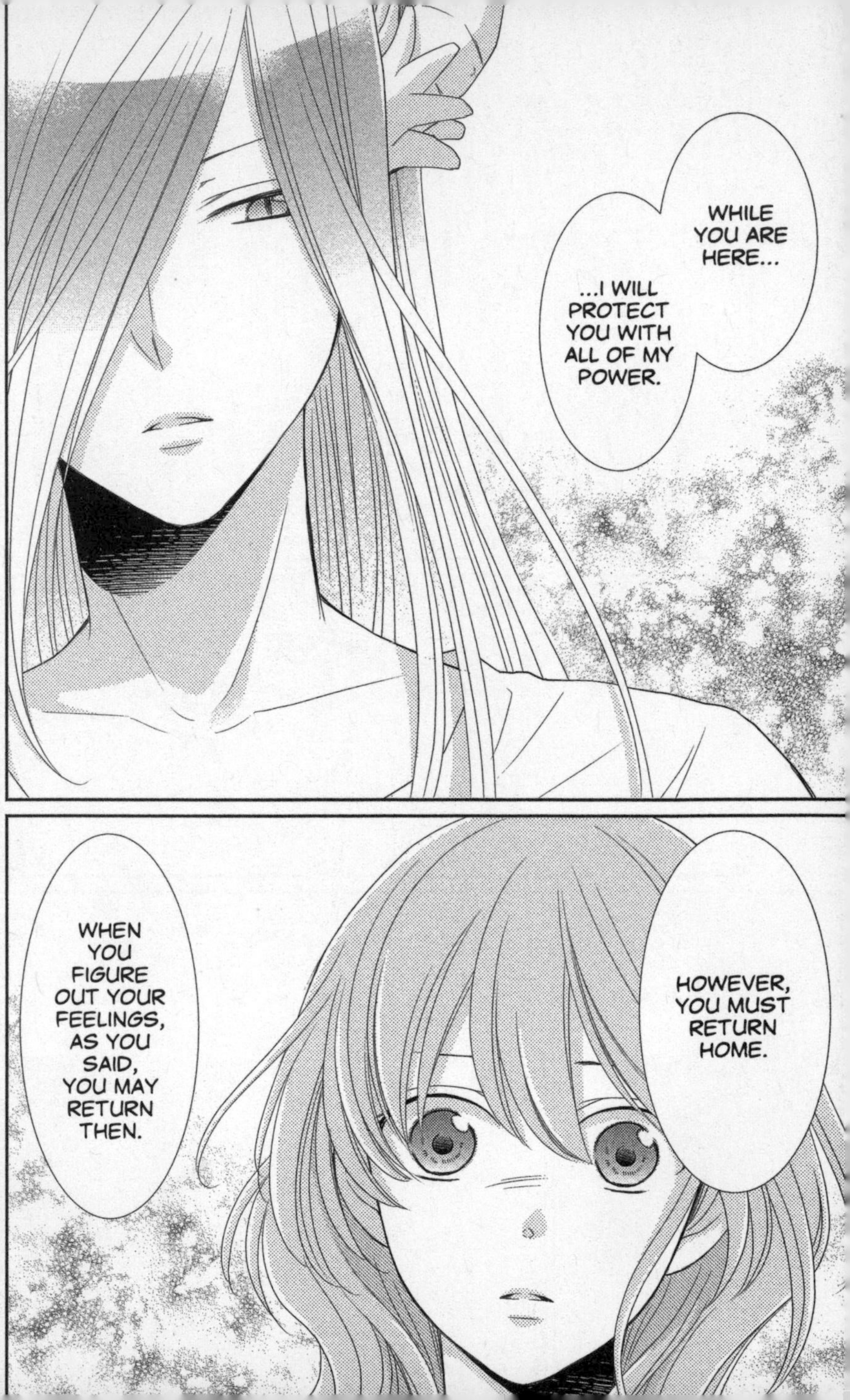
WHILE YOU ARE HERE...
...I WILL PROTECT YOU WITH ALL OF MY POWER.
HOWEVER, YOU MUST RETURN HOME.
WHEN YOU FIGURE OUT YOUR FEELINGS, AS YOU SAID, YOU MAY RETURN THEN.

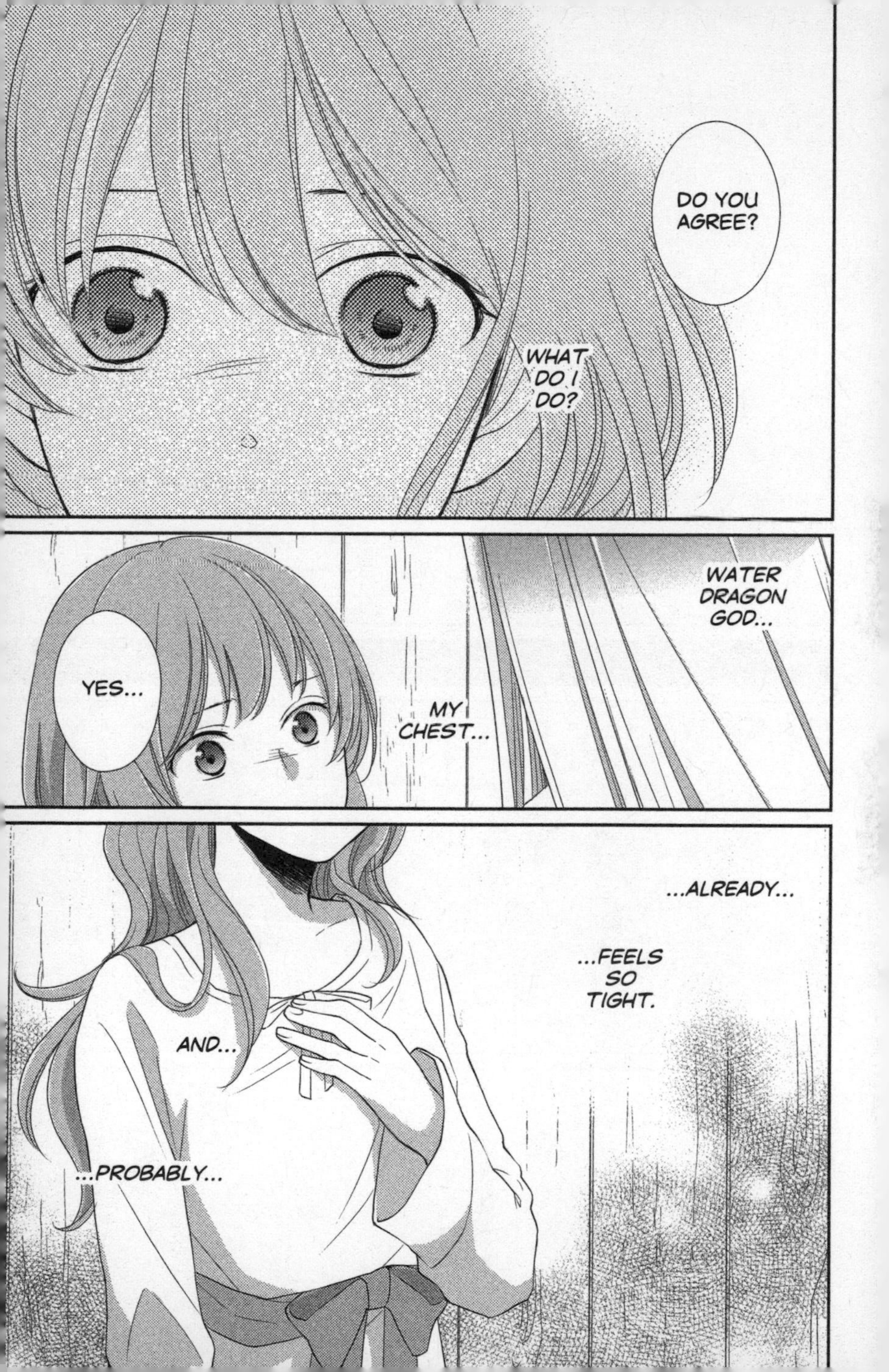
DO YOU AGREE?
WHAT DO I DO?
WATER DRAGON GOD...
YES...
MY CHEST...
...ALREADY...
...FEELS SO TIGHT.
AND...
...PROBABLY...

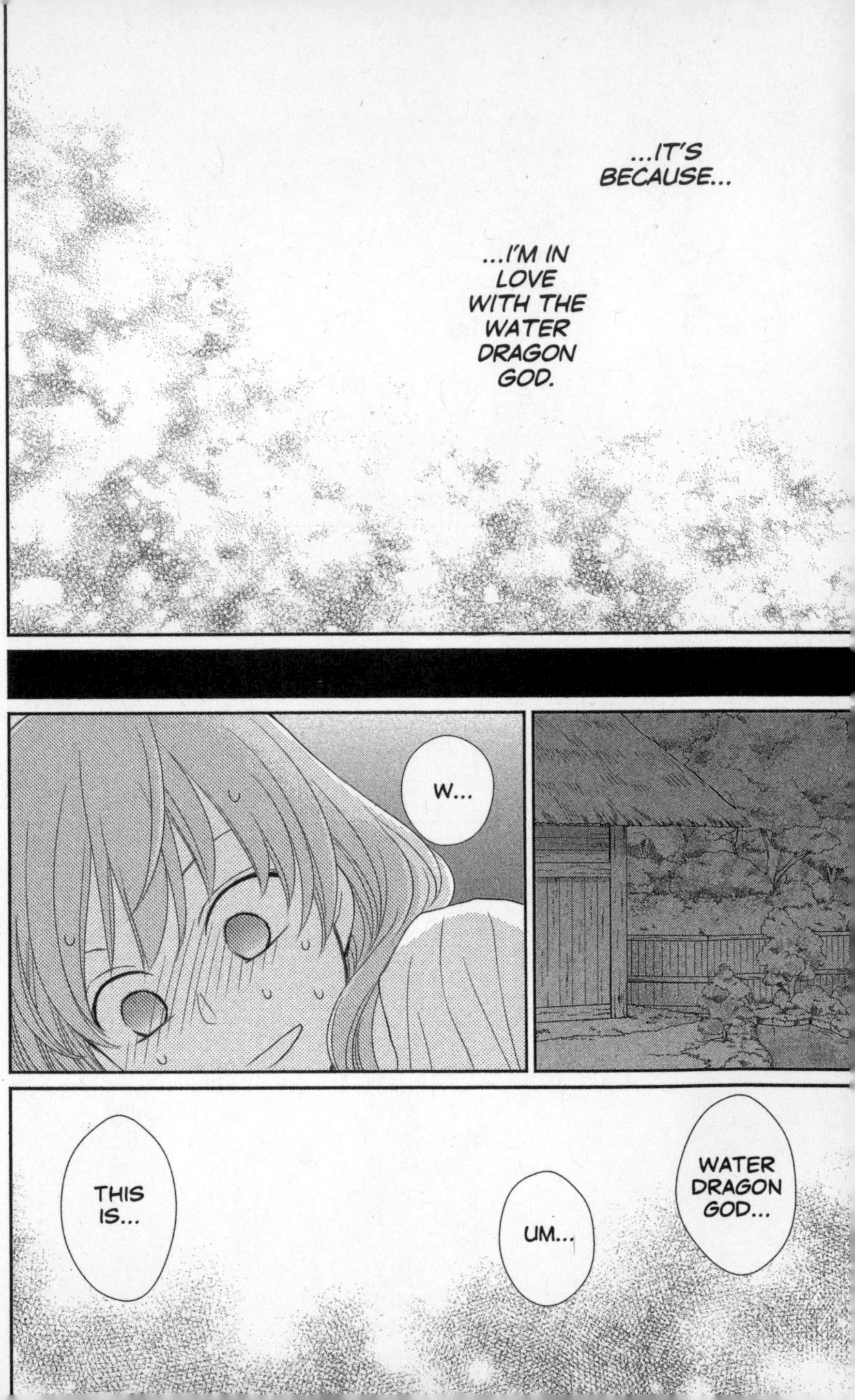
...IT'S BECAUSE...
...I'M IN LOVE WITH THE WATER DRAGON GOD.
W...
WATER DRAGON GOD...
UM...
THIS IS...

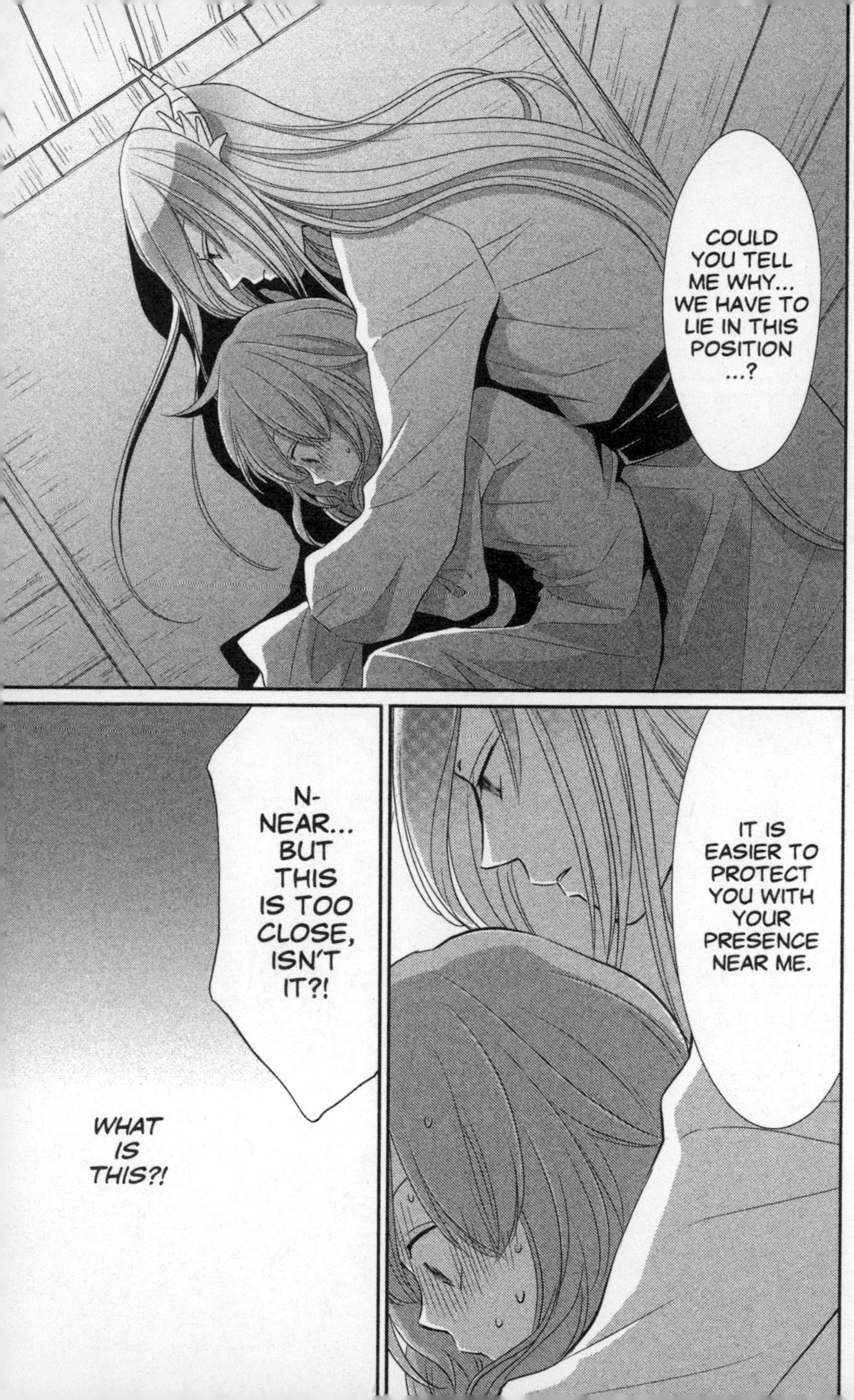
COULD YOU TELL ME WHY... WE HAVE TO LIE IN THIS POSITION ...?
IT IS EASIER TO PROTECT YOU WITH YOUR PRESENCE NEAR ME.
N-NEAR... BUT THIS IS TOO CLOSE, ISN'T IT?!
WHAT IS THIS?!

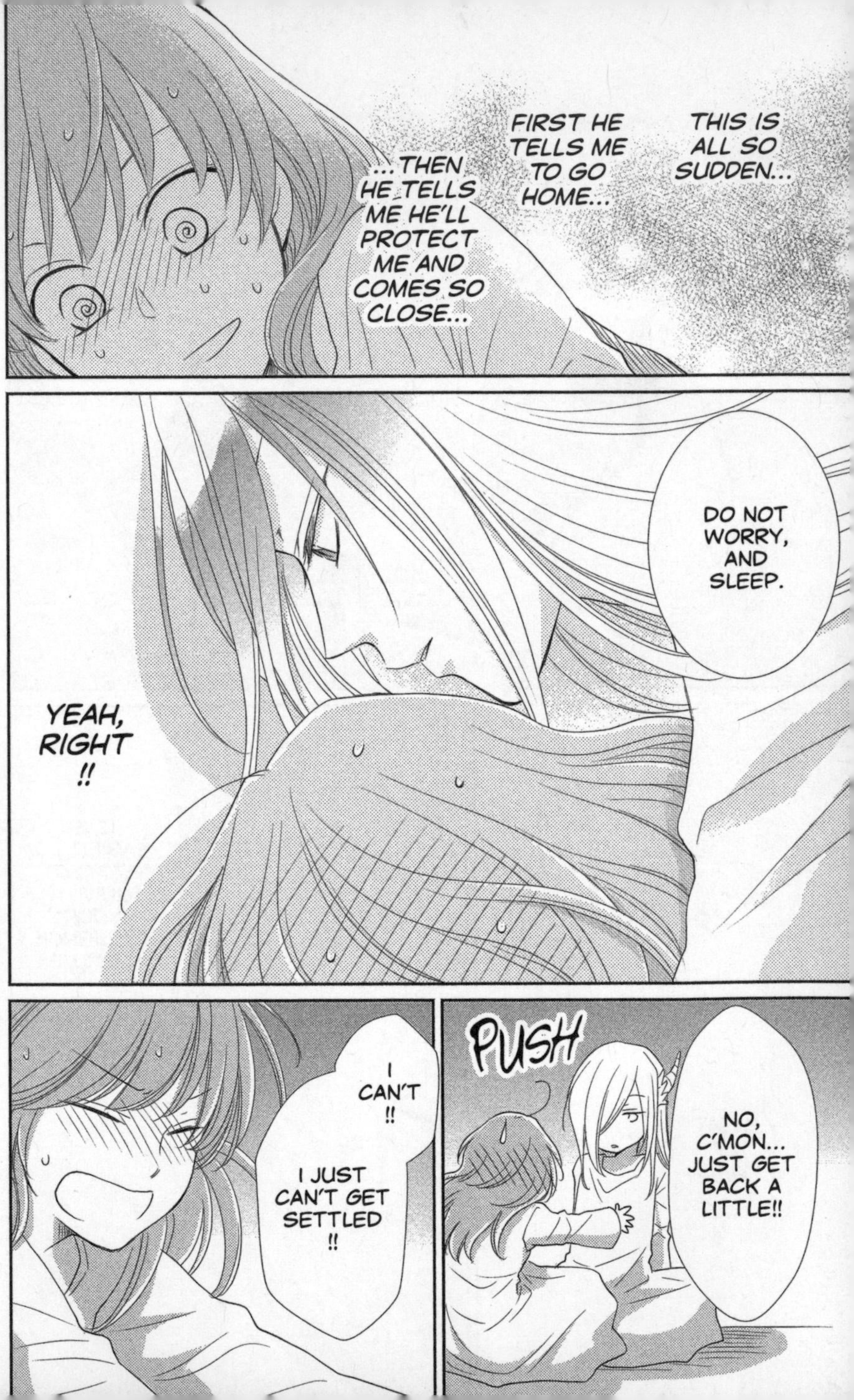
THIS IS ALL SO SUDDEN...
FIRST HE TELLS ME TO GO HOME...
...THEN HE TELLS ME HE'LL PROTECT ME AND COMES SO CLOSE...
DO NOT WORRY, AND SLEEP.
YEAH, RIGHT !!
NO, C'MON... JUST GET BACK A LITTLE!!
PUSH
I CAN'T !!
I JUST CAN'T GET SETTLED !!

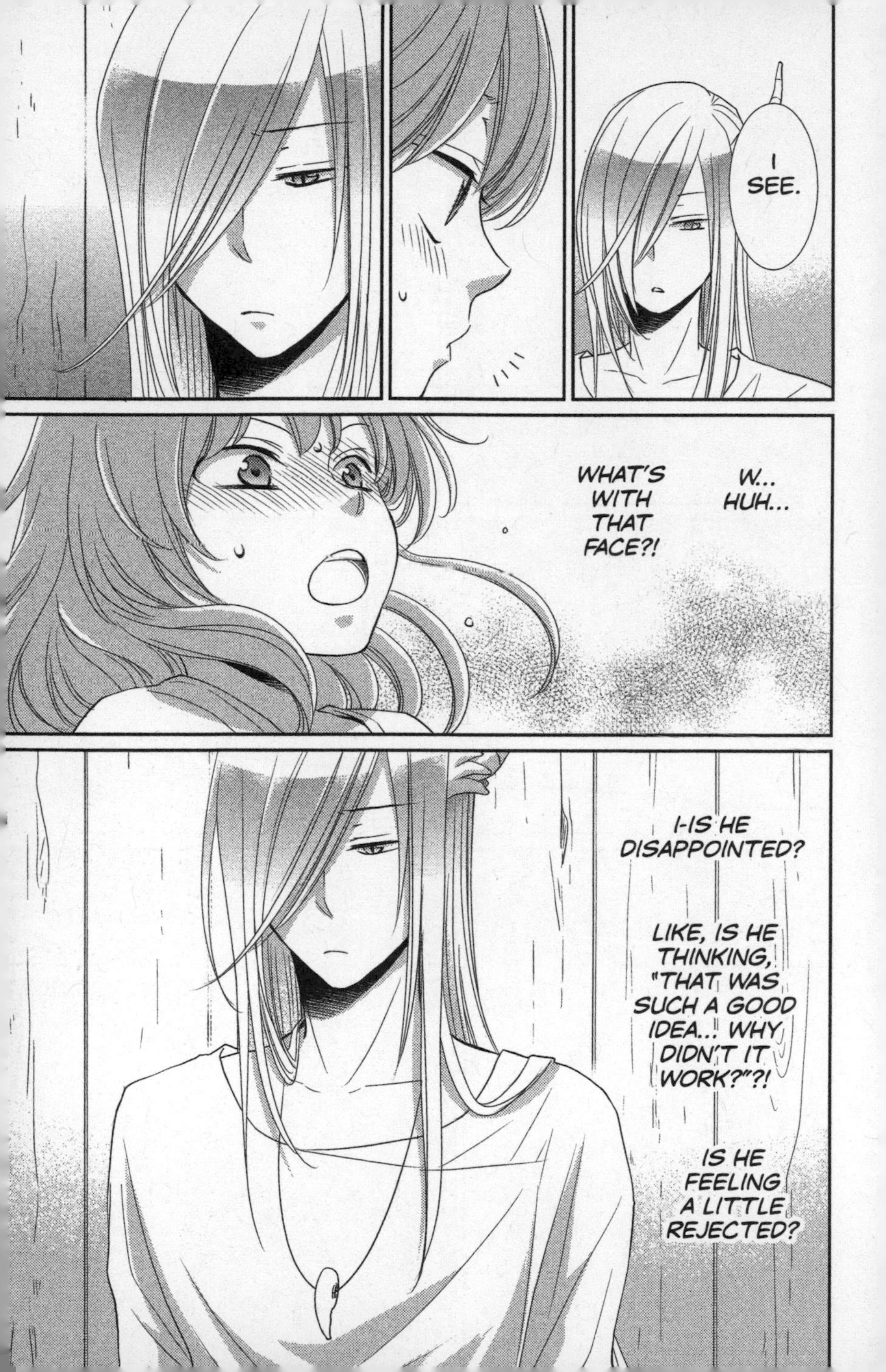
I SEE.
W... HUH...
WHAT'S WITH THAT FACE?!
I-IS HE DISAPPOINTED?
LIKE, IS HE THINKING, "THAT WAS SUCH A GOOD IDEA... WHY DIDN'T IT WORK?"?!
IS HE FEELING A LITTLE REJECTED?

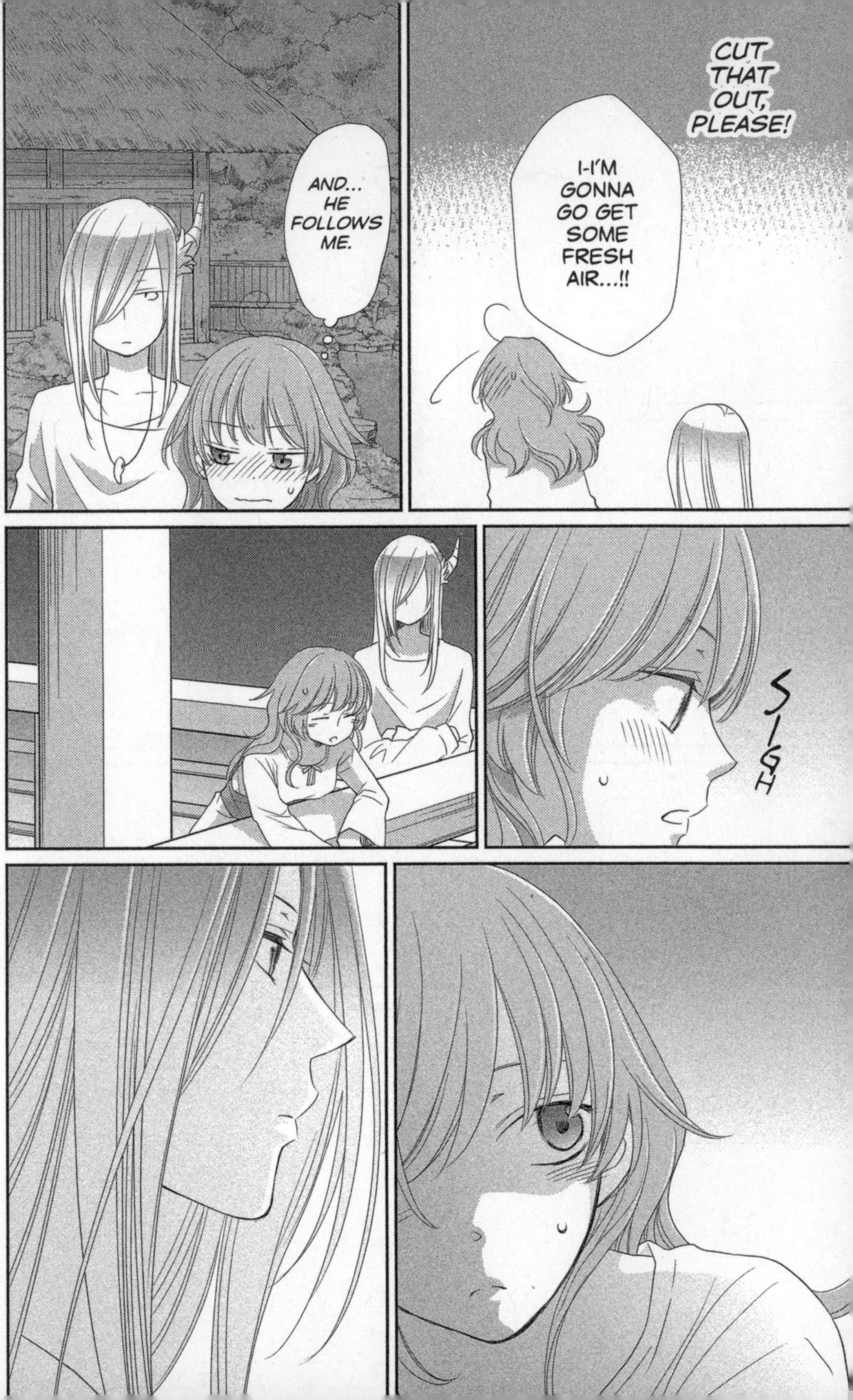
CUT THAT OUT, PLEASE!
I-I'M GONNA GO GET SOME FRESH AIR...!!
AND... HE FOLLOWS ME.
SIGH

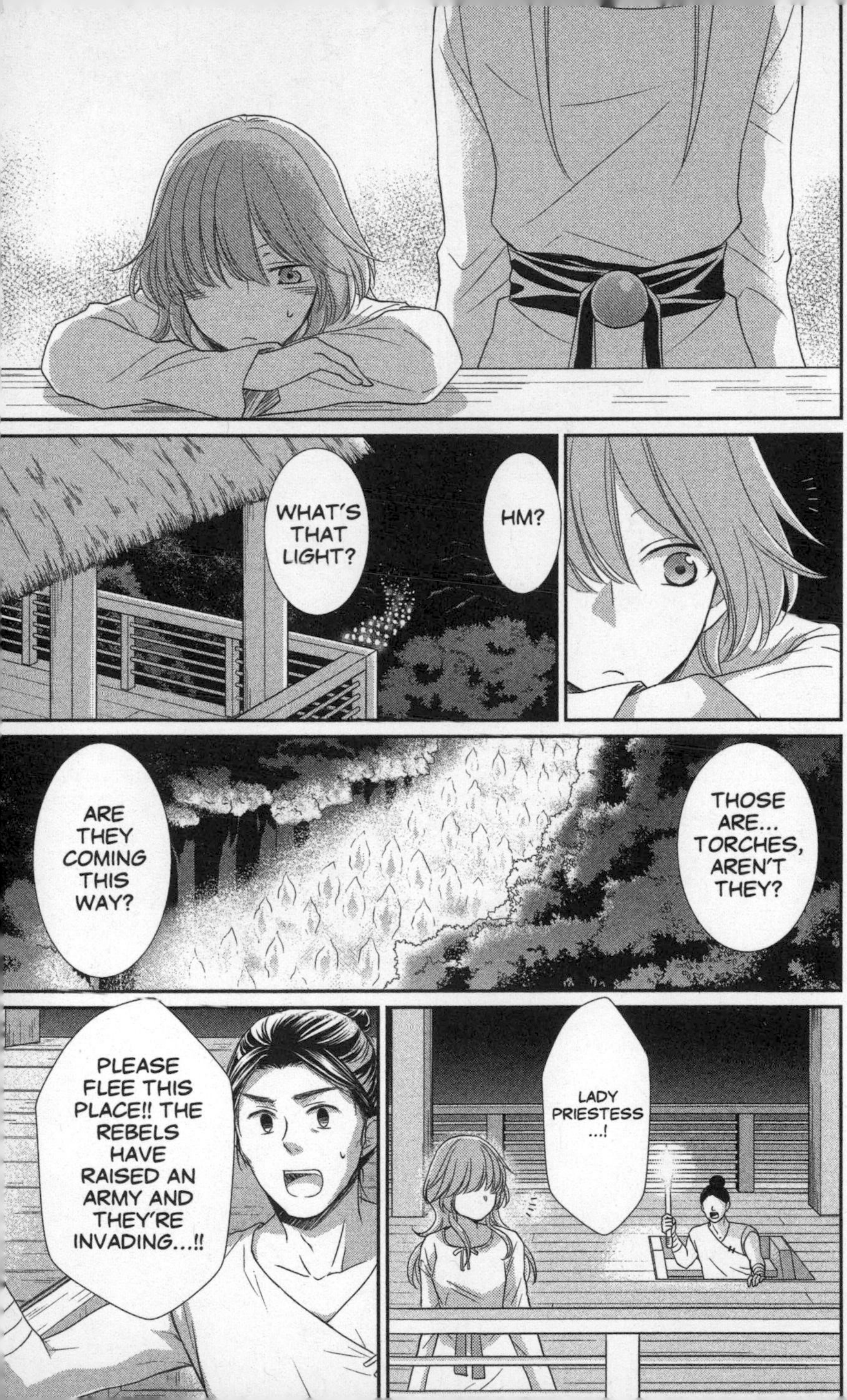

HM?
WHAT'S THAT LIGHT?
THOSE ARE... TORCHES, AREN'T THEY?
ARE THEY COMING THIS WAY?
LADY PRIESTESS ...!
PLEASE FLEE THIS PLACE!! THE REBELS HAVE RAISED AN ARMY AND THEY'RE INVADING...!!

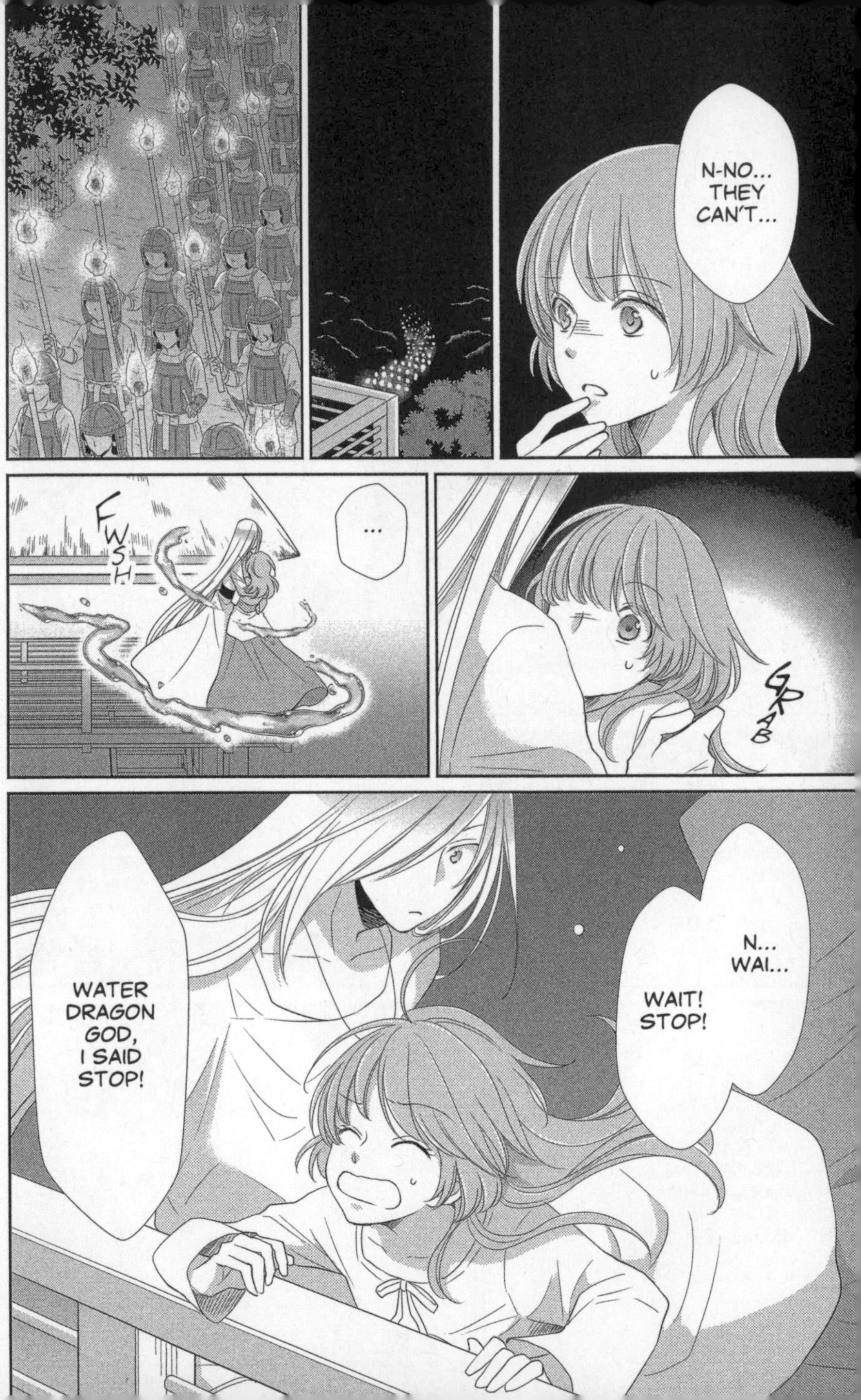
N-NO... THEY CAN'T...
GRAB
...
FWSH
N... WAI...
WAIT! STOP!
WATER DRAGON GOD, I SAID STOP!

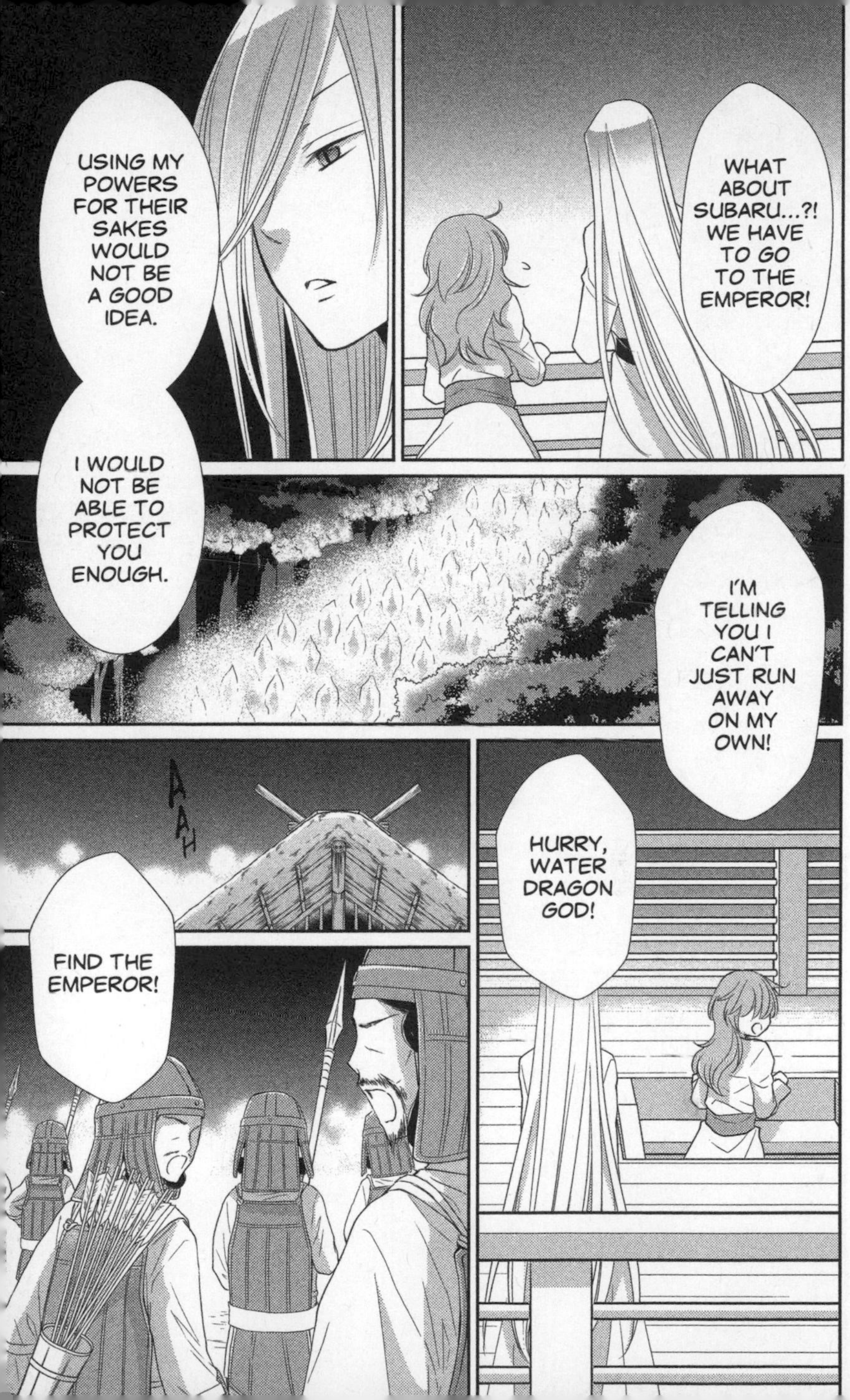
WHAT ABOUT SUBARU...?! WE HAVE TO GO TO THE EMPEROR!
USING MY POWERS FOR THEIR SAKES WOULD NOT BE A GOOD IDEA.
I WOULD NOT BE ABLE TO PROTECT YOU ENOUGH.
I'M TELLING YOU I CAN'T JUST RUN AWAY ON MY OWN!
HURRY, WATER DRAGON GOD!
AAH
FIND THE EMPEROR!

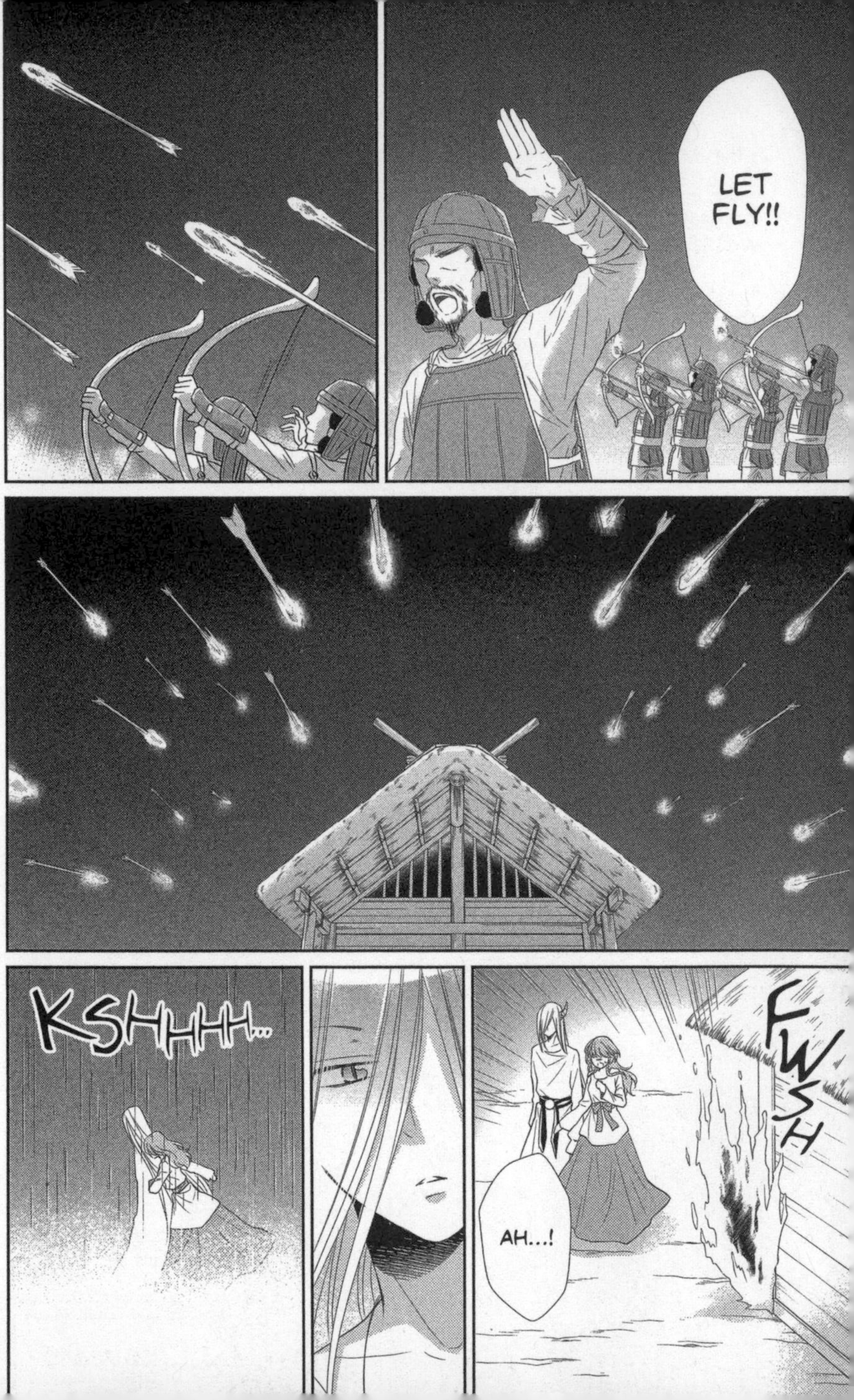
LET FLY!!
FWSH
AH...!
KSHHHH...

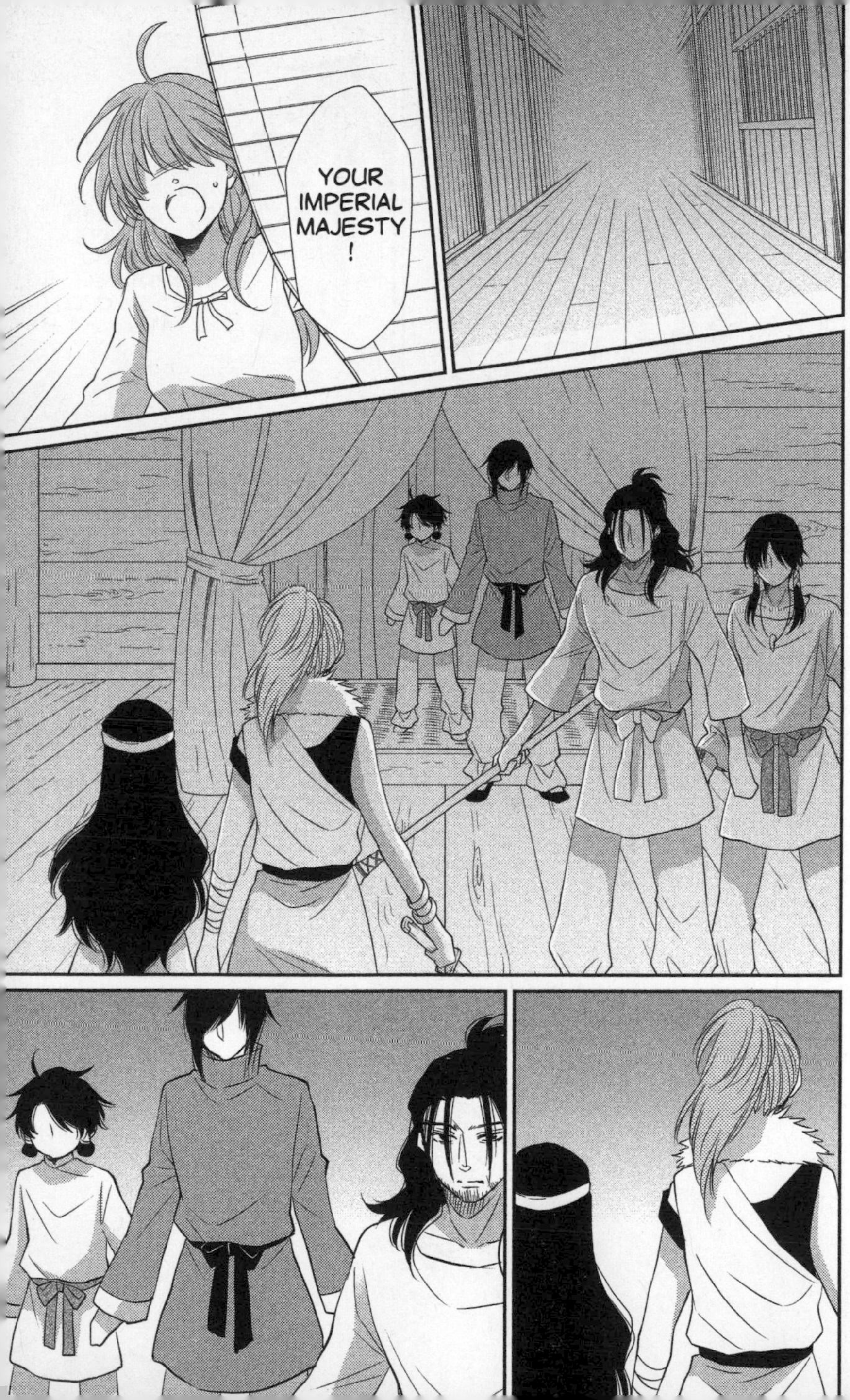
YOUR IMPERIAL MAJESTY!

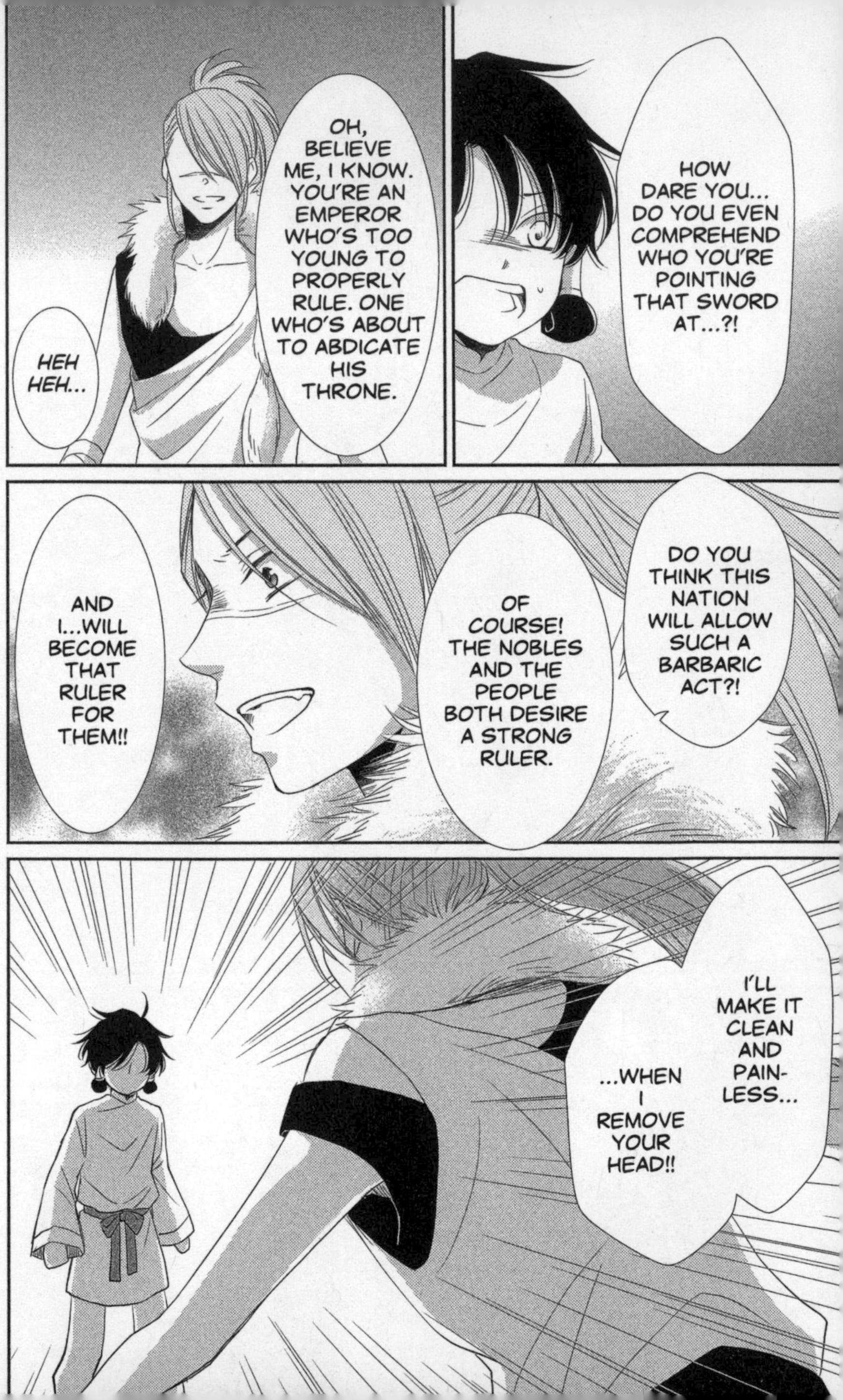
HOW DARE YOU... DO YOU EVEN COMPREHEND WHO YOU'RE POINTING THAT SWORD AT...?!
OH, BELIEVE ME, I KNOW. YOU'RE AN EMPEROR WHO'S TOO YOUNG TO PROPERLY RULE. ONE WHO'S ABOUT TO ABDICATE HIS THRONE.
HEH HEH...
DO YOU THINK THIS NATION WILL ALLOW SUCH A BARBARIC ACT?!
OF COURSE! THE NOBLES AND THE PEOPLE BOTH DESIRE A STRONG RULER.
AND I...WILL BECOME THAT RULER FOR THEM!!
I'LL MAKE IT CLEAN AND PAIN-LESS...
...WHEN I REMOVE YOUR HEAD!!

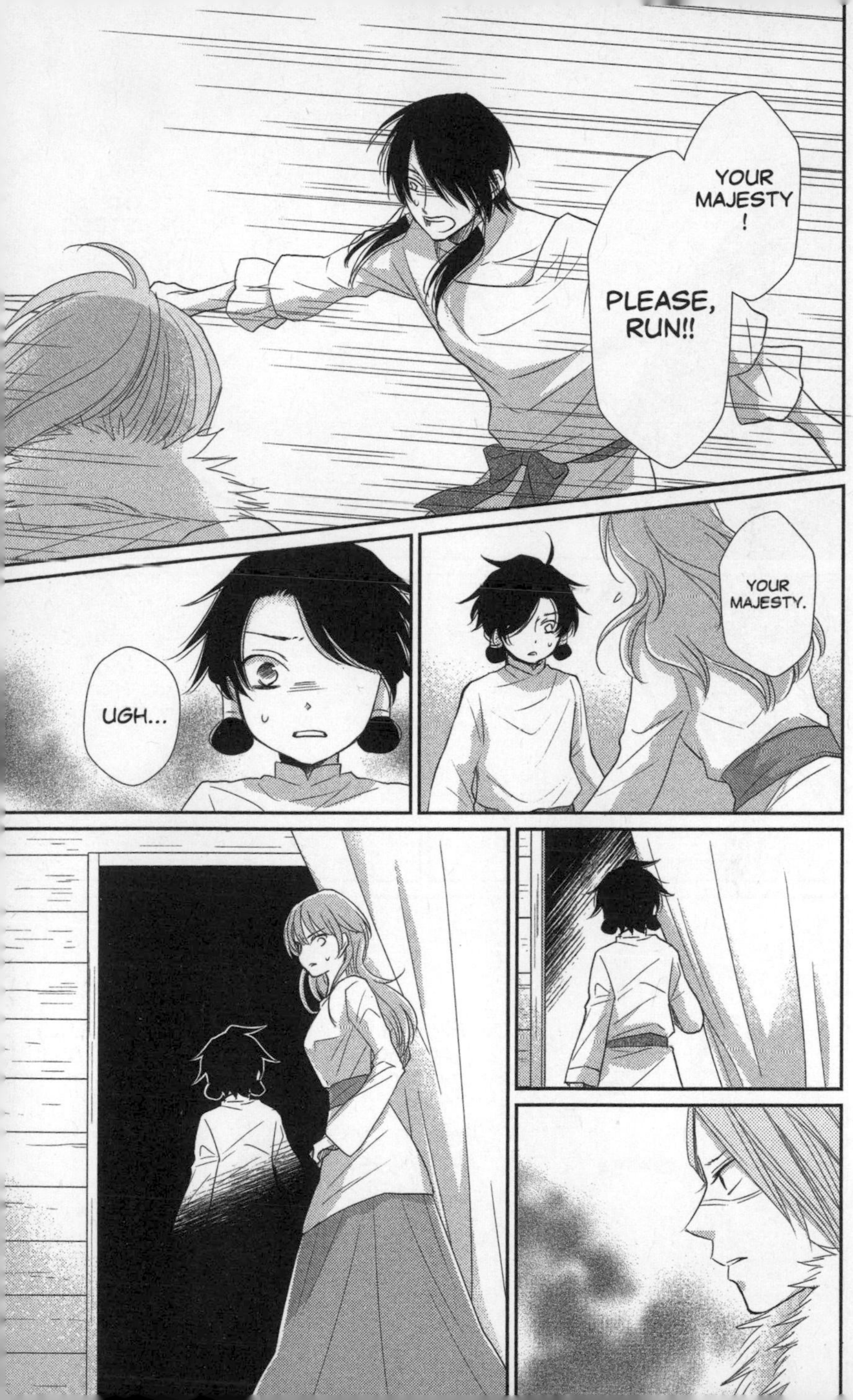
YOUR MAJESTY!
PLEASE, RUN!!
YOUR MAJESTY.
UGH...

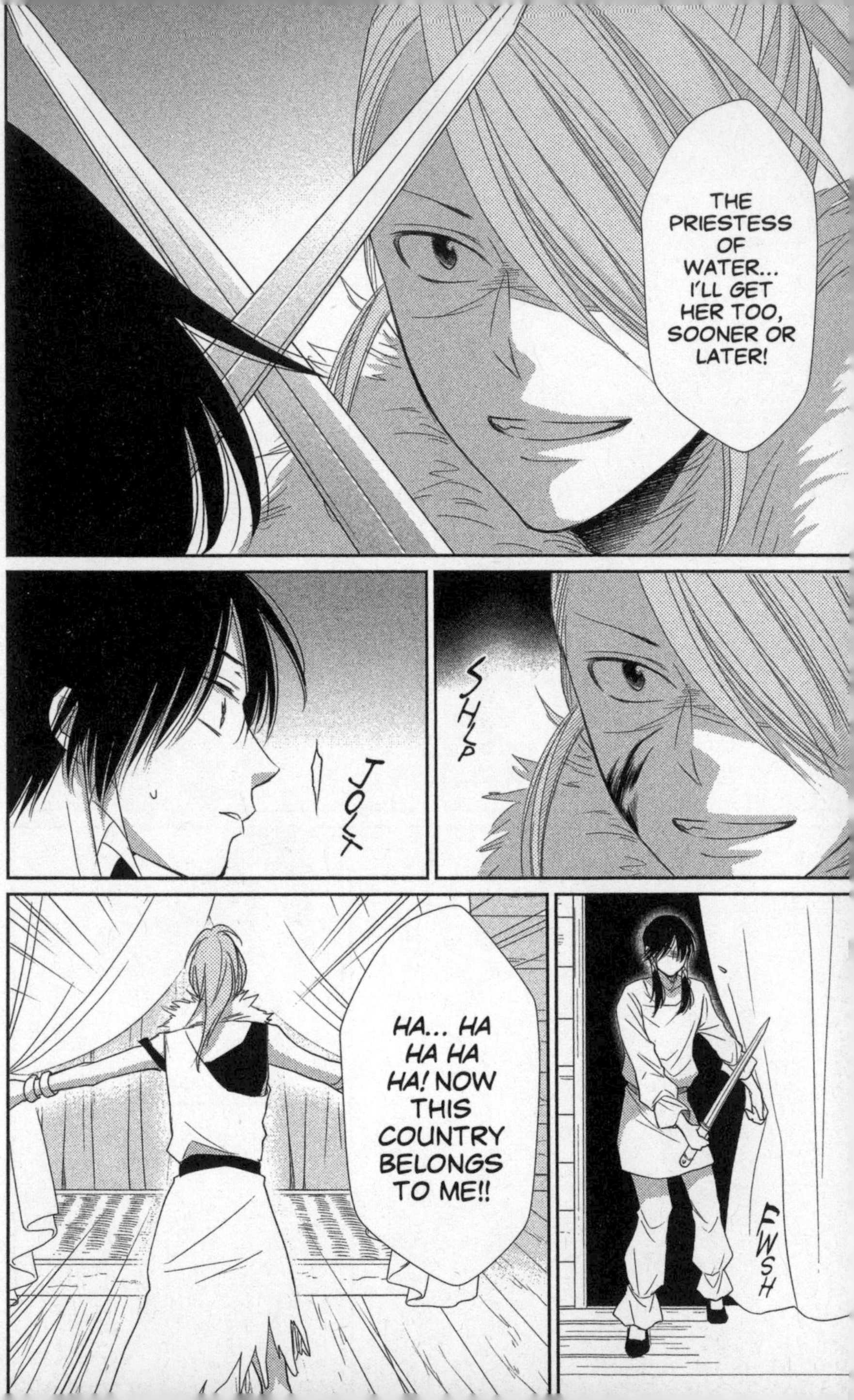
THE PRIESTESS OF WATER... I'LL GET HER TOO, SOONER OR LATER!
SHLP
JOLT
FWSH
HA... HA HA HA HA! NOW THIS COUNTRY BELONGS TO ME!!

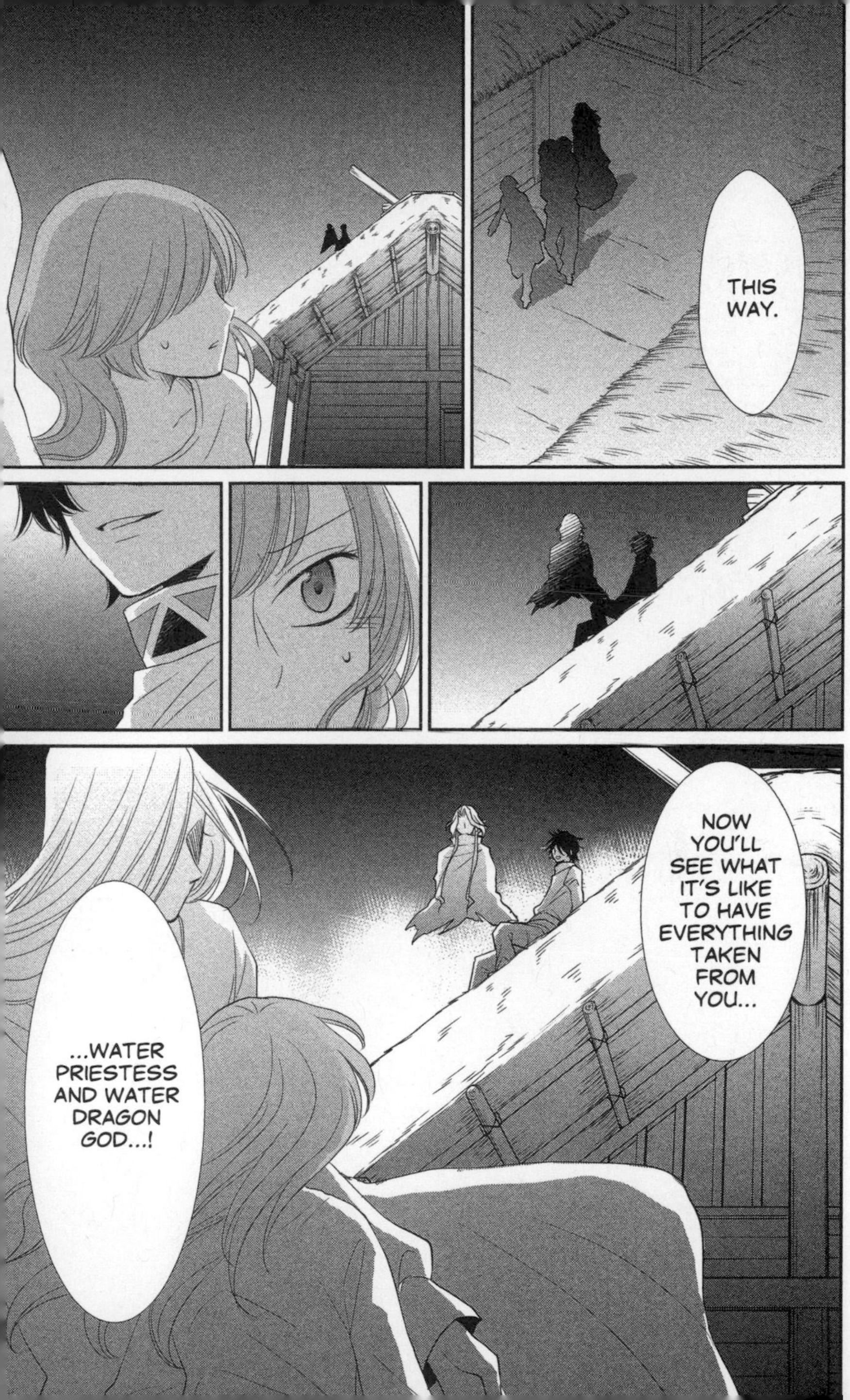
THIS WAY.
NOW YOU'LL SEE WHAT IT'S LIKE TO HAVE EVERYTHING TAKEN FROM YOU...
...WATER PRIESTESS AND WATER DRAGON GOD...!

Hello! It's Toma.

This is *The Water Dragon's Bride* volume 9. I'm drawing Kogahiko since he's gotten a good showing this time. He's a character I like a lot.

His image color is orange.

Kogahiko

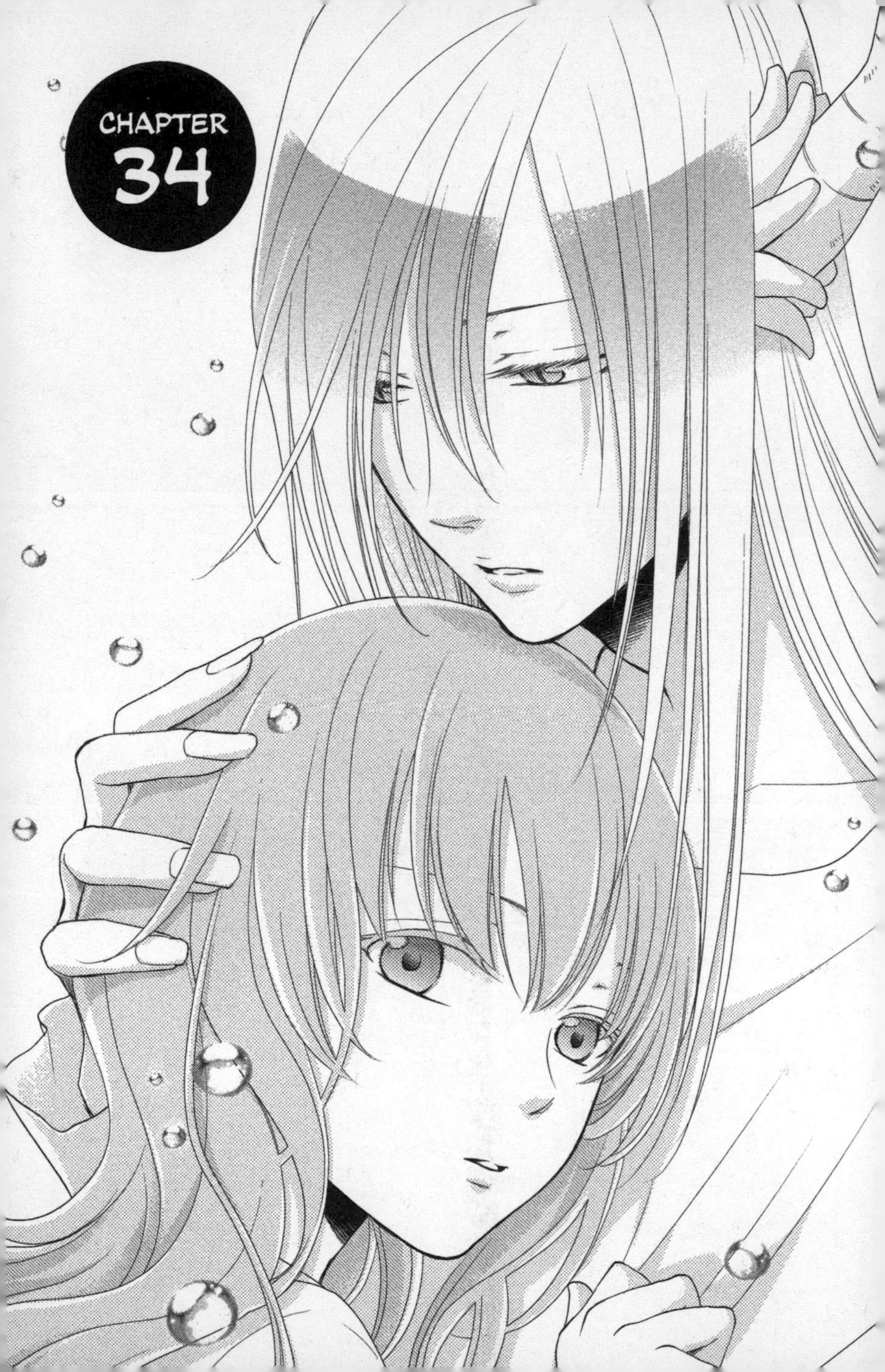
CHAPTER
34

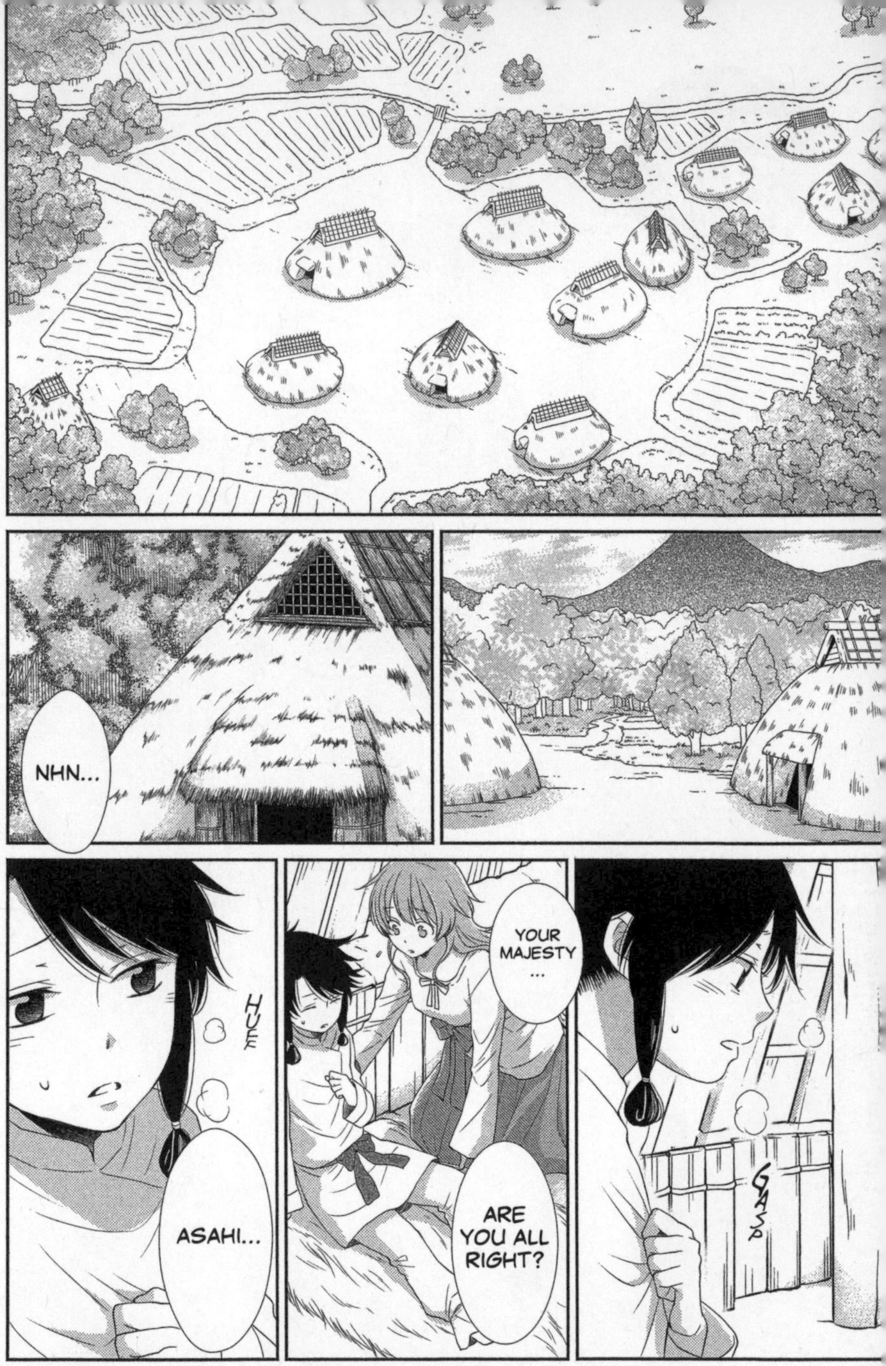
NHN...
GASP
YOUR MAJESTY ...
ARE YOU ALL RIGHT?
HUFF
ASAHI...

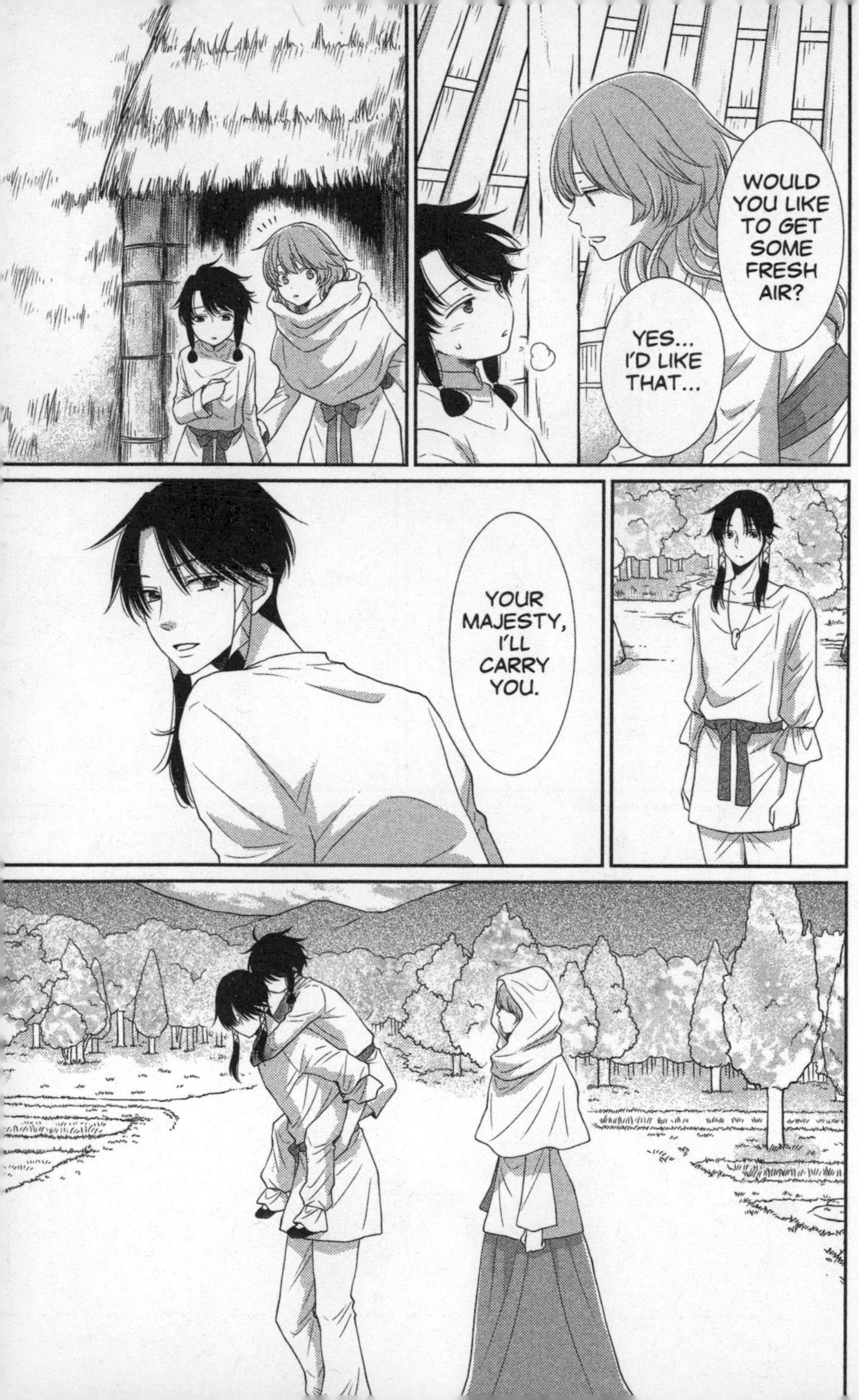
WOULD YOU LIKE TO GET SOME FRESH AIR?
YES... I'D LIKE THAT...
YOUR MAJESTY, I'LL CARRY YOU.

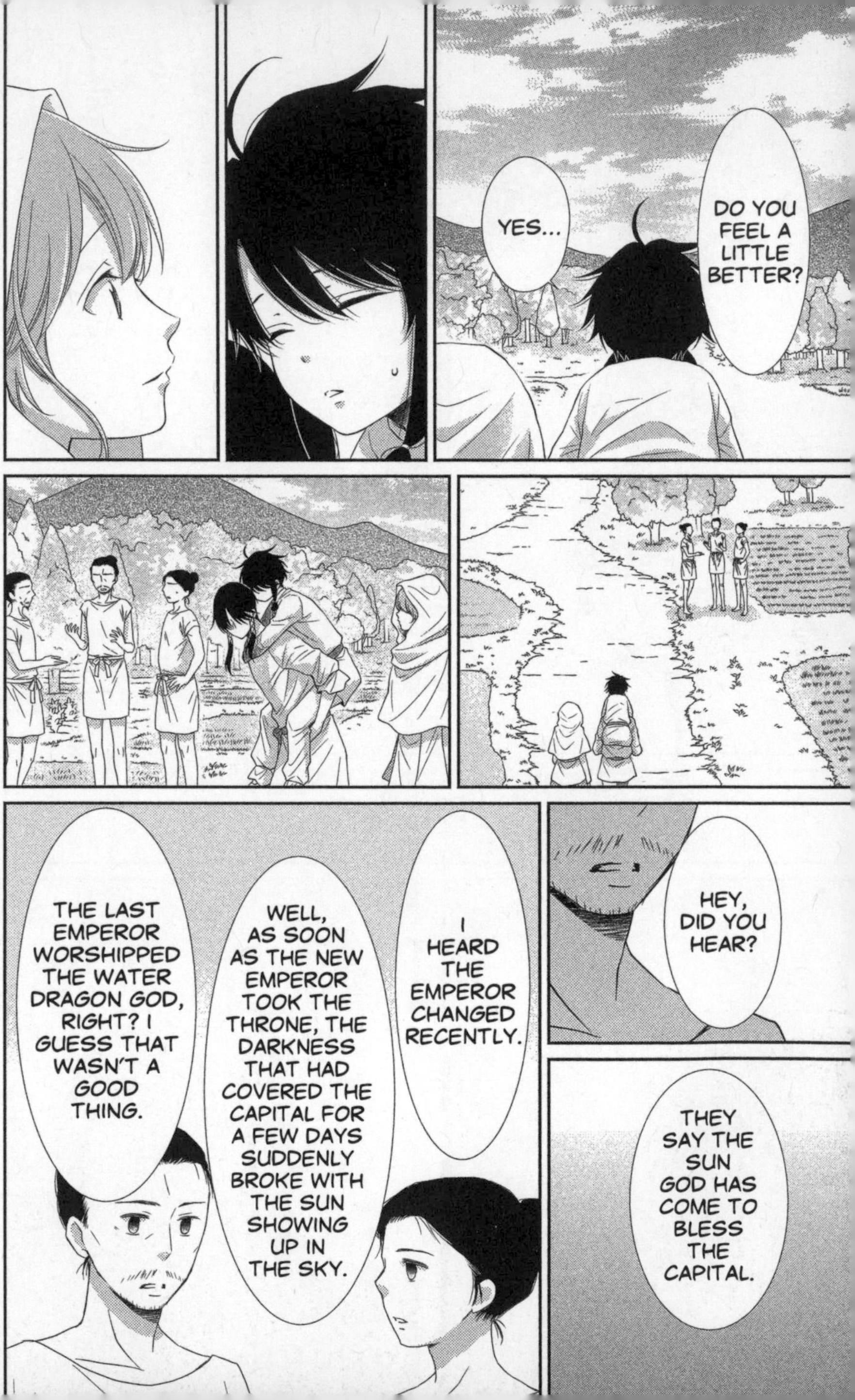
DO YOU FEEL A LITTLE BETTER?
YES...
HEY, DID YOU HEAR?
THEY SAY THE SUN GOD HAS COME TO BLESS THE CAPITAL.
I HEARD THE EMPEROR CHANGED RECENTLY.
WELL, AS SOON AS THE NEW EMPEROR TOOK THE THRONE, THE DARKNESS THAT HAD COVERED THE CAPITAL FOR A FEW DAYS SUDDENLY BROKE WITH THE SUN SHOWING UP IN THE SKY.
THE LAST EMPEROR WORSHIPPED THE WATER DRAGON GOD, RIGHT? I GUESS THAT WASN'T A GOOD THING.

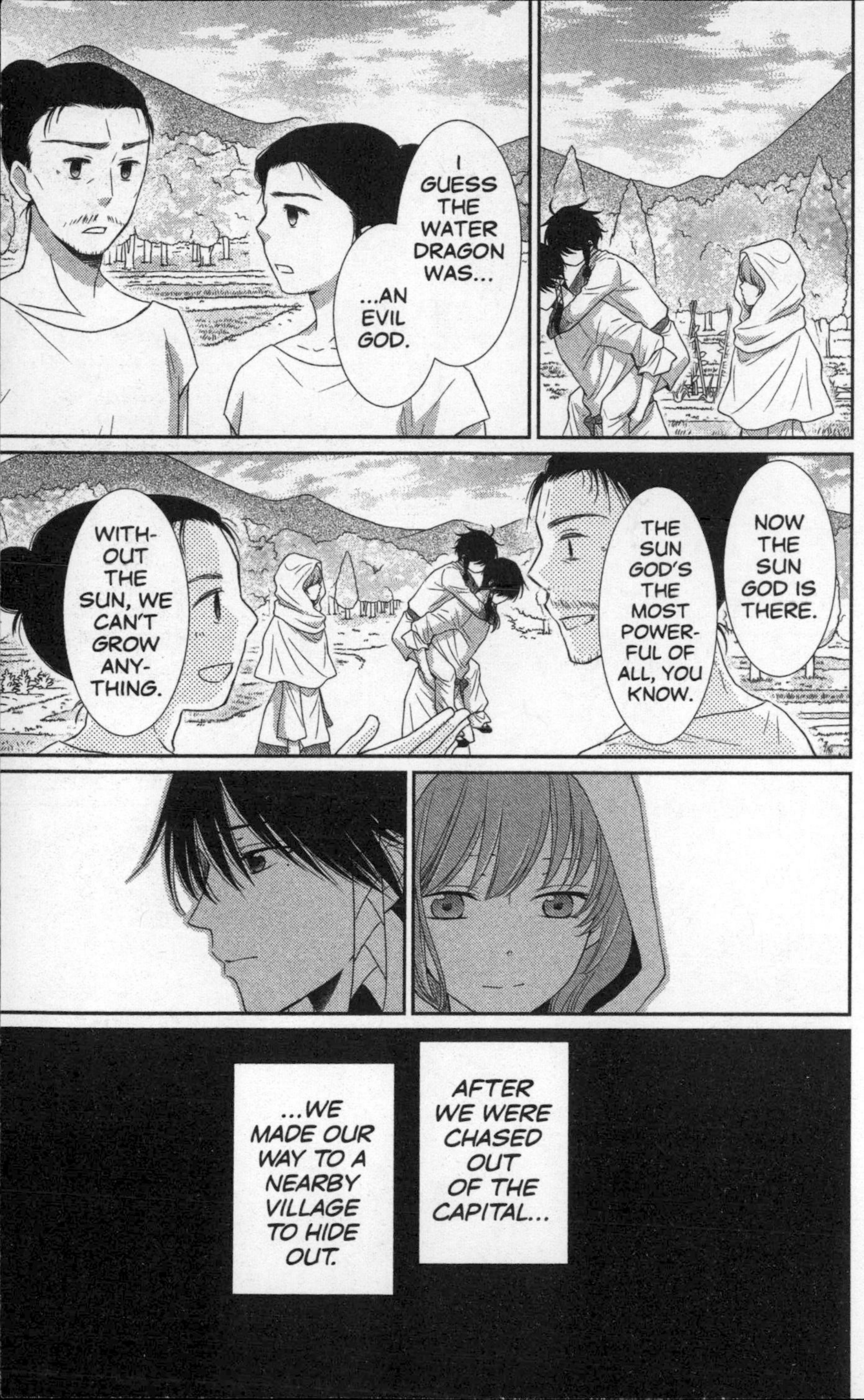
I GUESS THE WATER DRAGON WAS...
...AN EVIL GOD.
NOW THE SUN GOD IS THERE.
THE SUN GOD'S THE MOST POWERFUL OF ALL, YOU KNOW.
WITHOUT THE SUN, WE CAN'T GROW ANYTHING.
AFTER WE WERE CHASED OUT OF THE CAPITAL...
...WE MADE OUR WAY TO A NEARBY VILLAGE TO HIDE OUT.

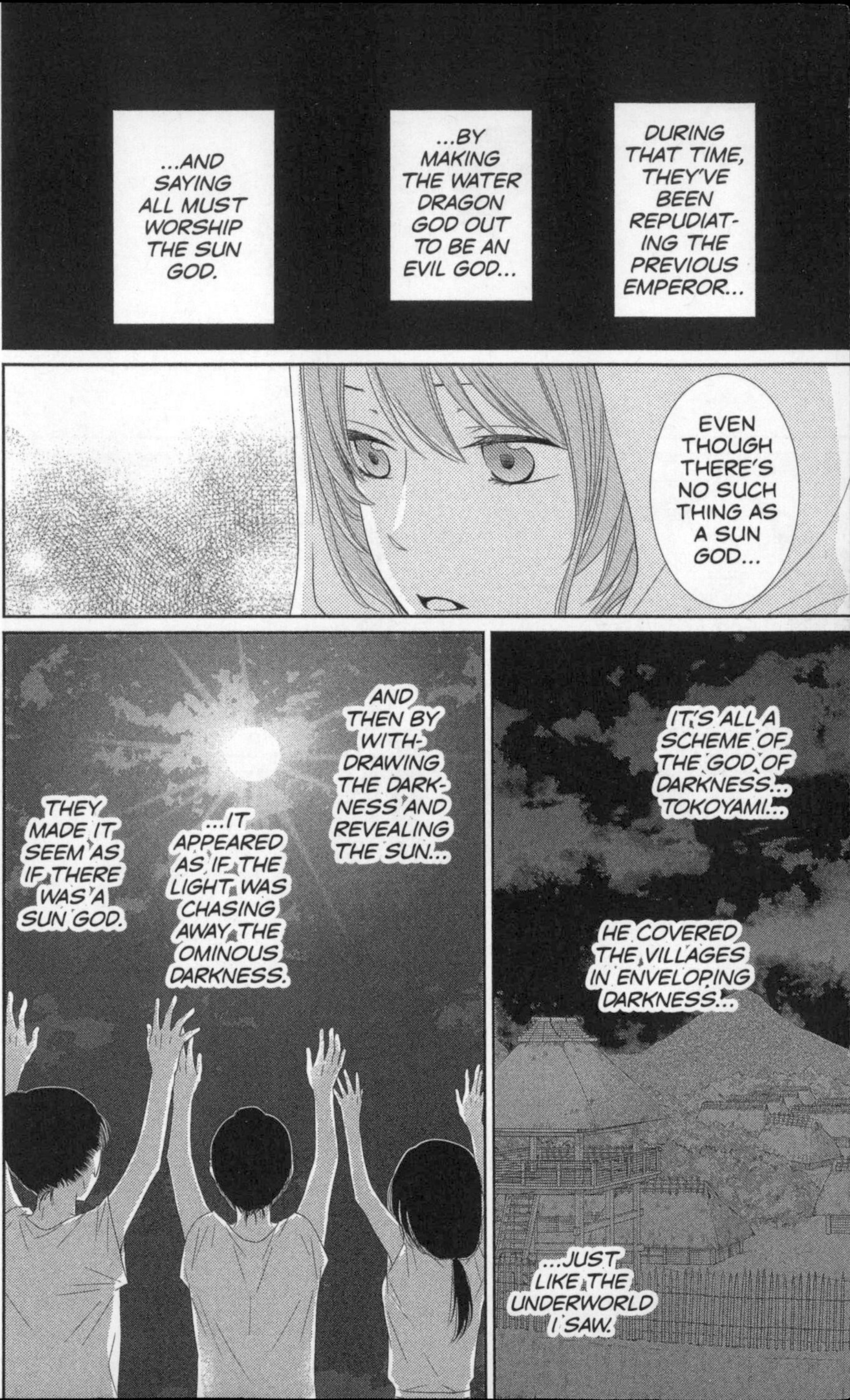
DURING THAT TIME, THEY'VE BEEN REPUDIATING THE PREVIOUS EMPEROR...
...BY MAKING THE WATER DRAGON GOD OUT TO BE AN EVIL GOD...
...AND SAYING ALL MUST WORSHIP THE SUN GOD.
EVEN THOUGH THERE'S NO SUCH THING AS A SUN GOD...
IT'S ALL A SCHEME OF THE GOD OF DARKNESS... TOKOYAMI...
HE COVERED THE VILLAGES IN ENVELOPING DARKNESS...
...JUST LIKE THE UNDERWORLD I SAW.
AND THEN BY WITHDRAWING THE DARKNESS AND REVEALING THE SUN...
...IT APPEARED AS IF THE LIGHT WAS CHASING AWAY THE OMINOUS DARKNESS.
THEY MADE IT SEEM AS IF THERE WAS A SUN GOD.

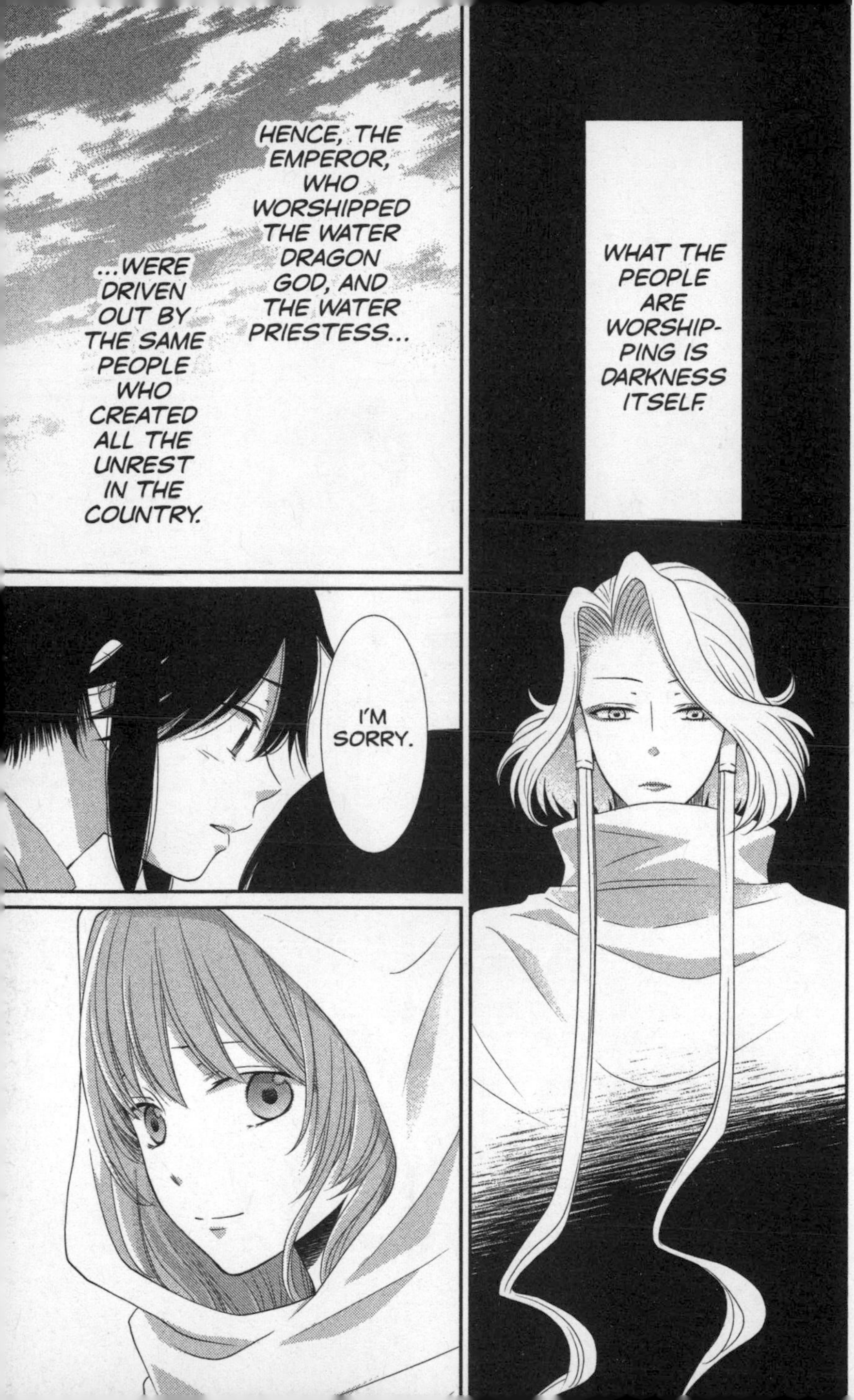
WHAT THE PEOPLE ARE WORSHIPPING IS DARKNESS ITSELF.
HENCE, THE EMPEROR, WHO WORSHIPPED THE WATER DRAGON GOD, AND THE WATER PRIESTESS...
...WERE DRIVEN OUT BY THE SAME PEOPLE WHO CREATED ALL THE UNREST IN THE COUNTRY.
I'M SORRY.

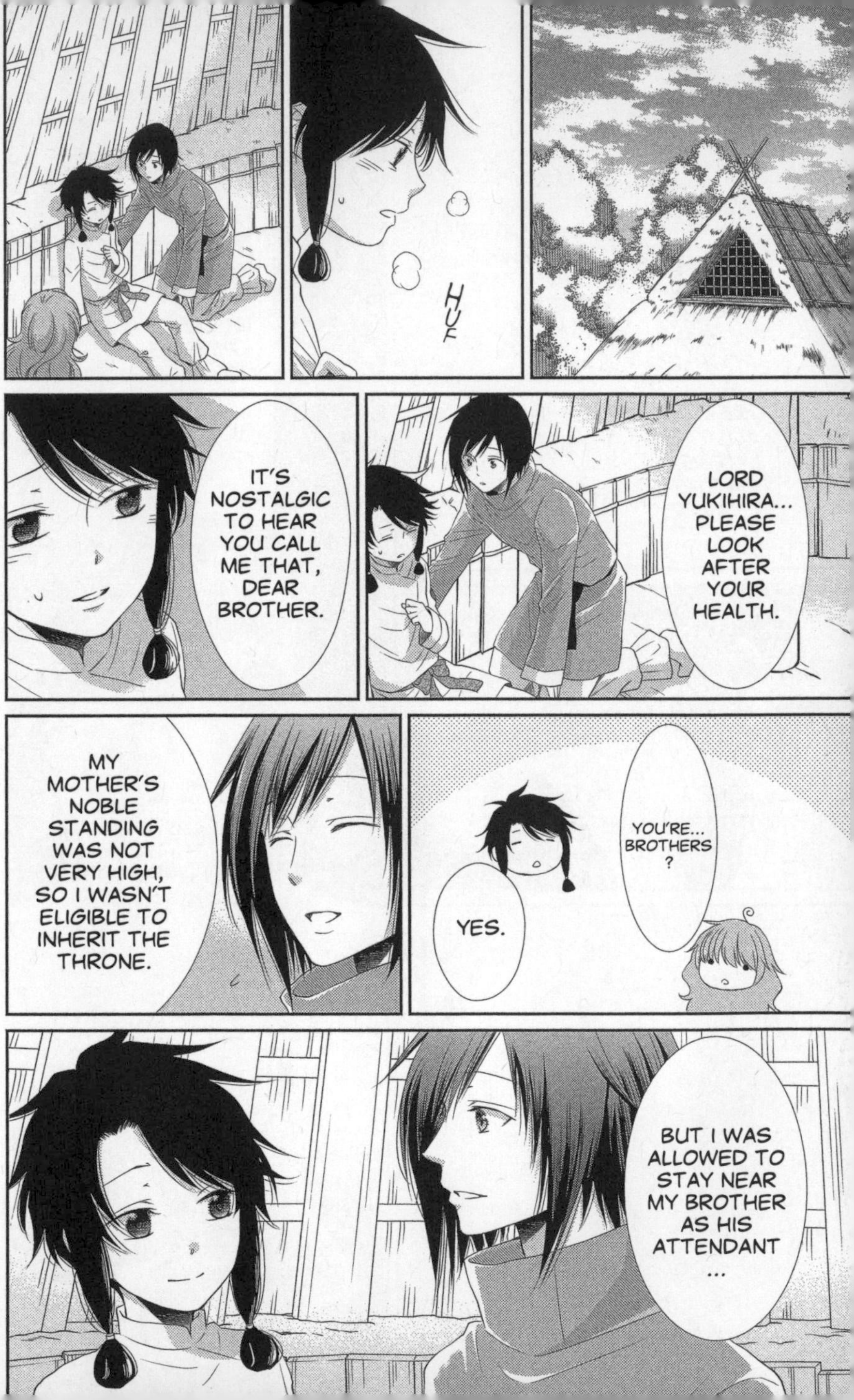
HUF
LORD YUKIHIRA... PLEASE LOOK AFTER YOUR HEALTH.
IT'S NOSTALGIC TO HEAR YOU CALL ME THAT, DEAR BROTHER.
YOU'RE... BROTHERS?
YES.
MY MOTHER'S NOBLE STANDING WAS NOT VERY HIGH, SO I WASN'T ELIGIBLE TO INHERIT THE THRONE.
BUT I WAS ALLOWED TO STAY NEAR MY BROTHER AS HIS ATTENDANT ...

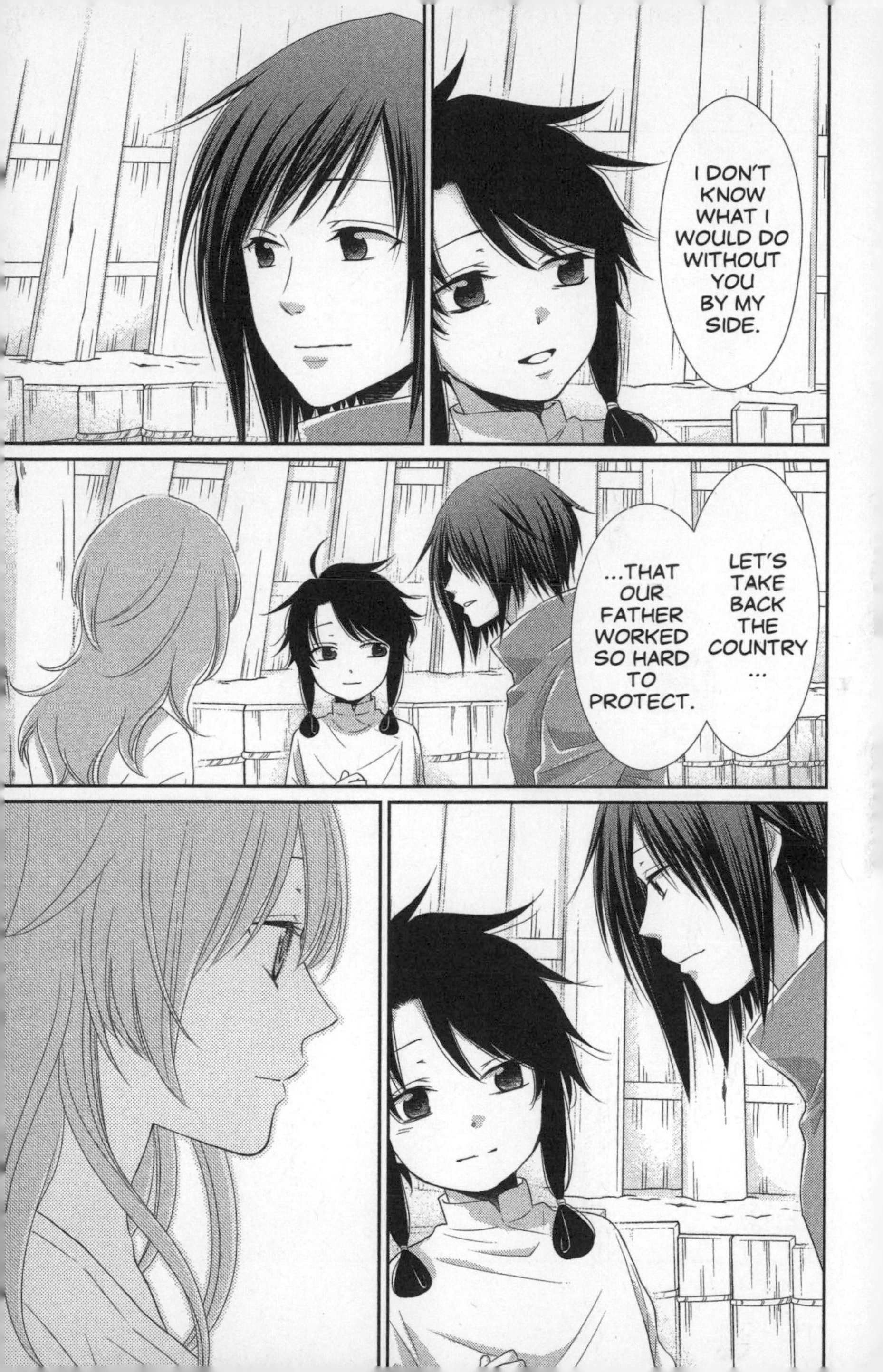
I DON'T KNOW WHAT I WOULD DO WITHOUT YOU BY MY SIDE.
LET'S TAKE BACK THE COUNTRY...
...THAT OUR FATHER WORKED SO HARD TO PROTECT.

HEY, COULD YOU BRING THAT FIREWOOD OVER HERE?

PHEW

...

HEY.

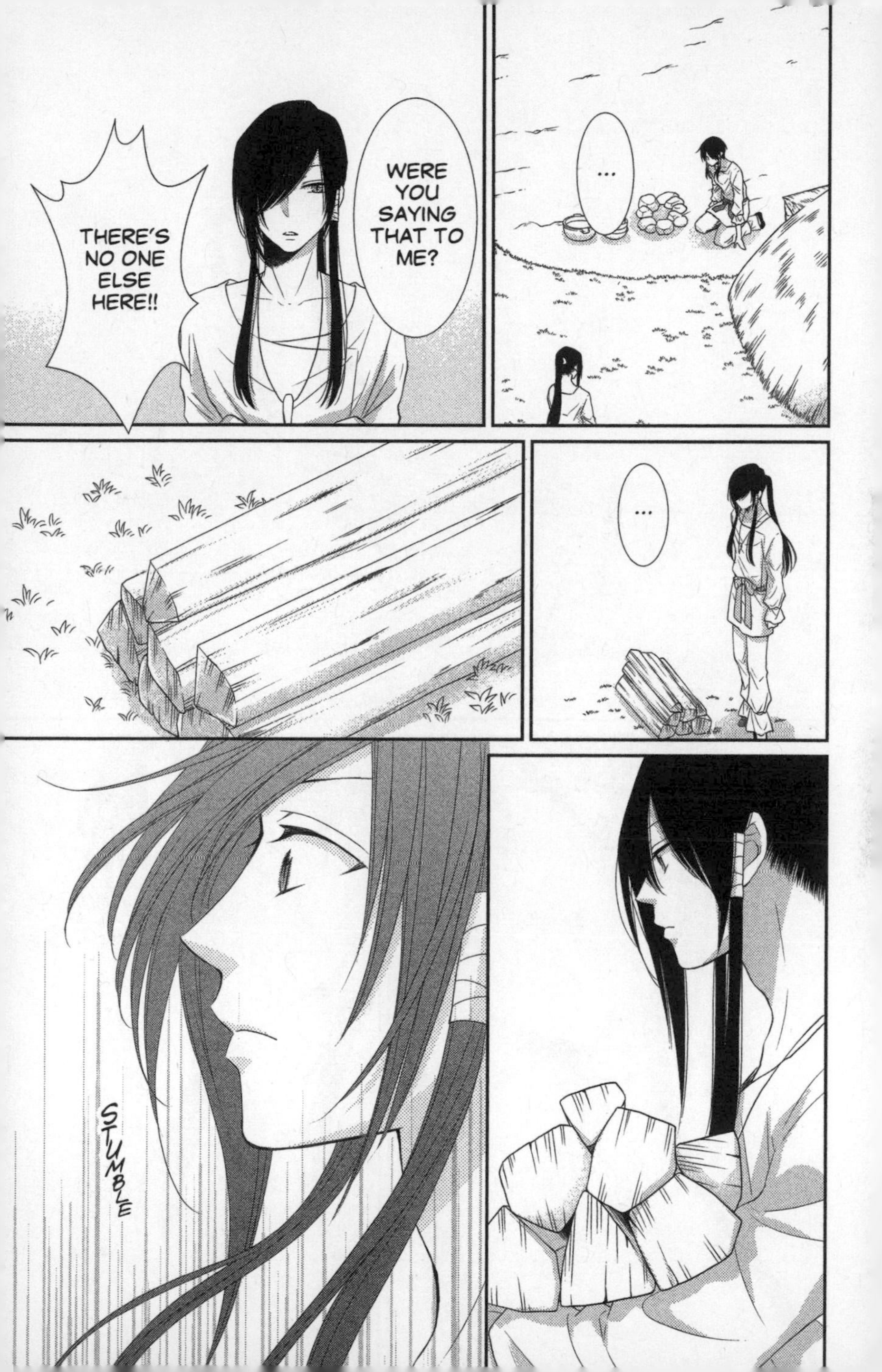
...
WERE YOU SAYING THAT TO ME?
THERE'S NO ONE ELSE HERE!!
...
STUMBLE

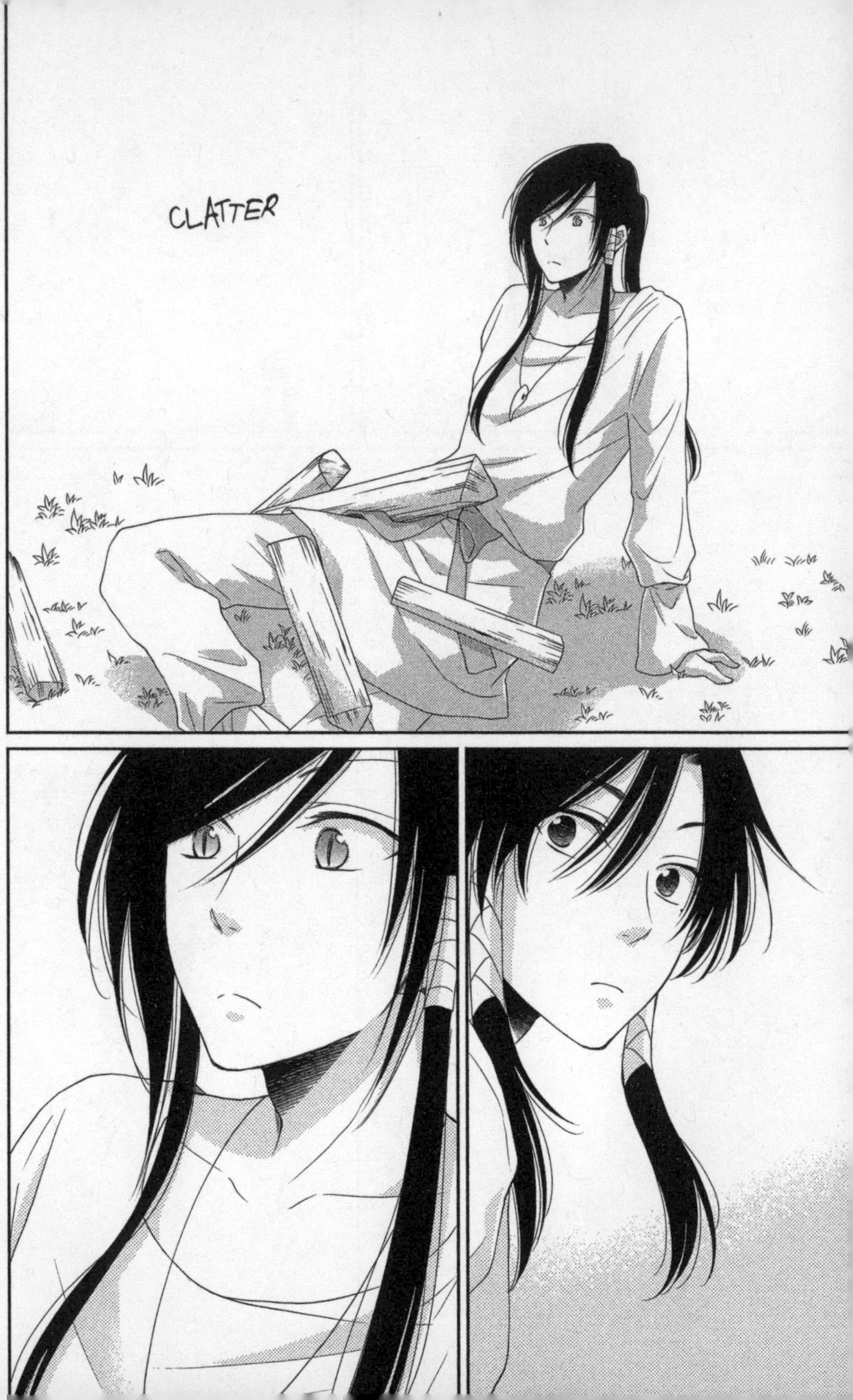
CLATTER

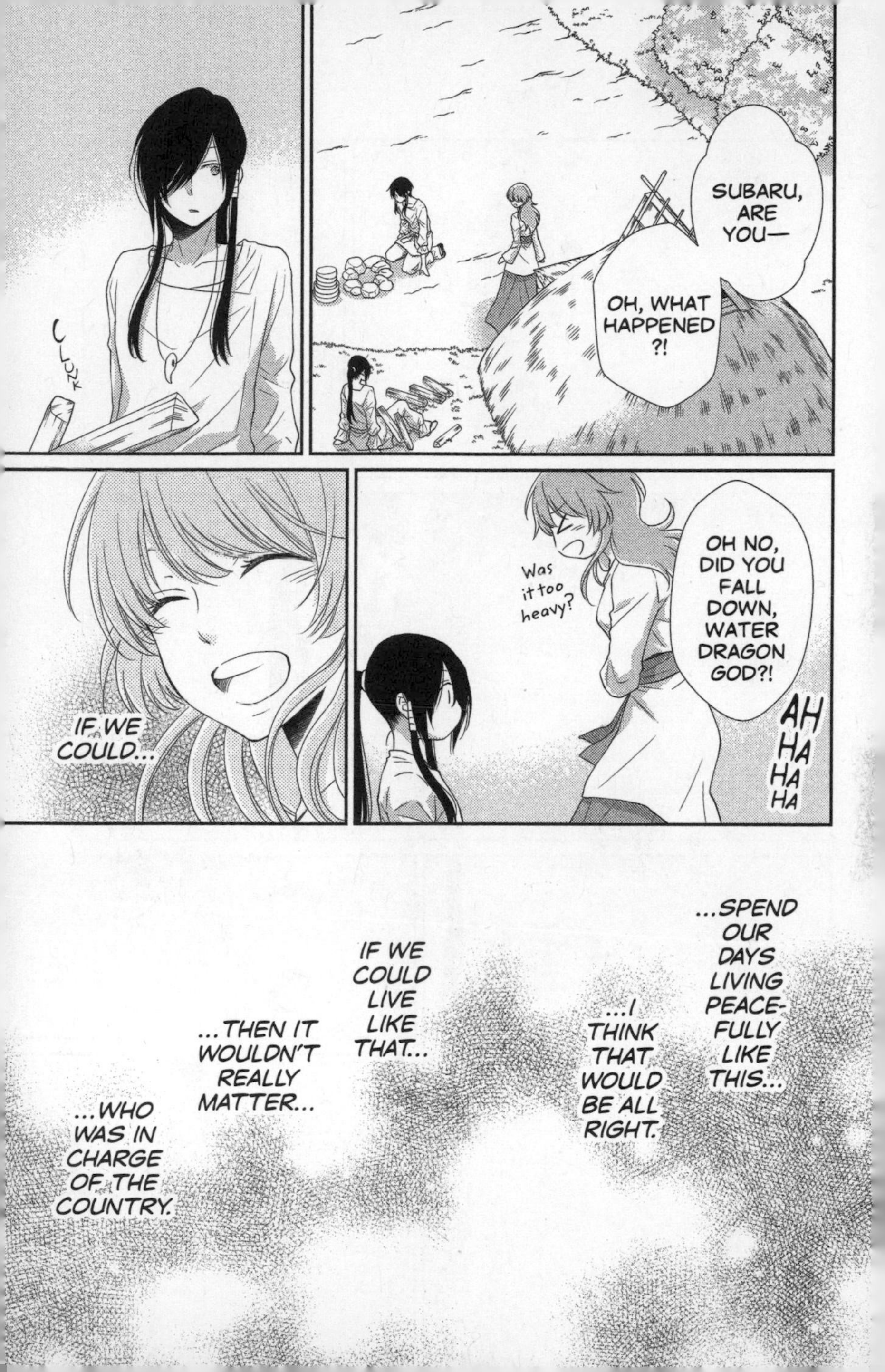
SUBARU, ARE YOU—
OH, WHAT HAPPENED?!
CLUNK
OH NO, DID YOU FALL DOWN, WATER DRAGON GOD?!
Was it too heavy?
AH HA HA HA
IF WE COULD...
...SPEND OUR DAYS LIVING PEACE-FULLY LIKE THIS...
...I THINK THAT WOULD BE ALL RIGHT.
IF WE COULD LIVE LIKE THAT...
...THEN IT WOULDN'T REALLY MATTER...
...WHO WAS IN CHARGE OF THE COUNTRY.

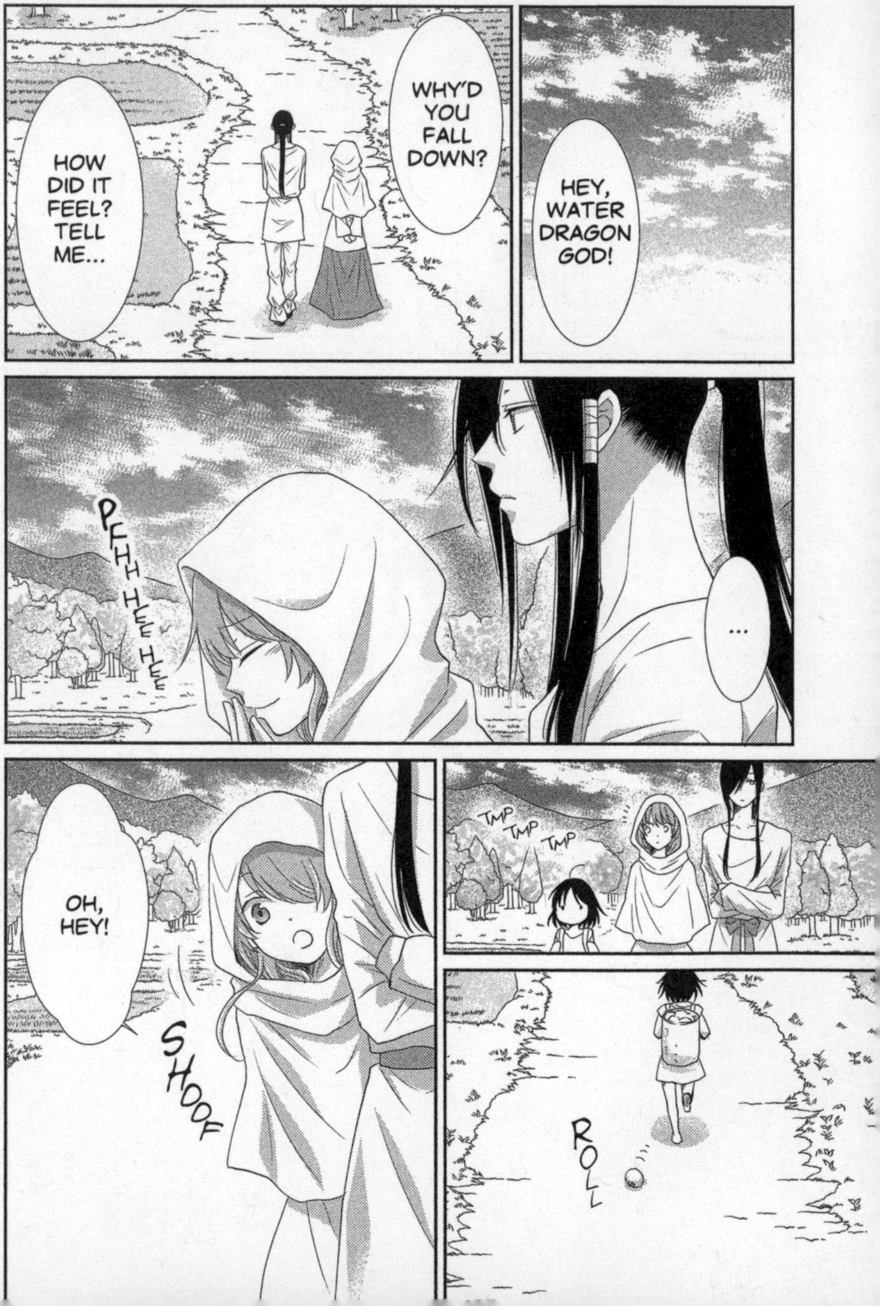
HEY, WATER DRAGON GOD!
WHY'D YOU FALL DOWN?
HOW DID IT FEEL? TELL ME...
...
PFHH HEE HEE
TMP TMP TMP
ROLL
OH, HEY!
SHOOF

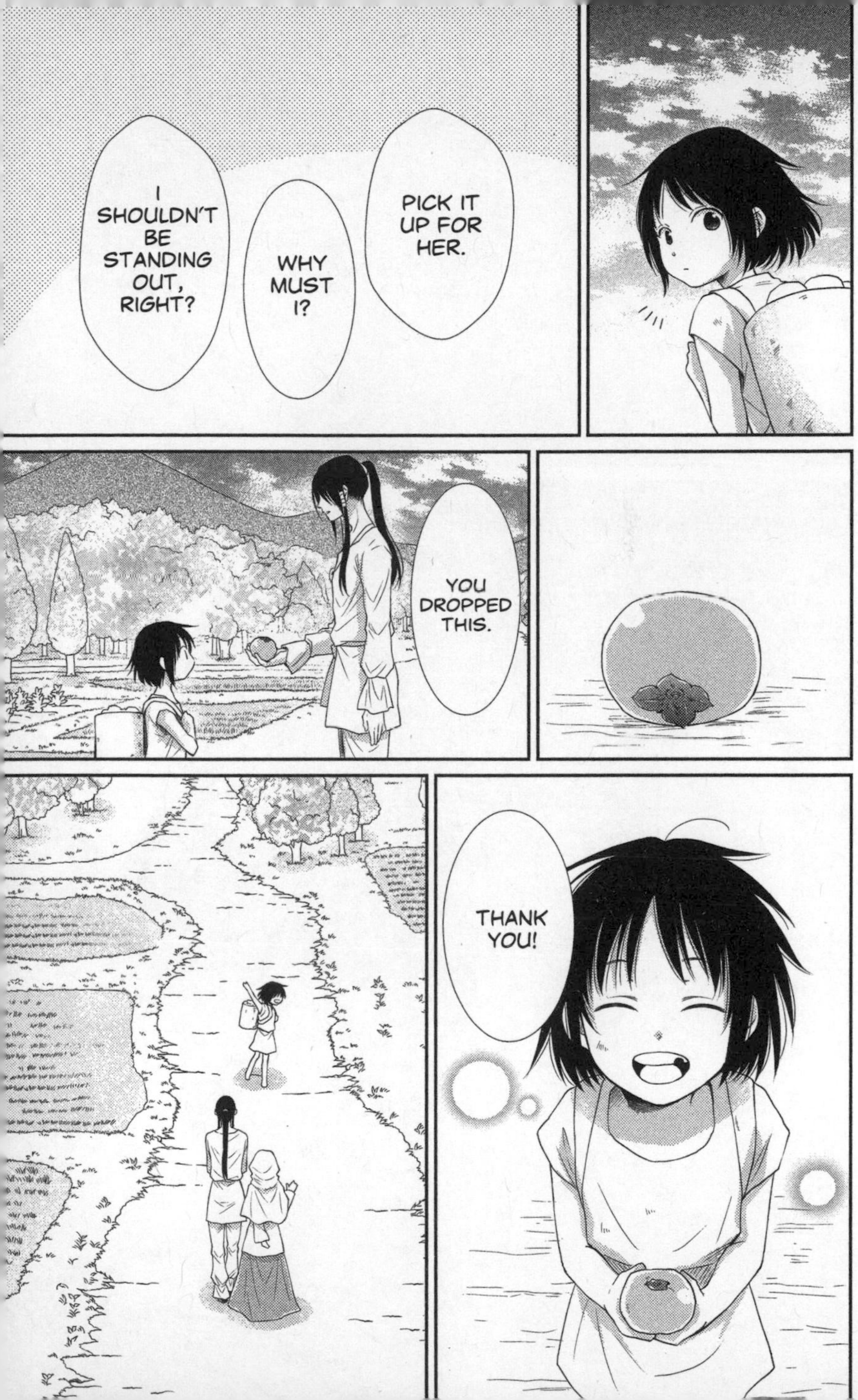
PICK IT UP FOR HER.
WHY MUST I?
I SHOULDN'T BE STANDING OUT, RIGHT?
YOU DROPPED THIS.
THANK YOU!

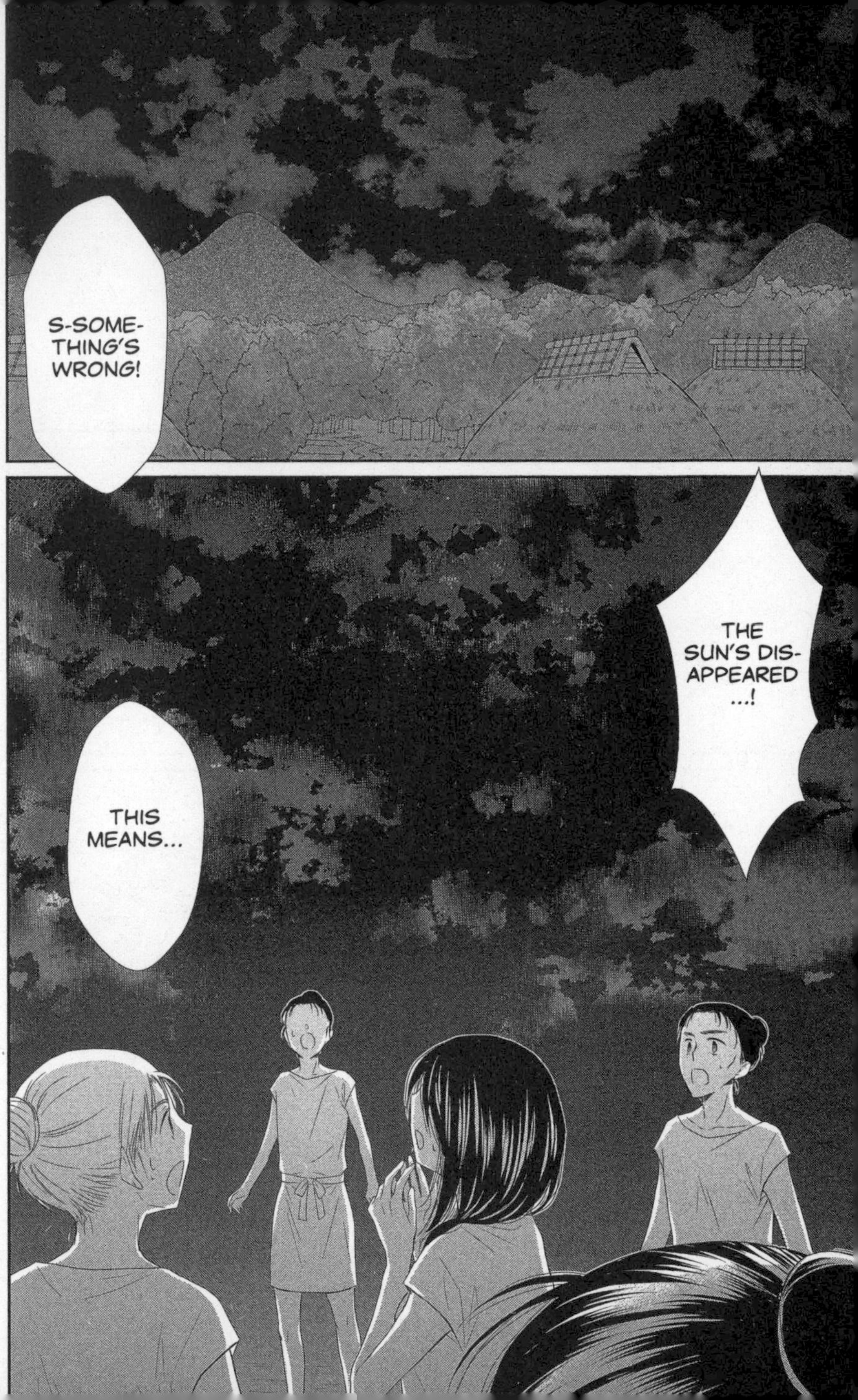
S-SOME-
THING'S
WRONG!
THE SUN'S DIS-
APPEARED
...!
THIS
MEANS...

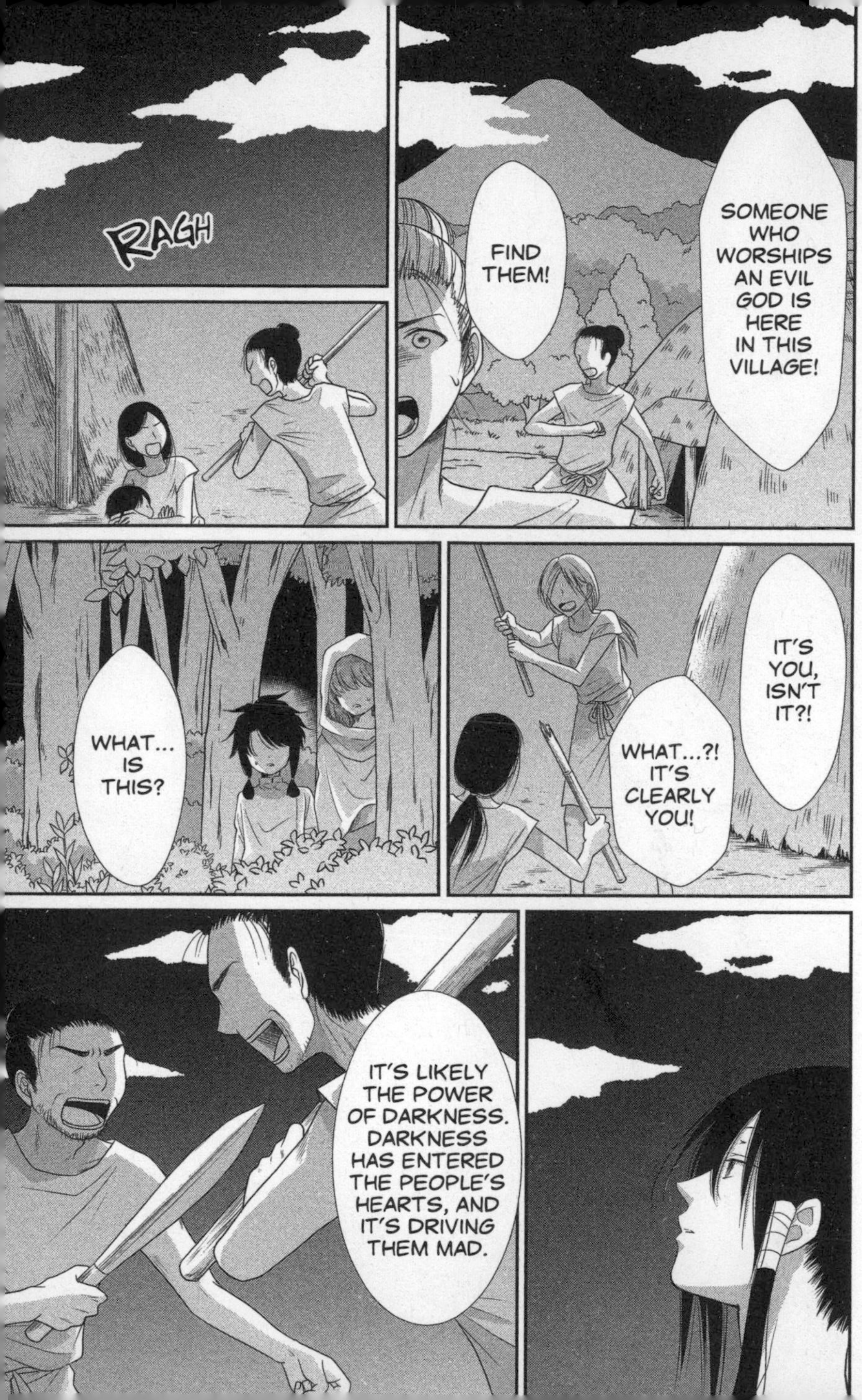
SOMEONE WHO WORSHIPS AN EVIL GOD IS HERE IN THIS VILLAGE!
FIND THEM!
RAGH
IT'S YOU, ISN'T IT?!
WHAT...?! IT'S CLEARLY YOU!
WHAT... IS THIS?
IT'S LIKELY THE POWER OF DARKNESS. DARKNESS HAS ENTERED THE PEOPLE'S HEARTS, AND IT'S DRIVING THEM MAD.

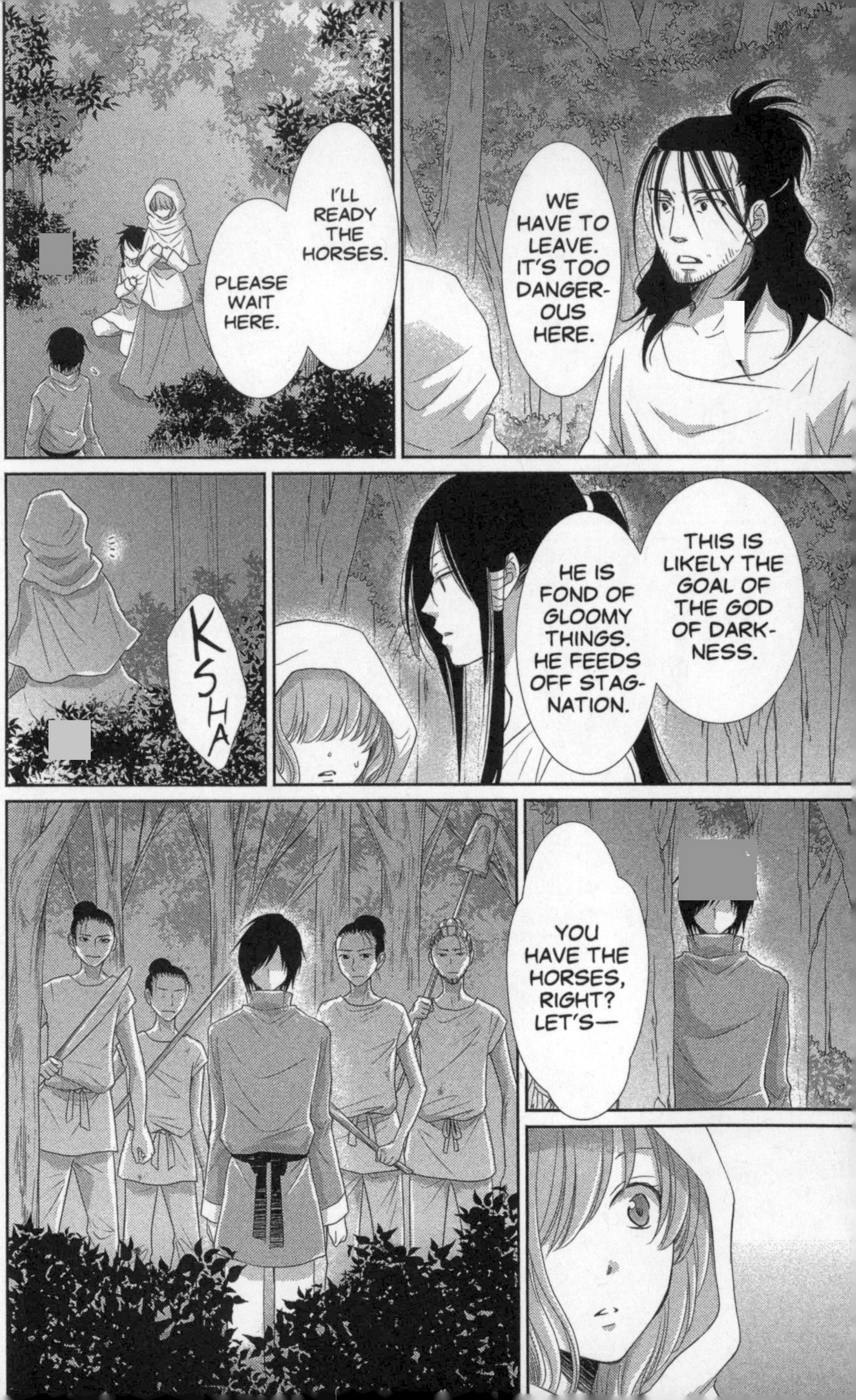
WE HAVE TO LEAVE. IT'S TOO DANGER-OUS HERE.
I'LL READY THE HORSES.
PLEASE WAIT HERE.
THIS IS LIKELY THE GOAL OF THE GOD OF DARK-NESS.
HE IS FOND OF GLOOMY THINGS. HE FEEDS OFF STAG-NATION.
KSHA
YOU HAVE THE HORSES, RIGHT? LET'S—

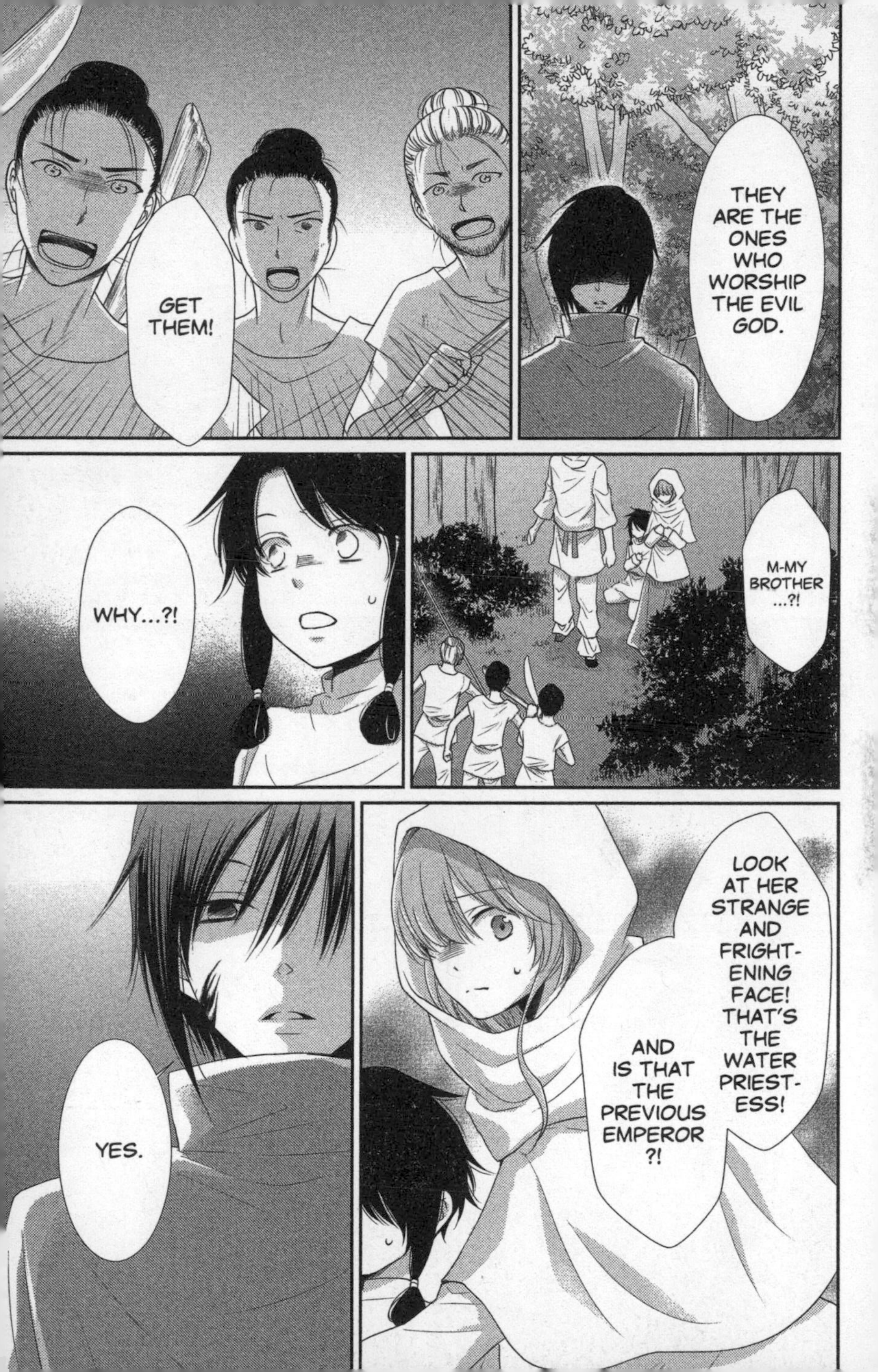
THEY ARE THE ONES WHO WORSHIP THE EVIL GOD.
GET THEM!
M-MY BROTHER ...?!
WHY...?!
LOOK AT HER STRANGE AND FRIGHT-ENING FACE! THAT'S THE WATER PRIEST-ESS!
AND IS THAT THE PREVIOUS EMPEROR ?!
YES.

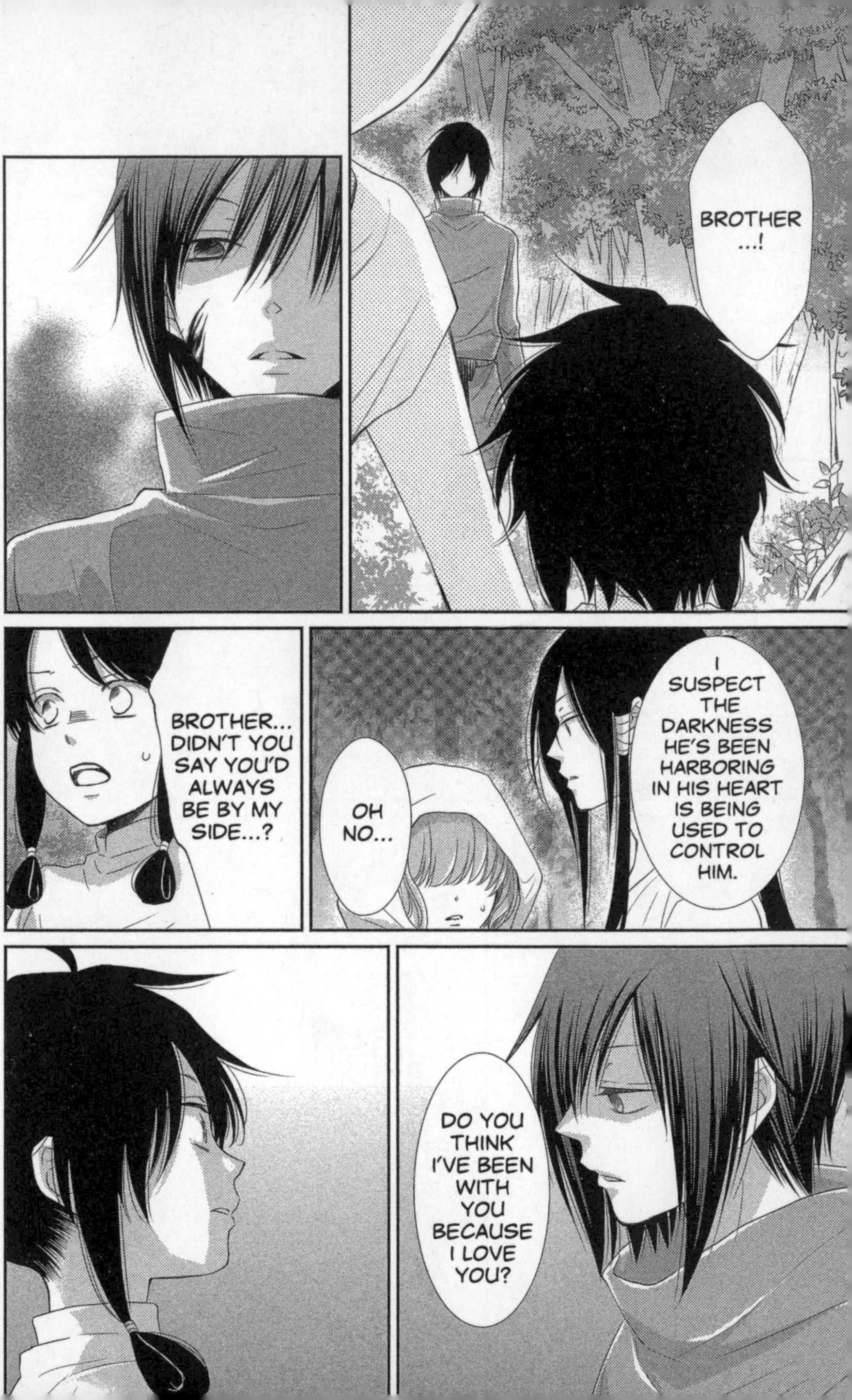
BROTHER ...!
I SUSPECT THE DARKNESS HE'S BEEN HARBORING IN HIS HEART IS BEING USED TO CONTROL HIM.
OH NO...
BROTHER... DIDN'T YOU SAY YOU'D ALWAYS BE BY MY SIDE...?
DO YOU THINK I'VE BEEN WITH YOU BECAUSE I LOVE YOU?

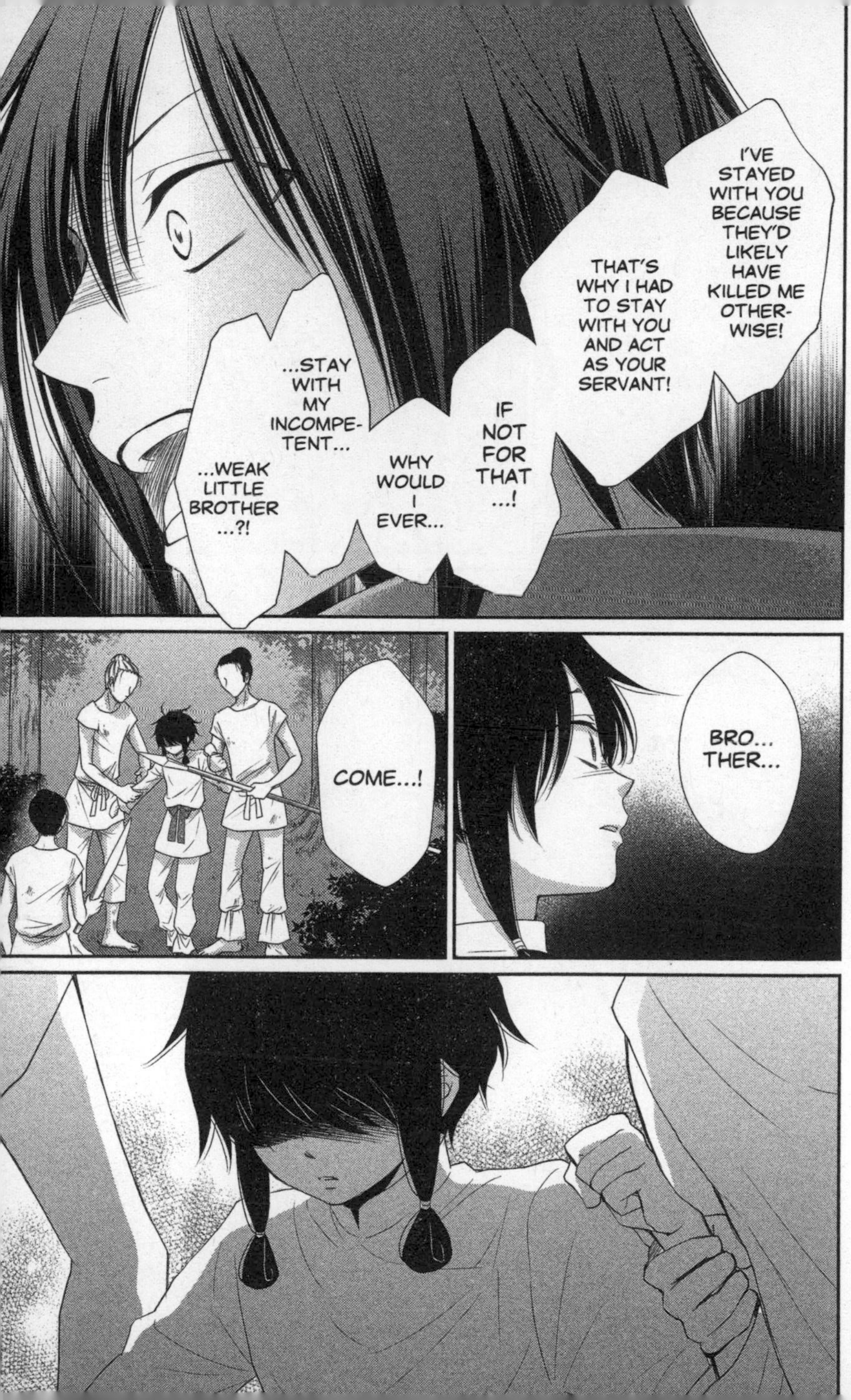
I'VE STAYED WITH YOU BECAUSE THEY'D LIKELY HAVE KILLED ME OTHER-WISE!
THAT'S WHY I HAD TO STAY WITH YOU AND ACT AS YOUR SERVANT!
IF NOT FOR THAT ...!
WHY WOULD I EVER...
...STAY WITH MY INCOMPE-TENT...
...WEAK LITTLE BROTHER ...?!
BRO... THER...
COME...!

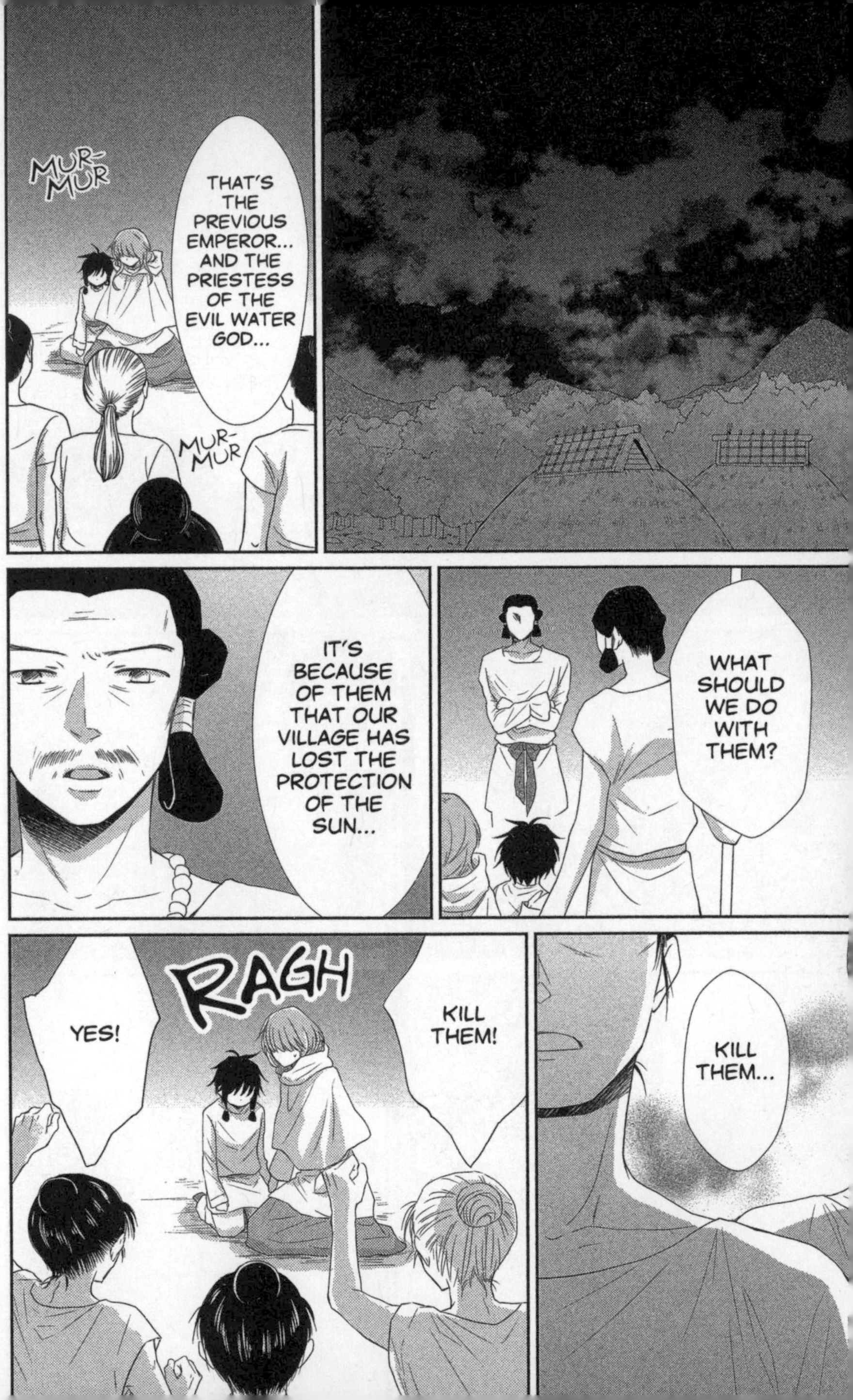
THAT'S THE PREVIOUS EMPEROR... AND THE PRIESTESS OF THE EVIL WATER GOD...
MUR-MUR
MUR-MUR
WHAT SHOULD WE DO WITH THEM?
IT'S BECAUSE OF THEM THAT OUR VILLAGE HAS LOST THE PROTECTION OF THE SUN...
KILL THEM...
KILL THEM!
RAGH
YES!

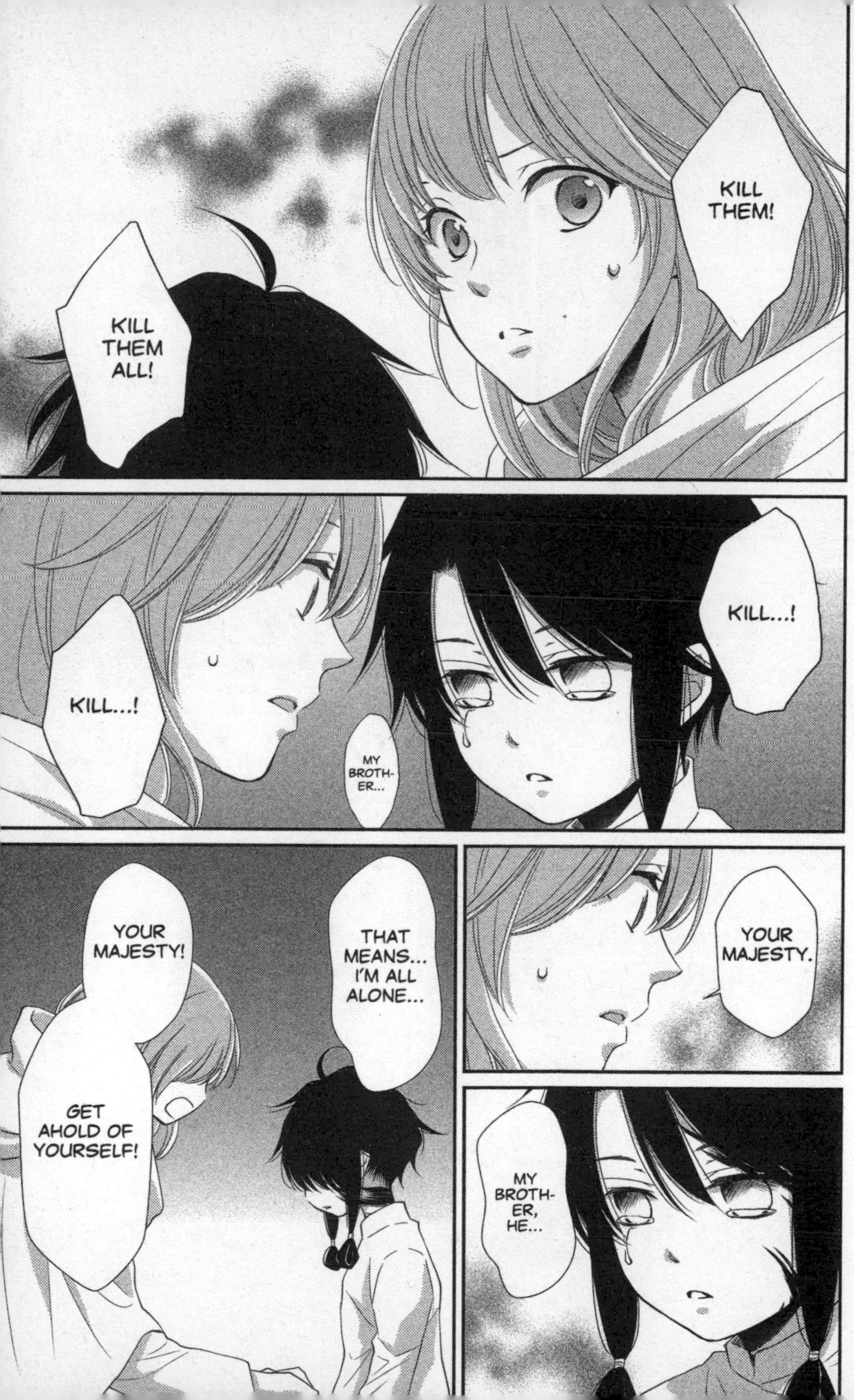
KILL THEM!
KILL THEM ALL!
KILL...!
MY BROTH-ER...
KILL...!
YOUR MAJESTY.
MY BROTH-ER, HE...
THAT MEANS... I'M ALL ALONE...
YOUR MAJESTY!
GET AHOLD OF YOURSELF!

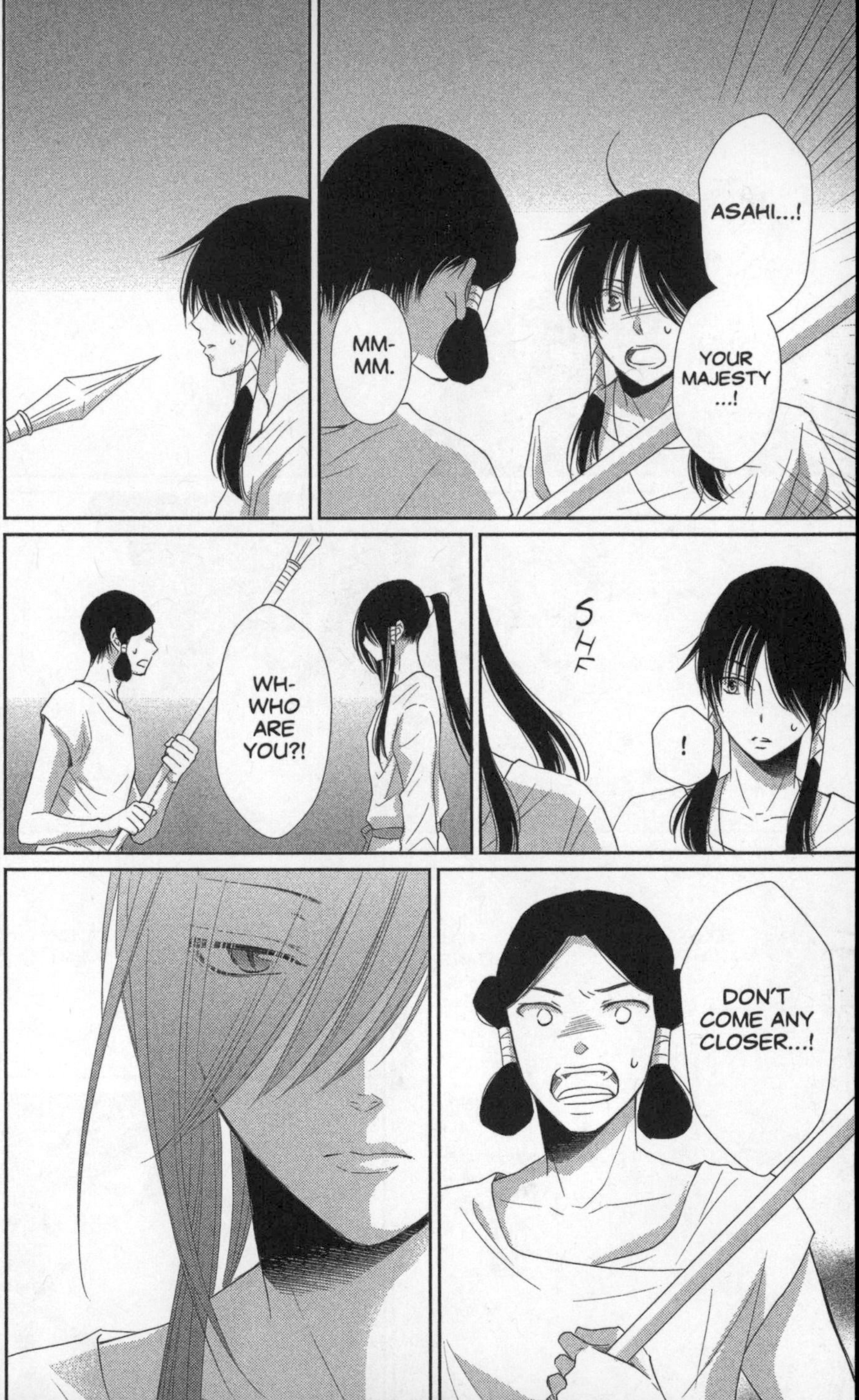
ASAHI...!
YOUR MAJESTY ...!
MM-MM.
SHF
!
WH-WHO ARE YOU?!
DON'T COME ANY CLOSER...!

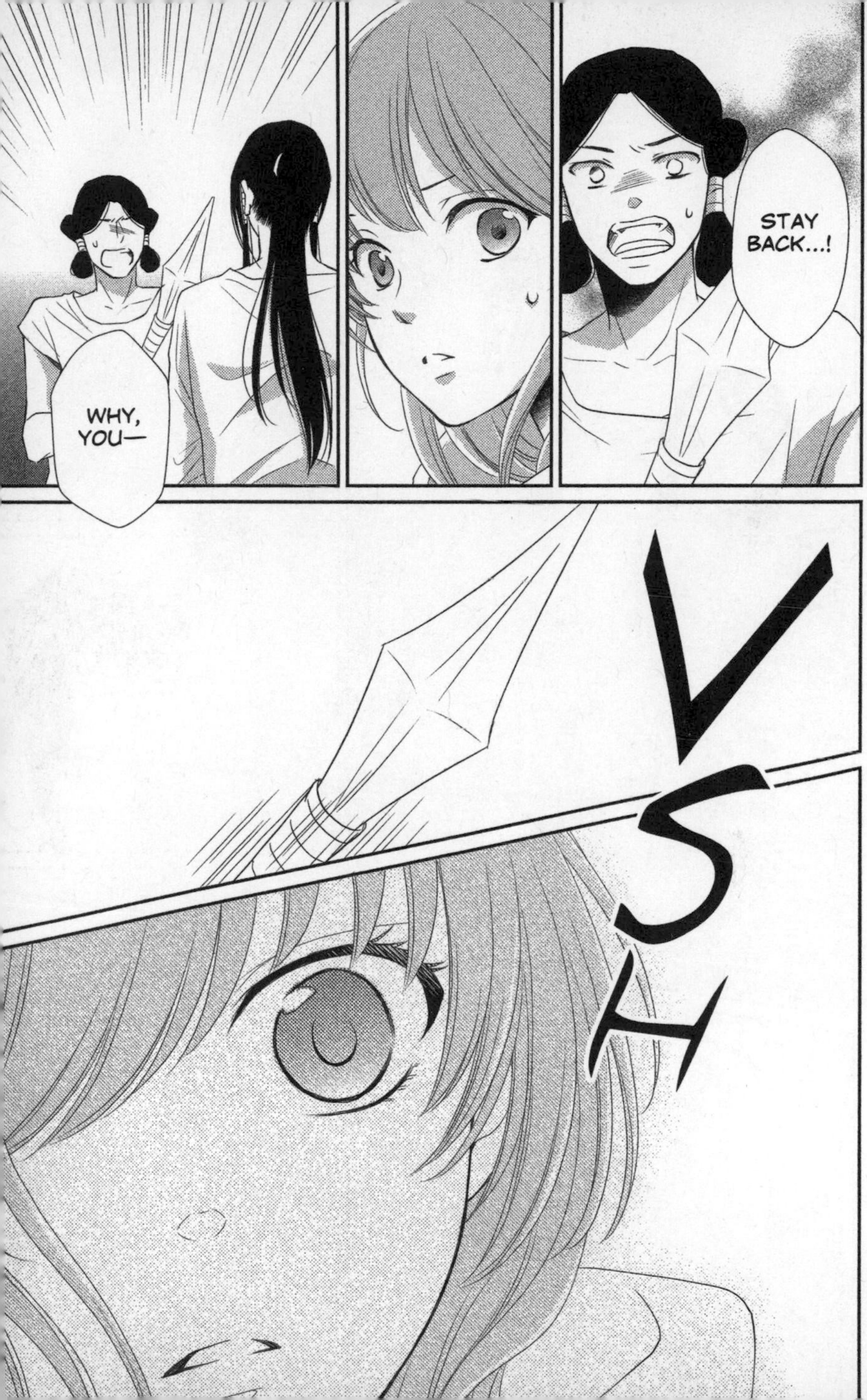
STAY BACK...!
WHY, YOU—
VSH

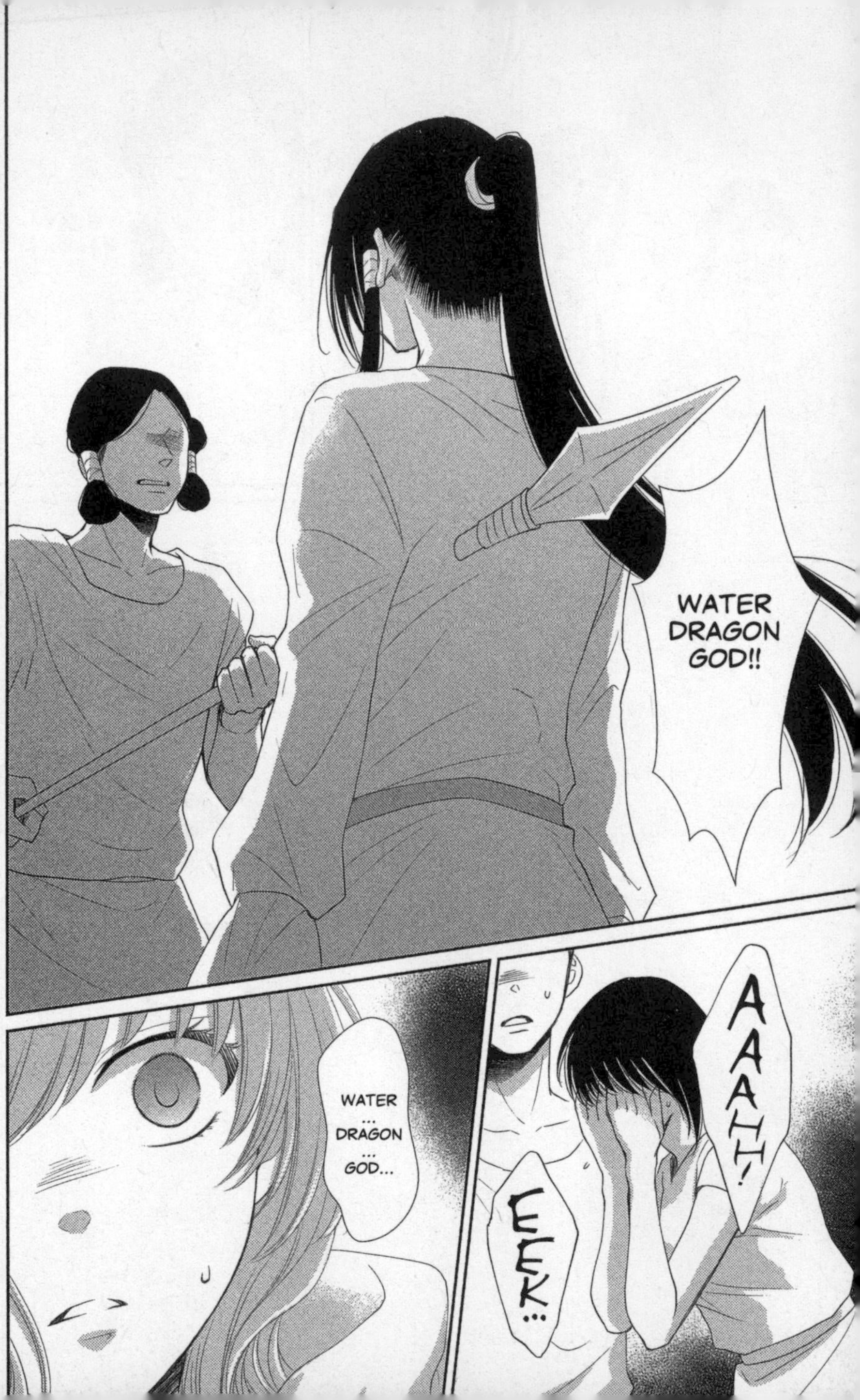
WATER DRAGON GOD!!
AAAAH!
EEEK...
WATER ... DRAGON ... GOD...

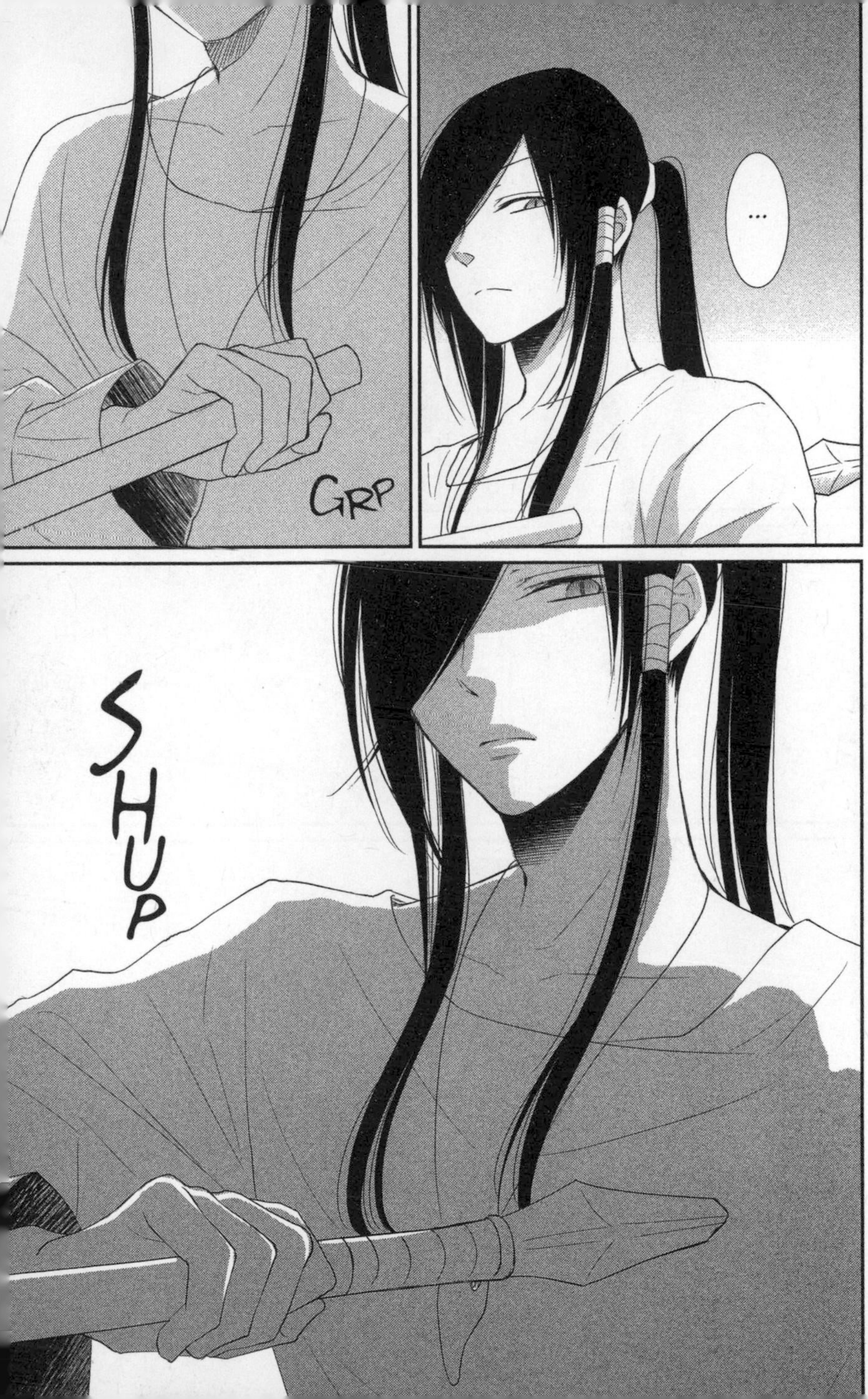
...
GRP
SHUP

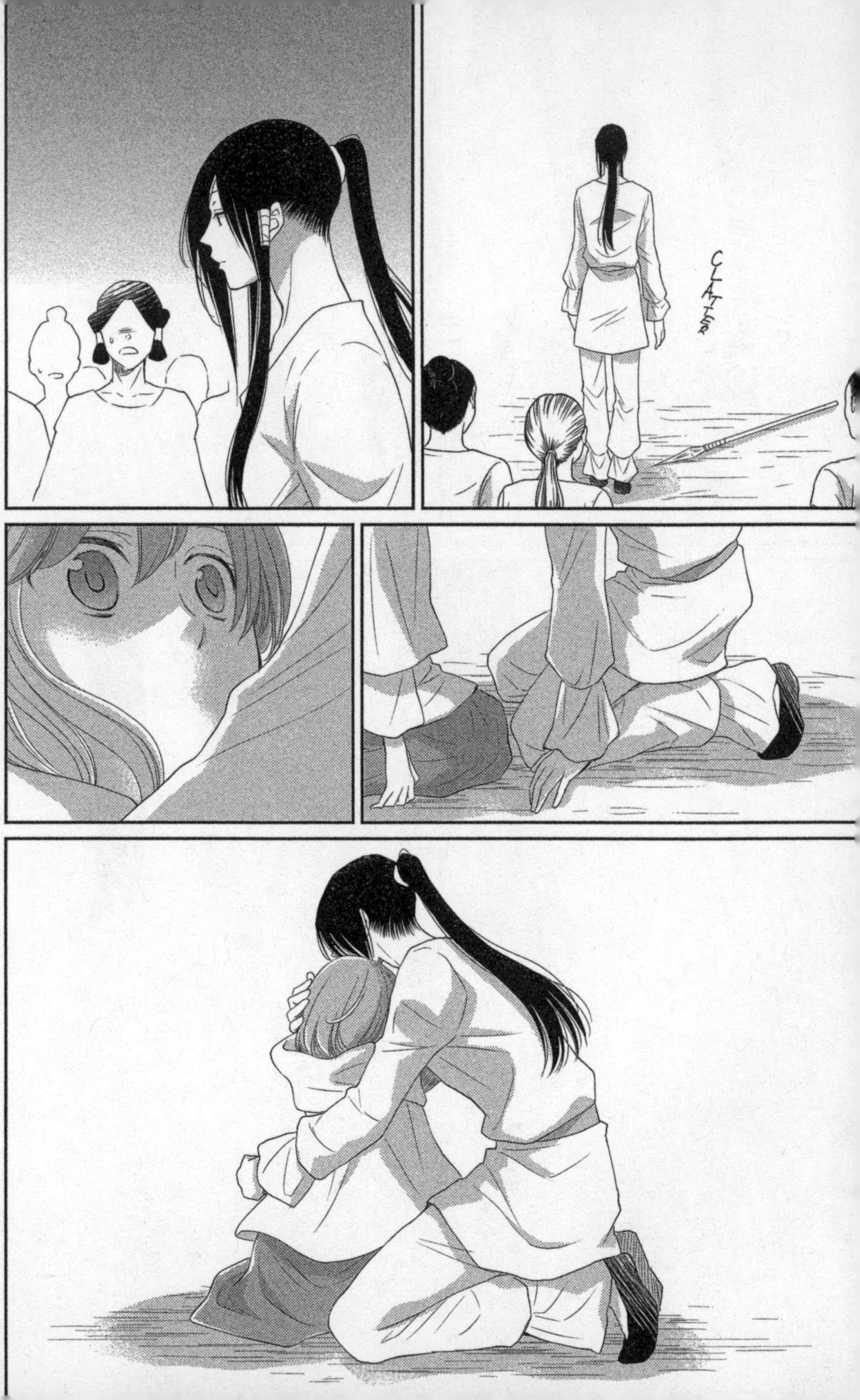
CLATTER

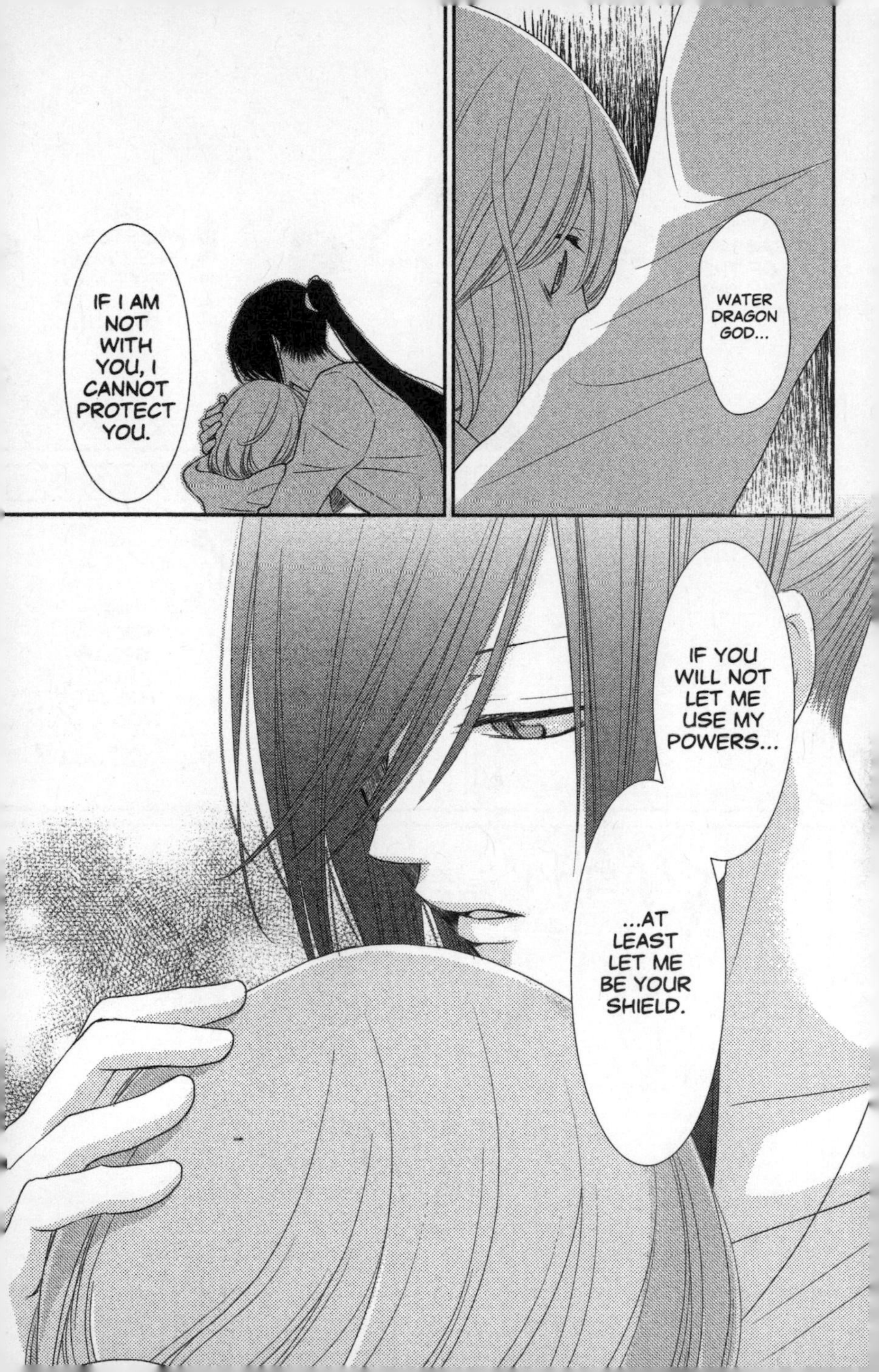
WATER DRAGON GOD...
IF I AM NOT WITH YOU, I CANNOT PROTECT YOU.
IF YOU WILL NOT LET ME USE MY POWERS...
...AT LEAST LET ME BE YOUR SHIELD.

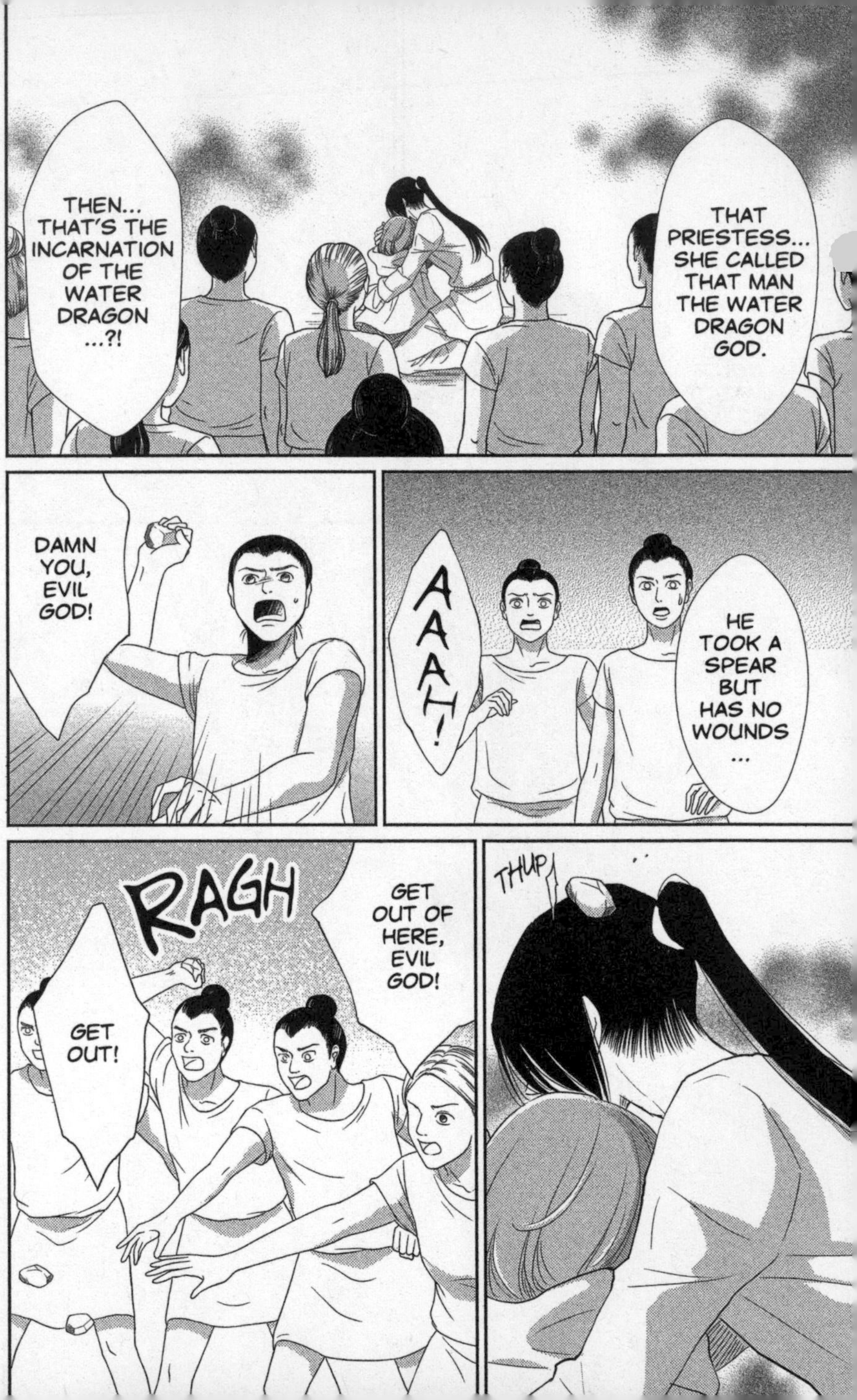
THAT PRIESTESS... SHE CALLED THAT MAN THE WATER DRAGON GOD.
THEN... THAT'S THE INCARNATION OF THE WATER DRAGON ...?!
HE TOOK A SPEAR BUT HAS NO WOUNDS ...
AAAH!
DAMN YOU, EVIL GOD!
THUP
GET OUT OF HERE, EVIL GOD!
RAGH
GET OUT!

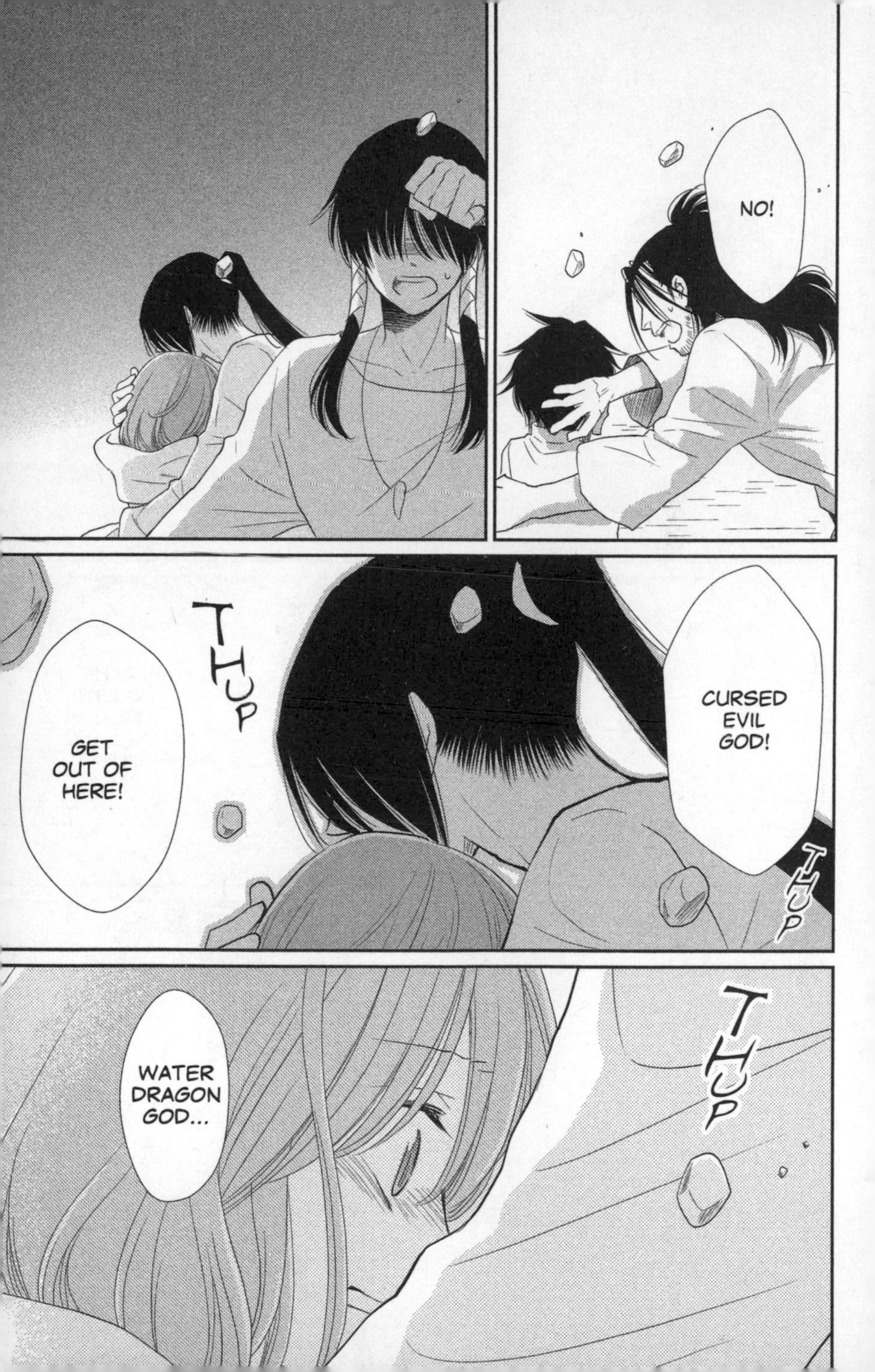
NO!
CURSED EVIL GOD!
THUP
THUP
GET OUT OF HERE!
THUP
WATER DRAGON GOD...

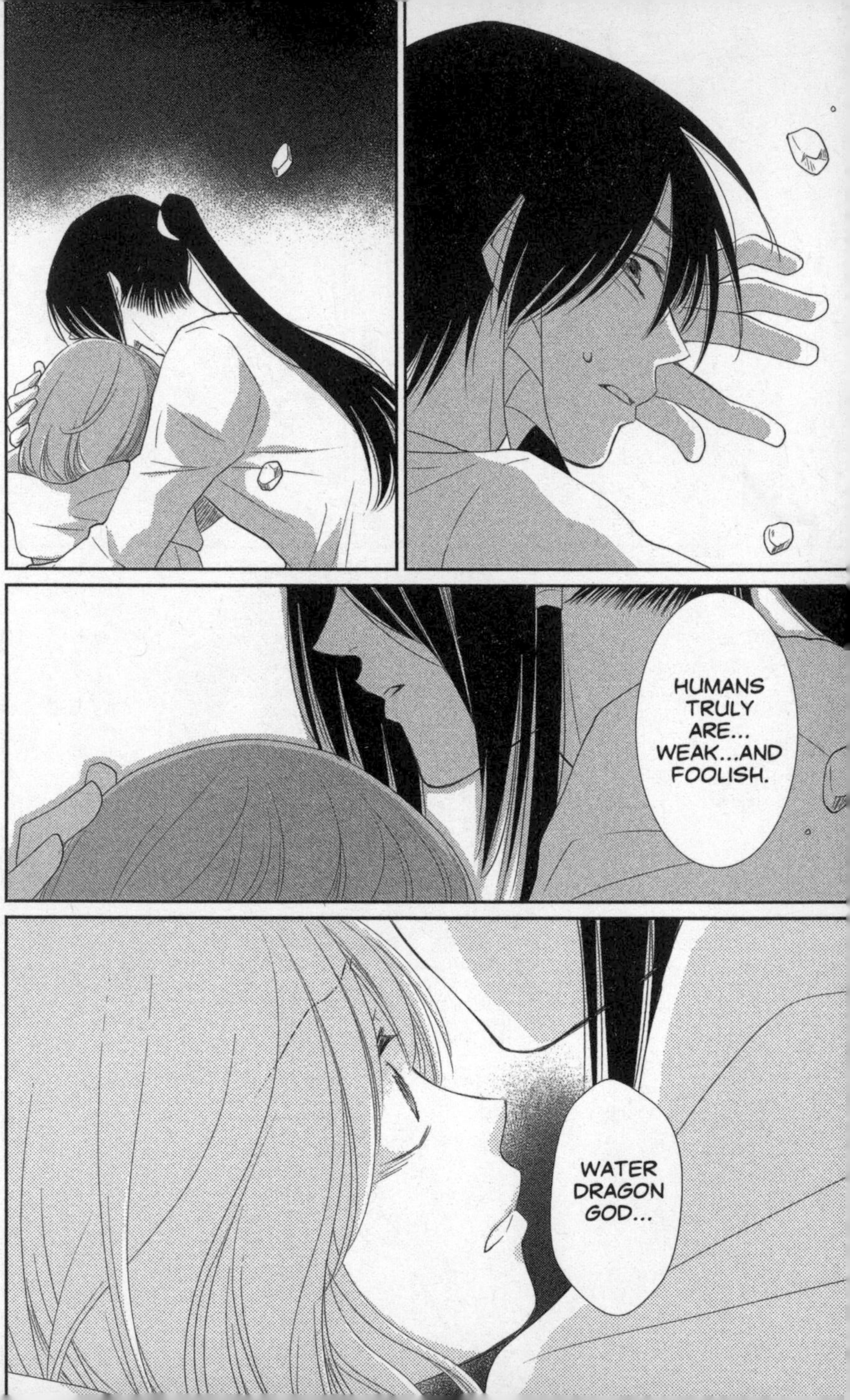
HUMANS TRULY ARE... WEAK...AND FOOLISH.
WATER DRAGON GOD...

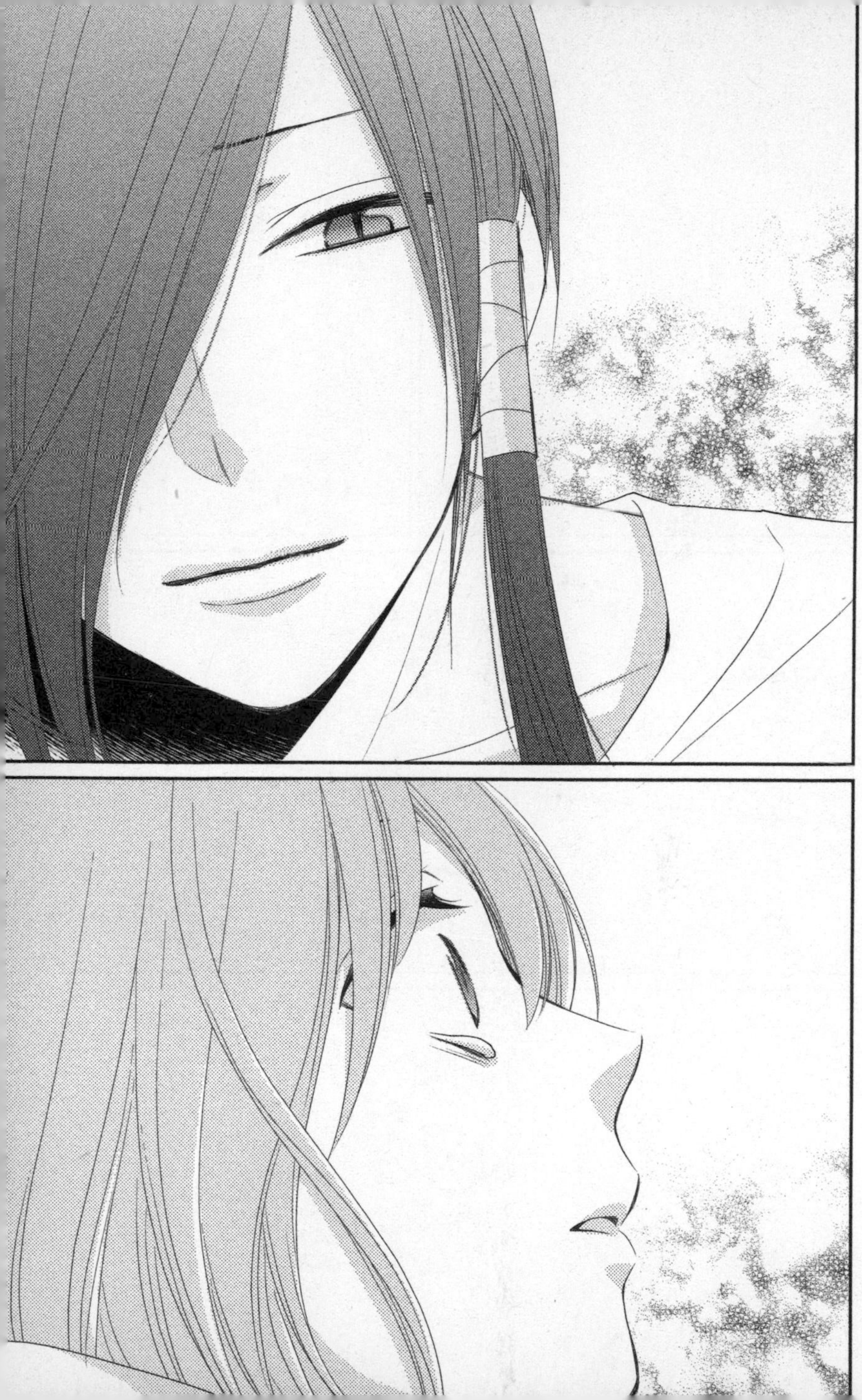

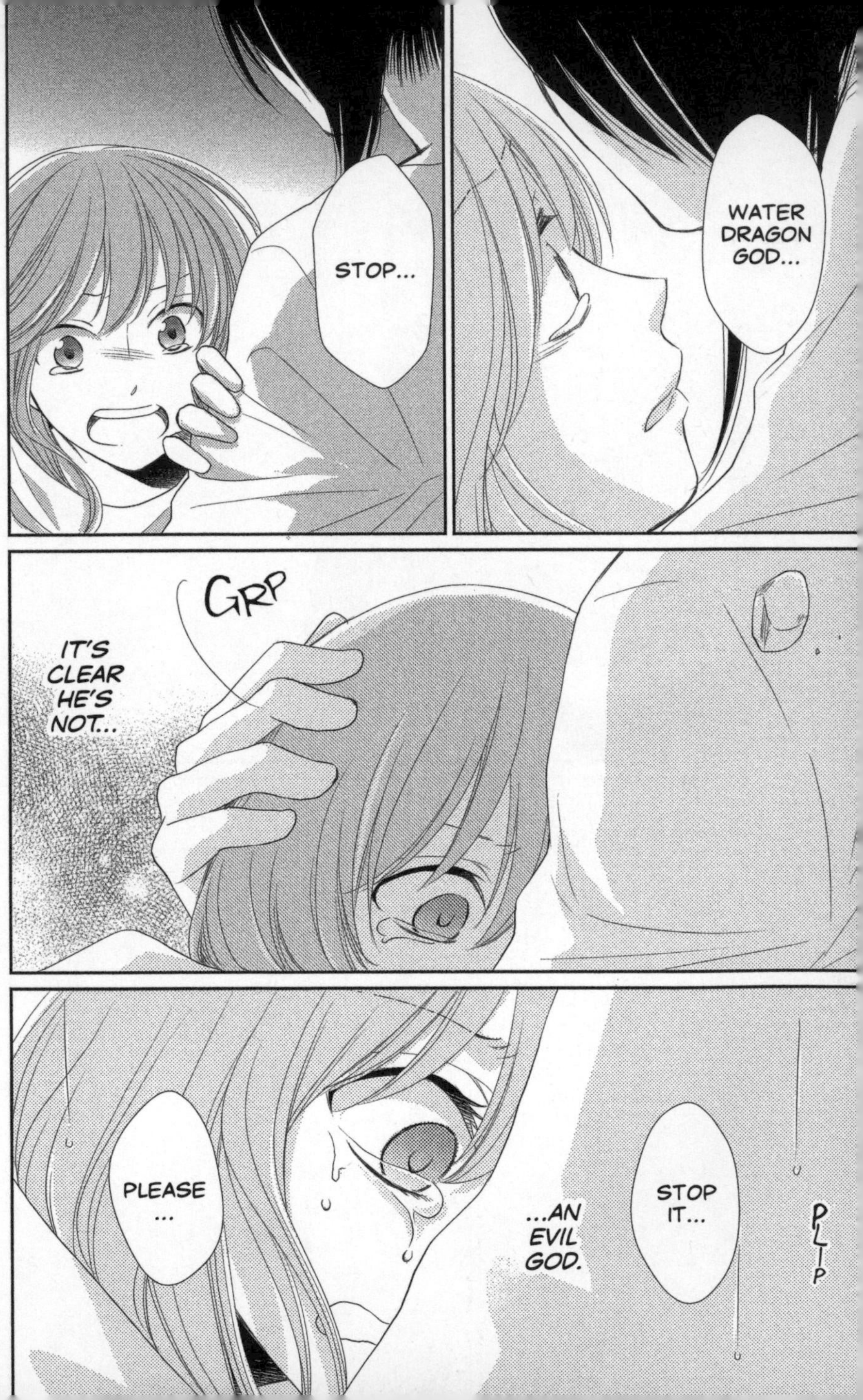
WATER DRAGON GOD...
STOP...
GRP
IT'S CLEAR HE'S NOT...
PLIP
STOP IT...
...AN EVIL GOD.
PLEASE ...

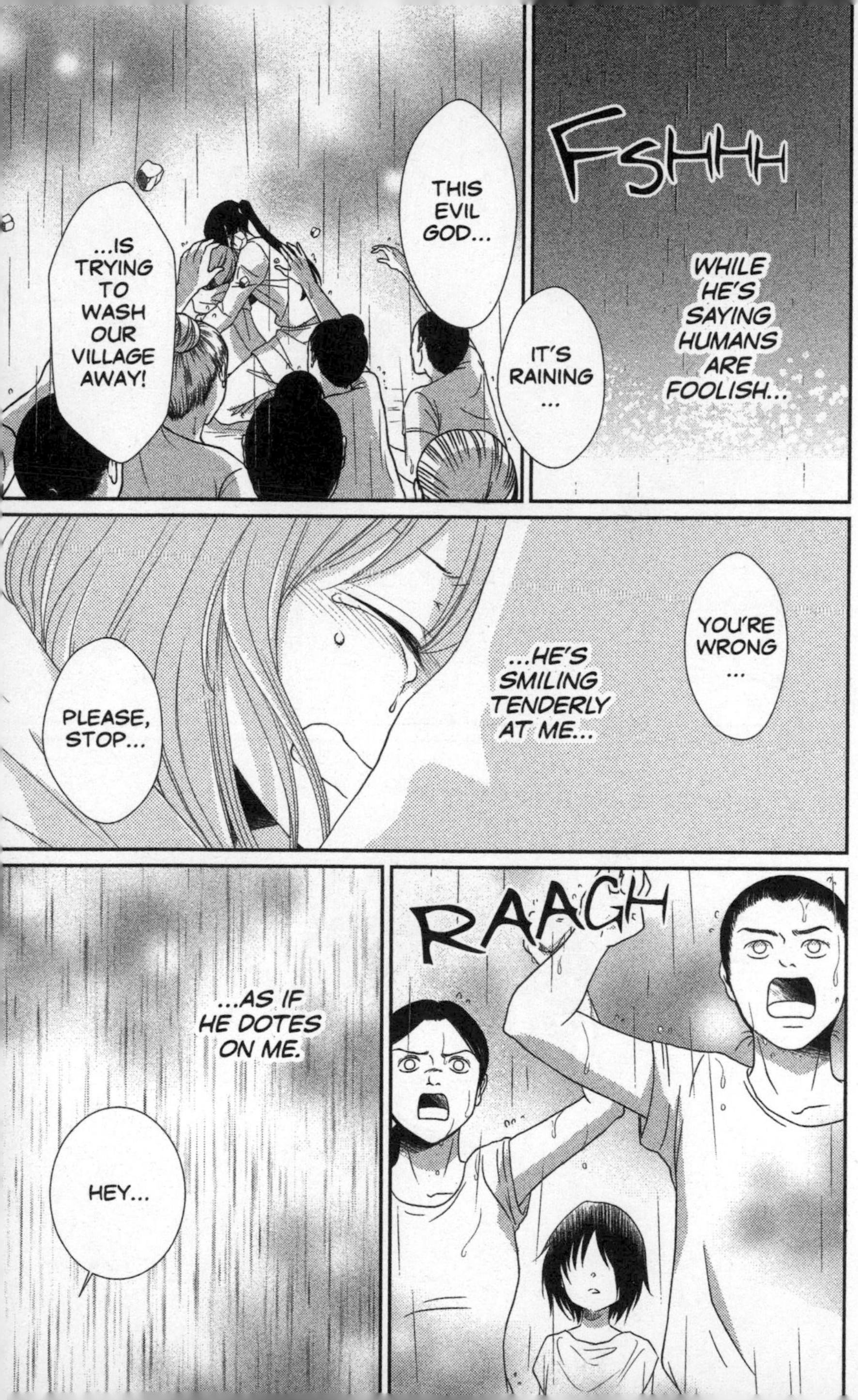
FSHHH
WHILE HE'S SAYING HUMANS ARE FOOLISH...
IT'S RAINING...
THIS EVIL GOD...
...IS TRYING TO WASH OUR VILLAGE AWAY!
YOU'RE WRONG...
...HE'S SMILING TENDERLY AT ME...
PLEASE, STOP...
RAAGH
...AS IF HE DOTES ON ME.
HEY...

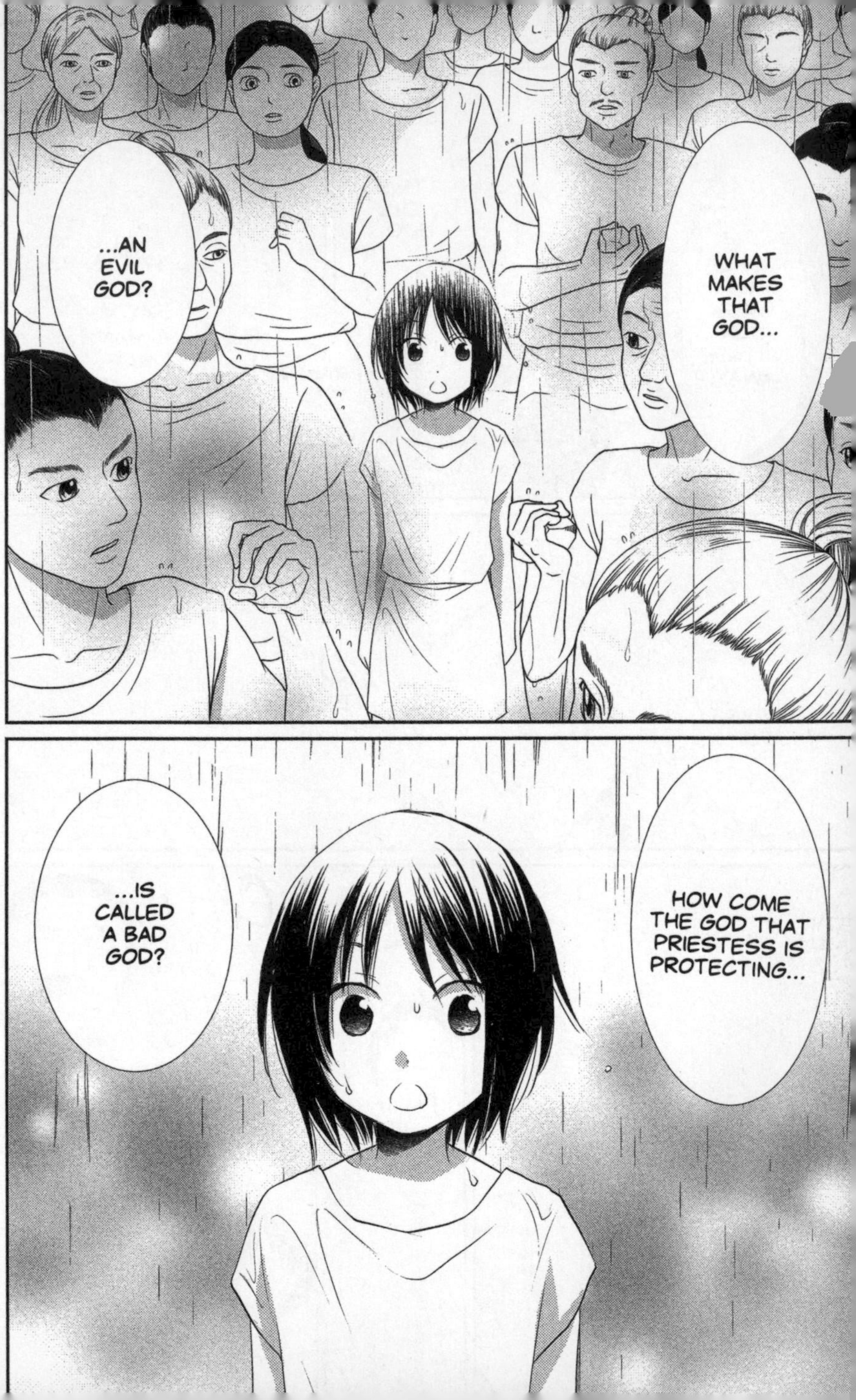
WHAT MAKES THAT GOD...
...AN EVIL GOD?
HOW COME THE GOD THAT PRIESTESS IS PROTECTING...
...IS CALLED A BAD GOD?

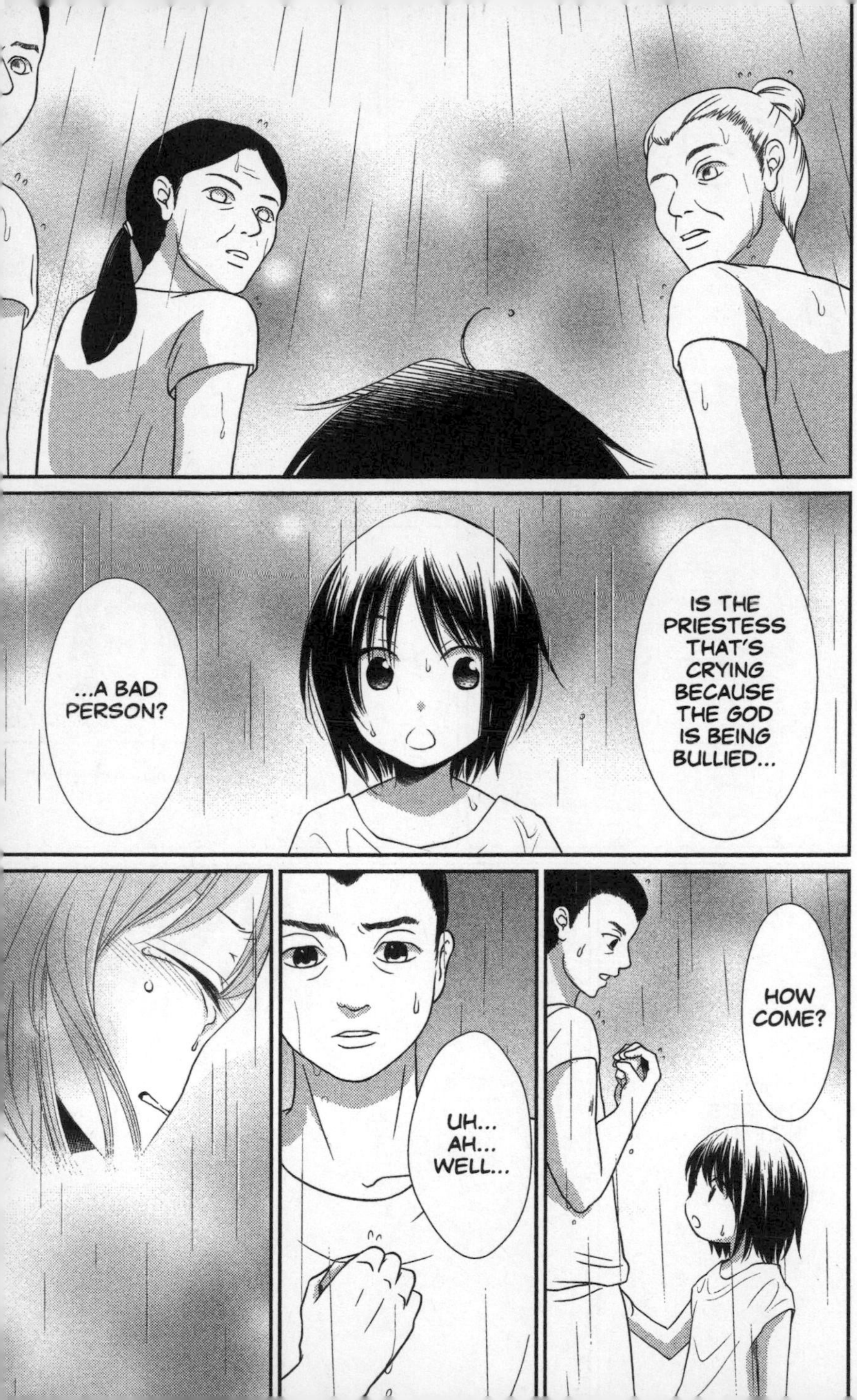
IS THE PRIESTESS THAT'S CRYING BECAUSE THE GOD IS BEING BULLIED...
...A BAD PERSON?
HOW COME?
UH... AH... WELL...

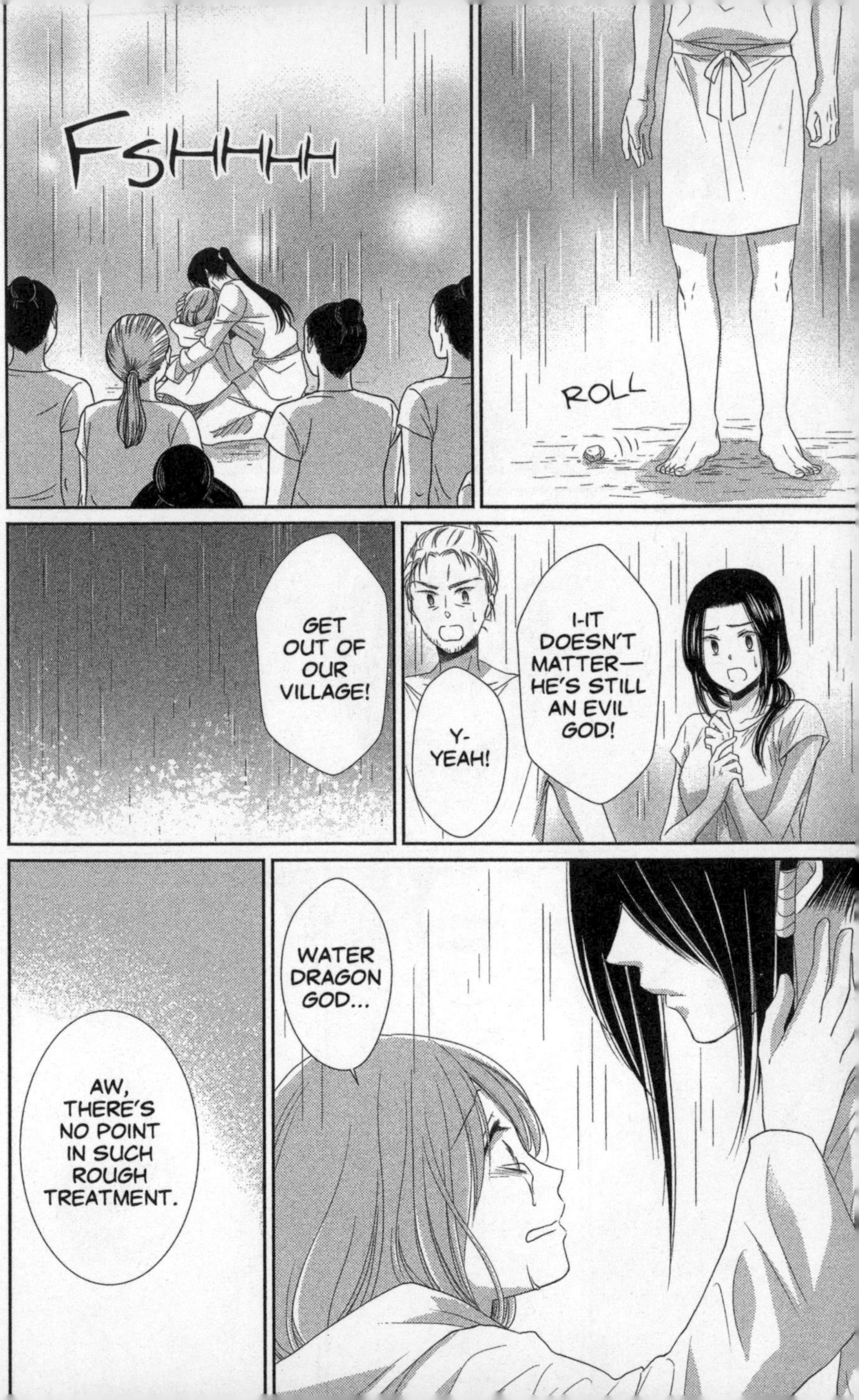
ROLL
FSHHHH
I-IT DOESN'T MATTER—HE'S STILL AN EVIL GOD!
Y-YEAH!
GET OUT OF OUR VILLAGE!
WATER DRAGON GOD...
AW, THERE'S NO POINT IN SUCH ROUGH TREATMENT.

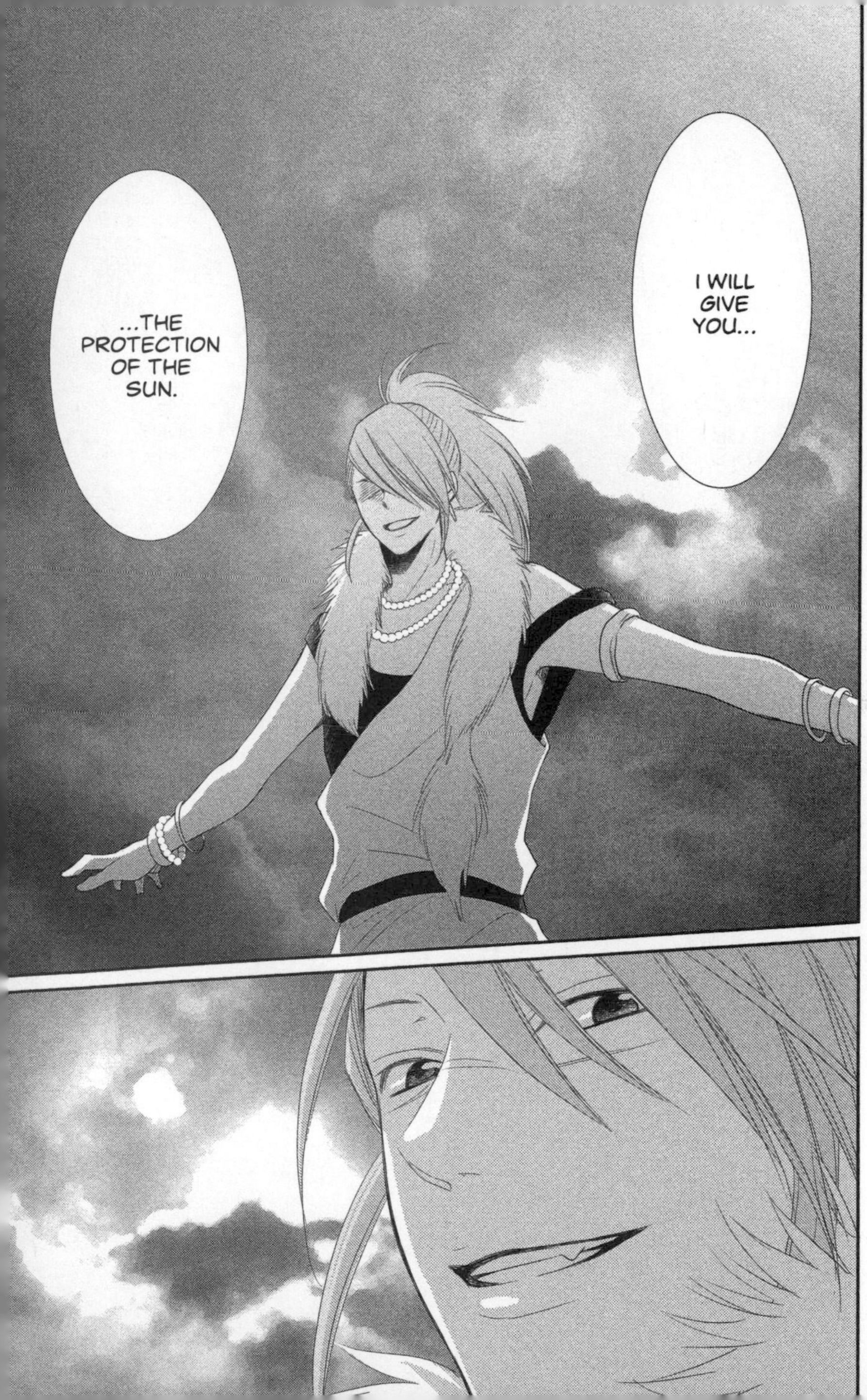
I WILL GIVE YOU...
...THE PROTECTION OF THE SUN.

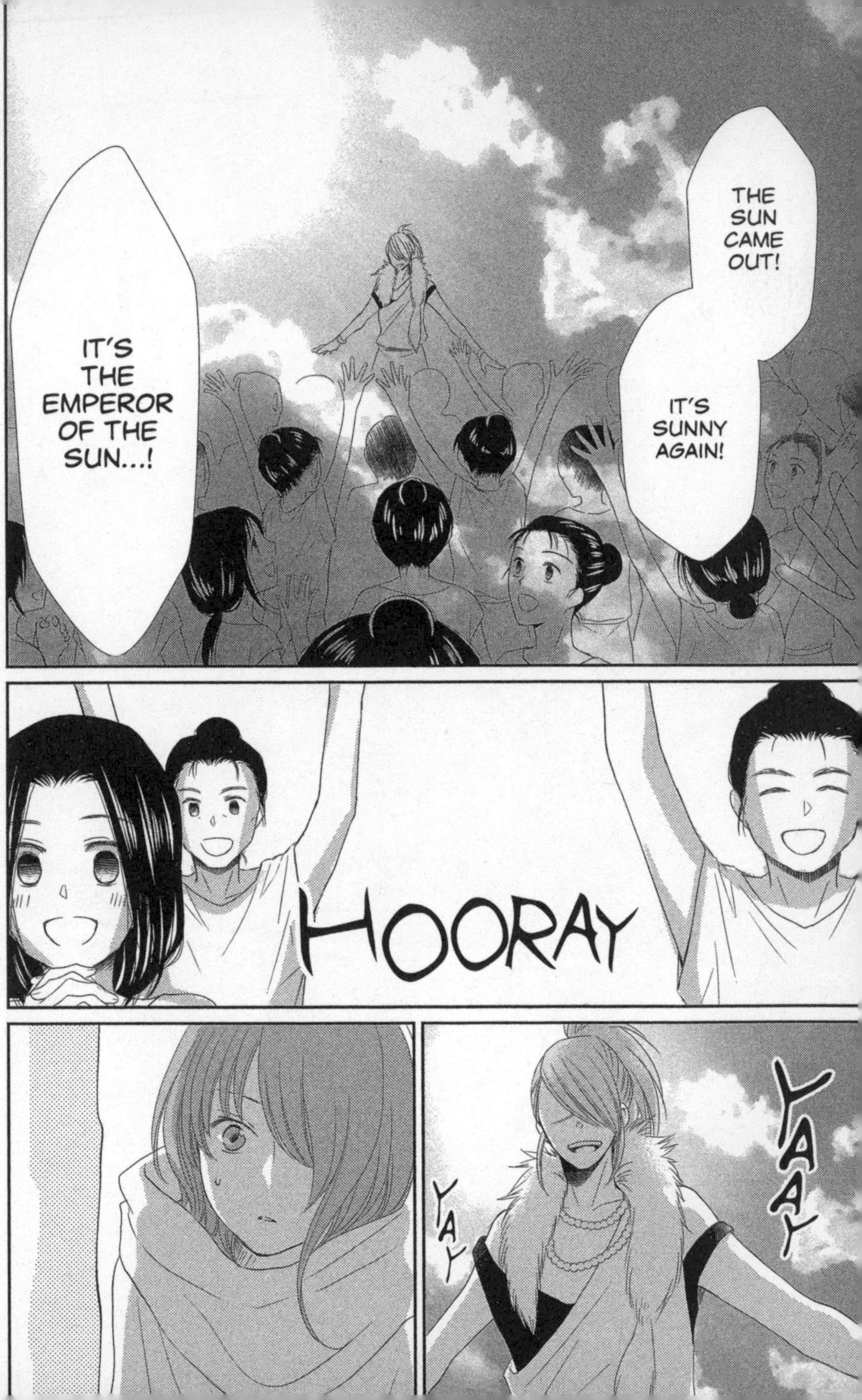
THE SUN CAME OUT!
IT'S SUNNY AGAIN!
IT'S THE EMPEROR OF THE SUN...!
HOORAY
YAAAY
YAY

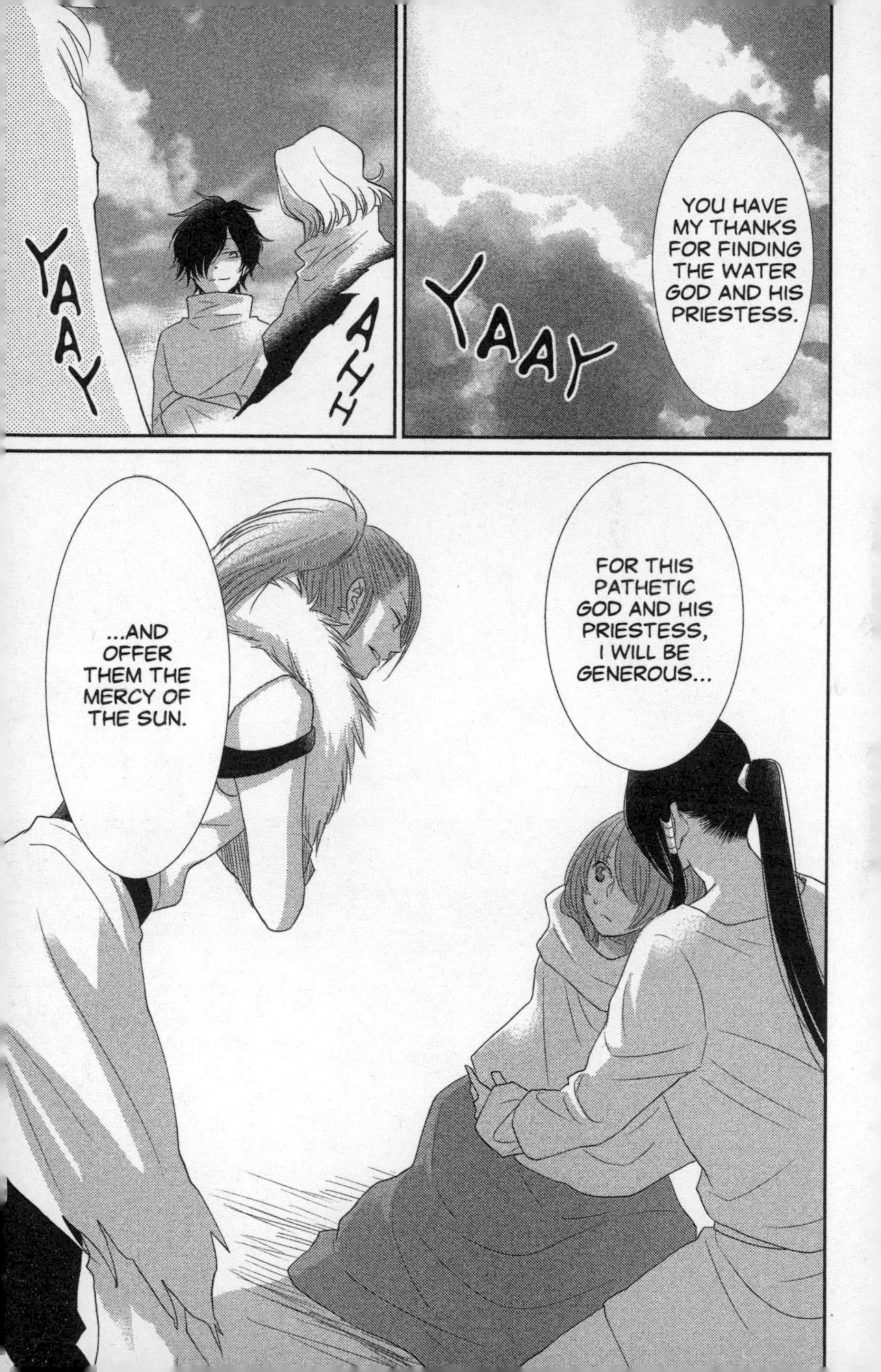
YOU HAVE MY THANKS FOR FINDING THE WATER GOD AND HIS PRIESTESS.
YAAY
YAAY
AHH
FOR THIS PATHETIC GOD AND HIS PRIESTESS, I WILL BE GENEROUS...
...AND OFFER THEM THE MERCY OF THE SUN.

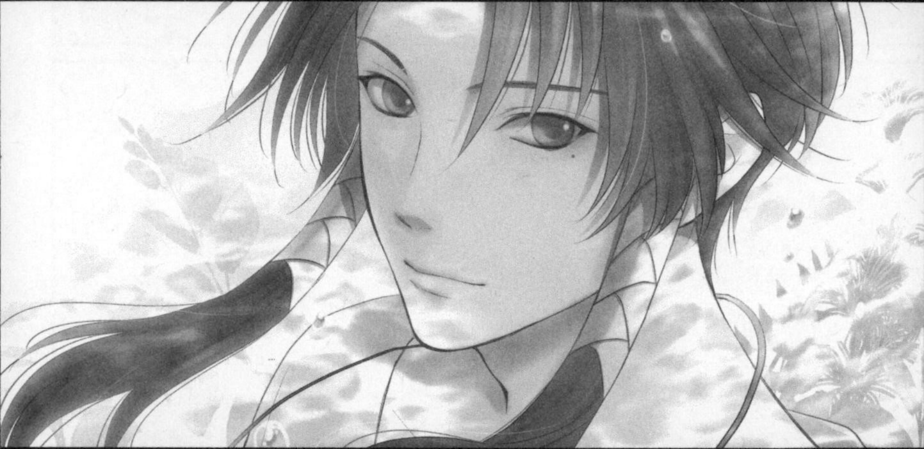

THIS TIME I DREW JUST SUBARU. I WAS THIS CLOSE TO FORGETTING TO DRAW IN HIS TEARDROP MOLE. I ALWAYS TRY TO BE SO CAREFUL WHEN IT COMES TIME TO DO THE FINAL DRAFT ITSELF, BUT EVEN SO I STILL HAVE A TENDENCY TO FORGET IT.

CHAPTER 35

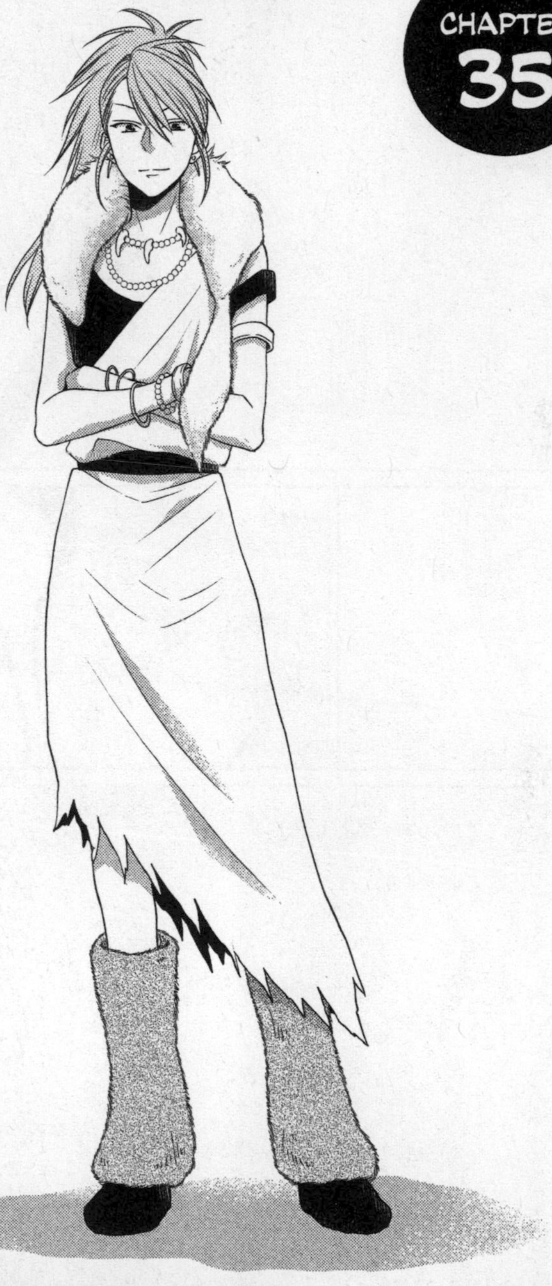

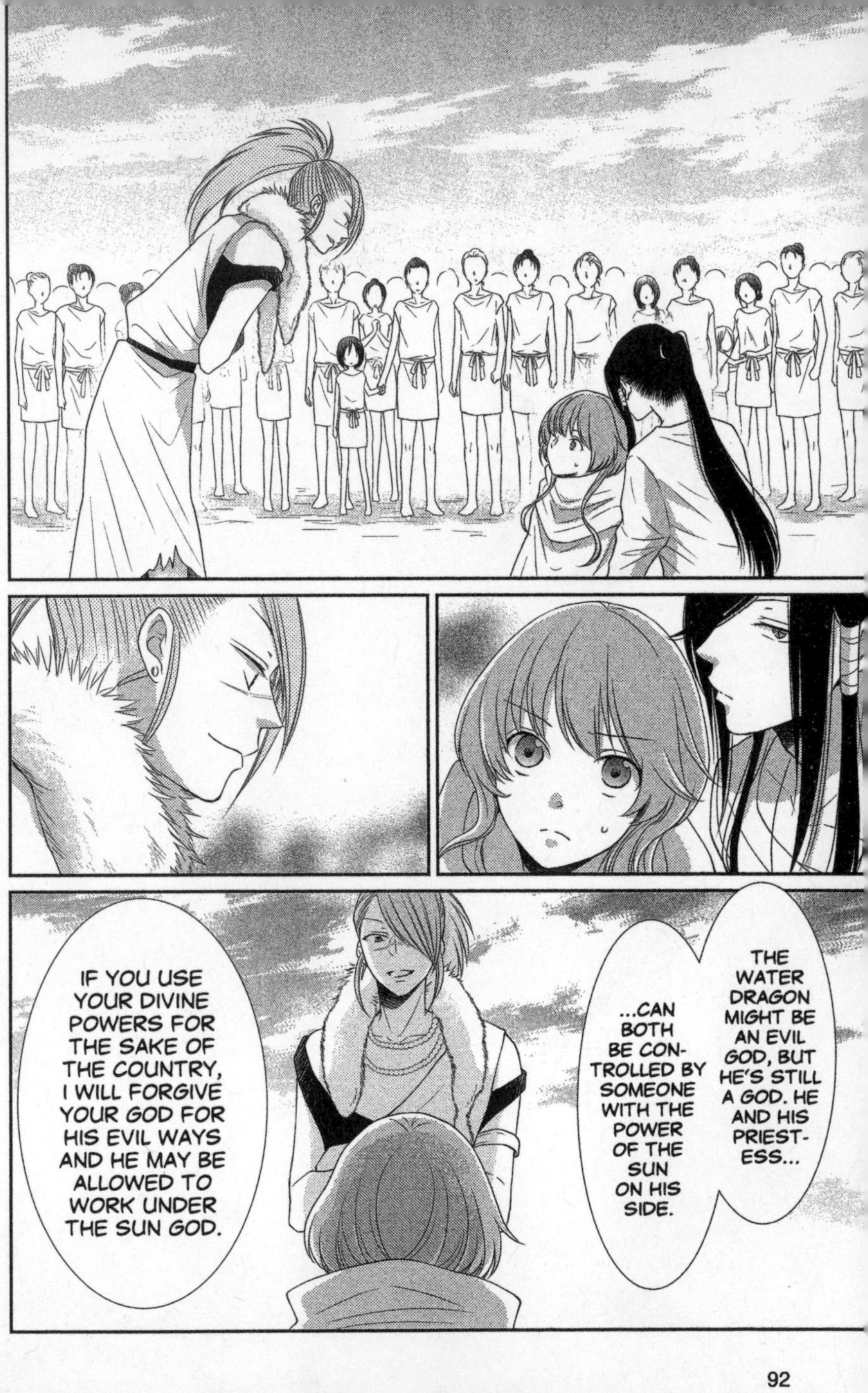
THE WATER DRAGON MIGHT BE AN EVIL GOD, BUT HE'S STILL A GOD. HE AND HIS PRIEST-ESS...
...CAN BOTH BE CON-TROLLED BY SOMEONE WITH THE POWER OF THE SUN ON HIS SIDE.
IF YOU USE YOUR DIVINE POWERS FOR THE SAKE OF THE COUNTRY, I WILL FORGIVE YOUR GOD FOR HIS EVIL WAYS AND HE MAY BE ALLOWED TO WORK UNDER THE SUN GOD.

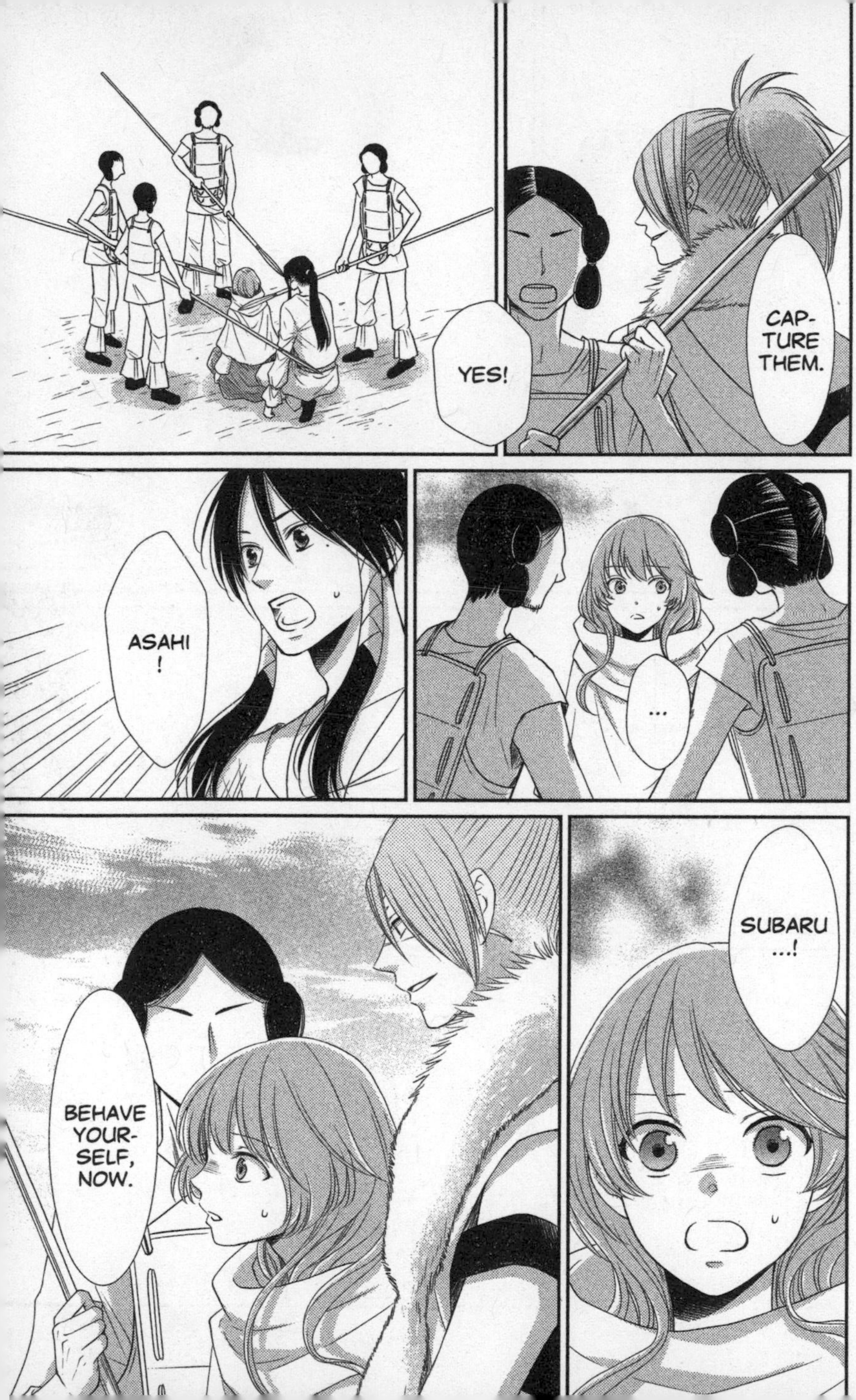
CAP-TURE THEM.
YES!
...
ASAHI!
SUBARU...!
BEHAVE YOUR-SELF, NOW.

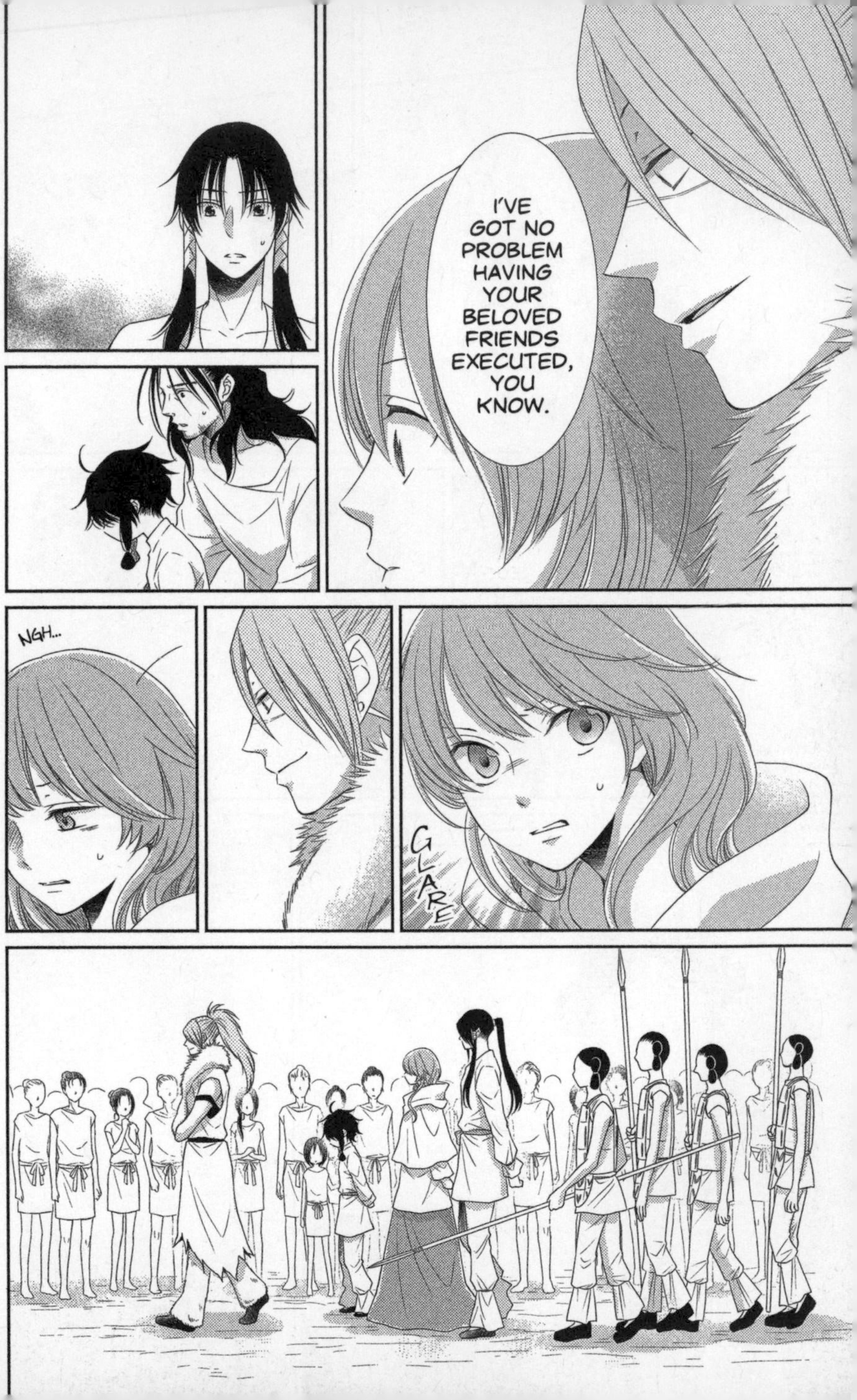
I'VE GOT NO PROBLEM HAVING YOUR BELOVED FRIENDS EXECUTED, YOU KNOW.
GLARE
NGH...

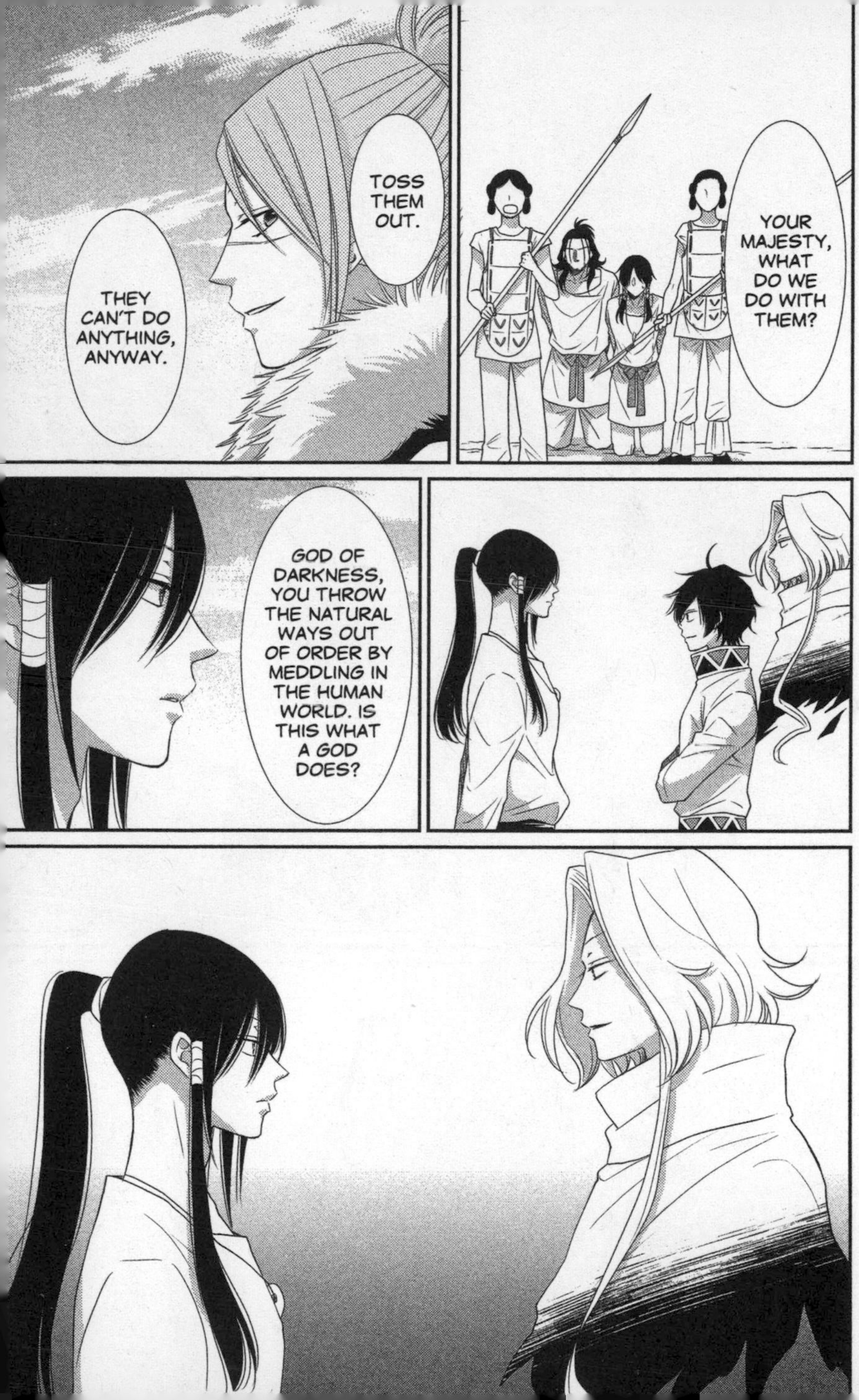
YOUR MAJESTY, WHAT DO WE DO WITH THEM?
TOSS THEM OUT.
THEY CAN'T DO ANYTHING, ANYWAY.
GOD OF DARKNESS, YOU THROW THE NATURAL WAYS OUT OF ORDER BY MEDDLING IN THE HUMAN WORLD. IS THIS WHAT A GOD DOES?

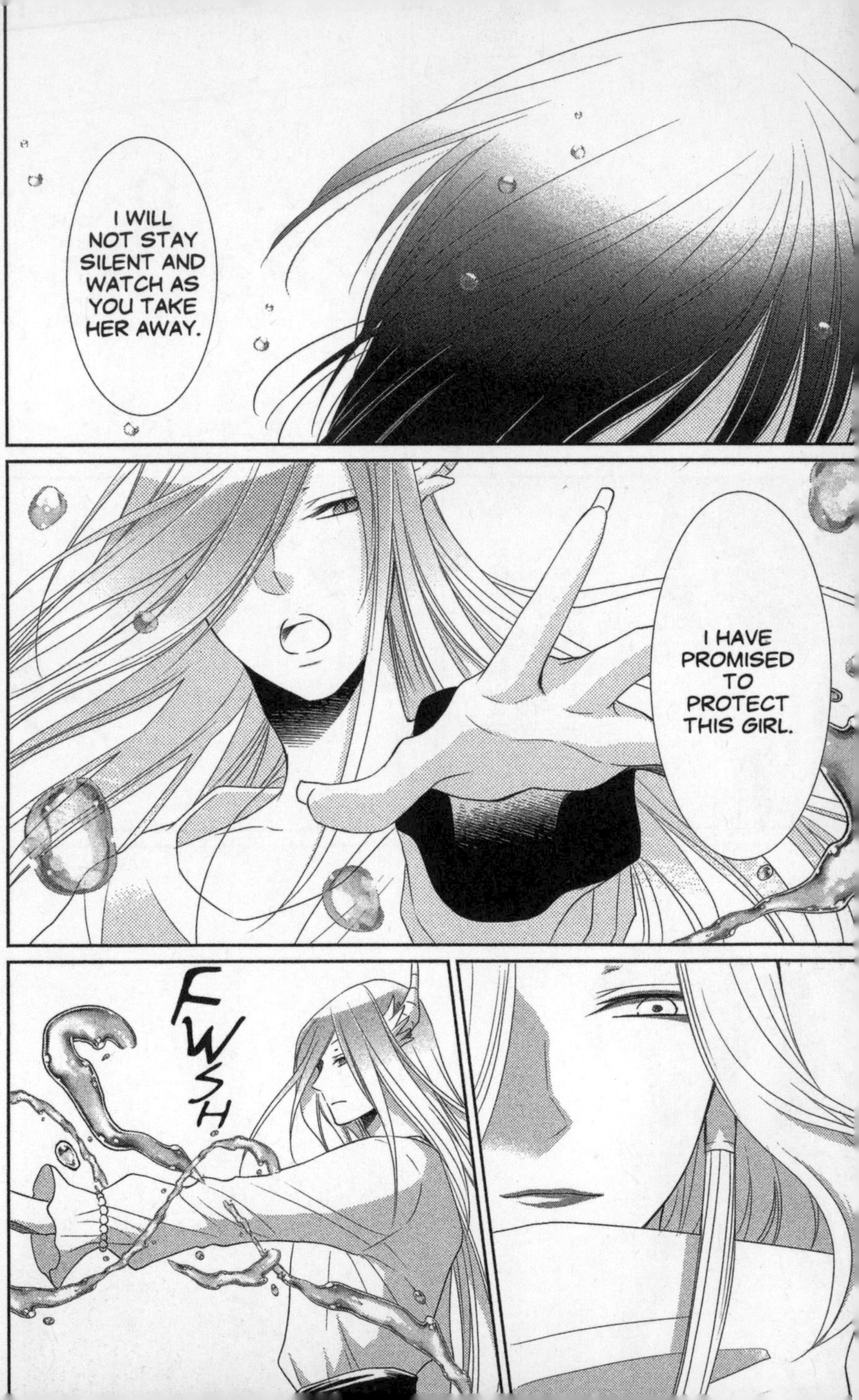
I WILL NOT STAY SILENT AND WATCH AS YOU TAKE HER AWAY.
I HAVE PROMISED TO PROTECT THIS GIRL.
FWSH

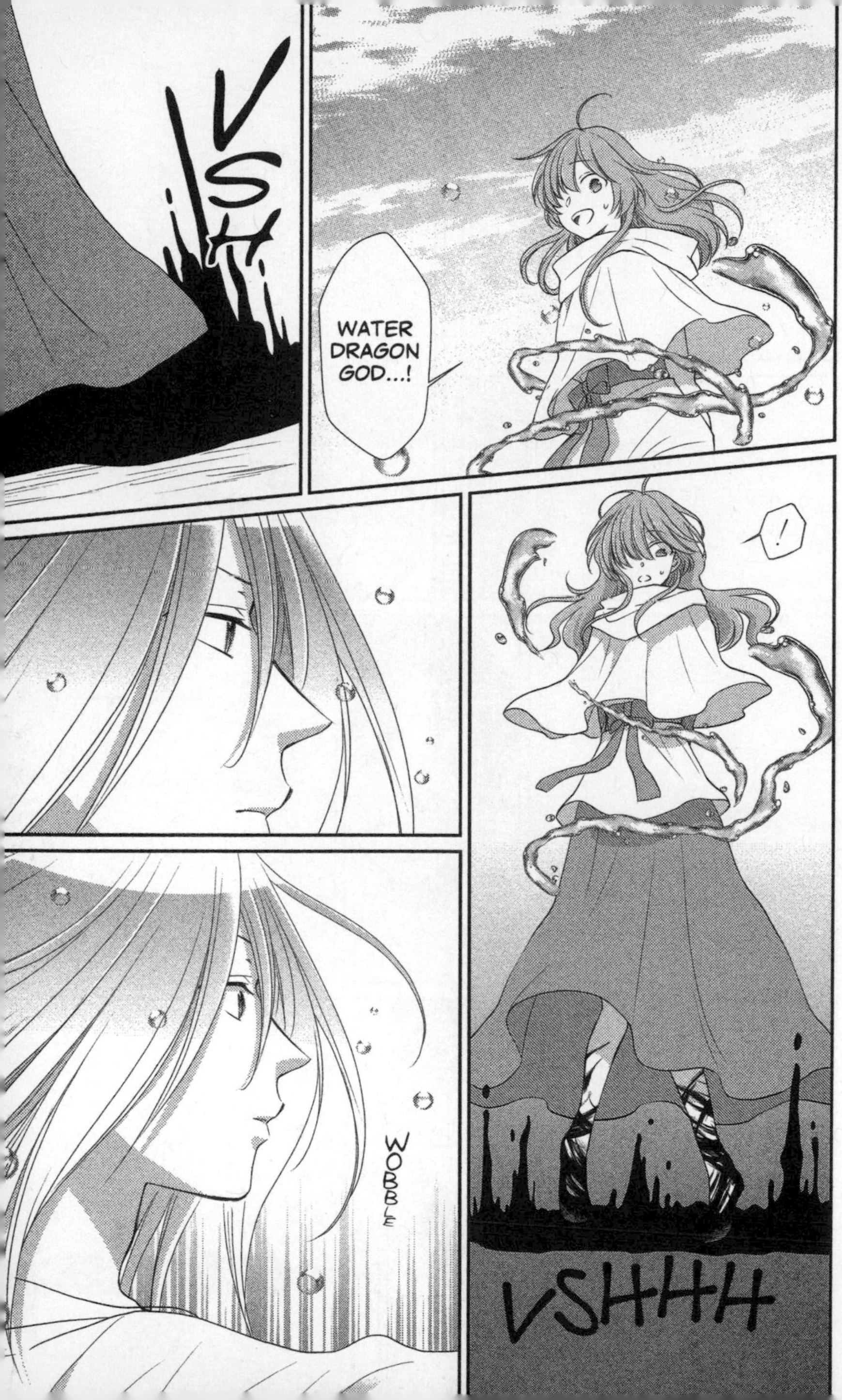
WATER DRAGON GOD...!
VSH
!
VSHHH
WOBBLE

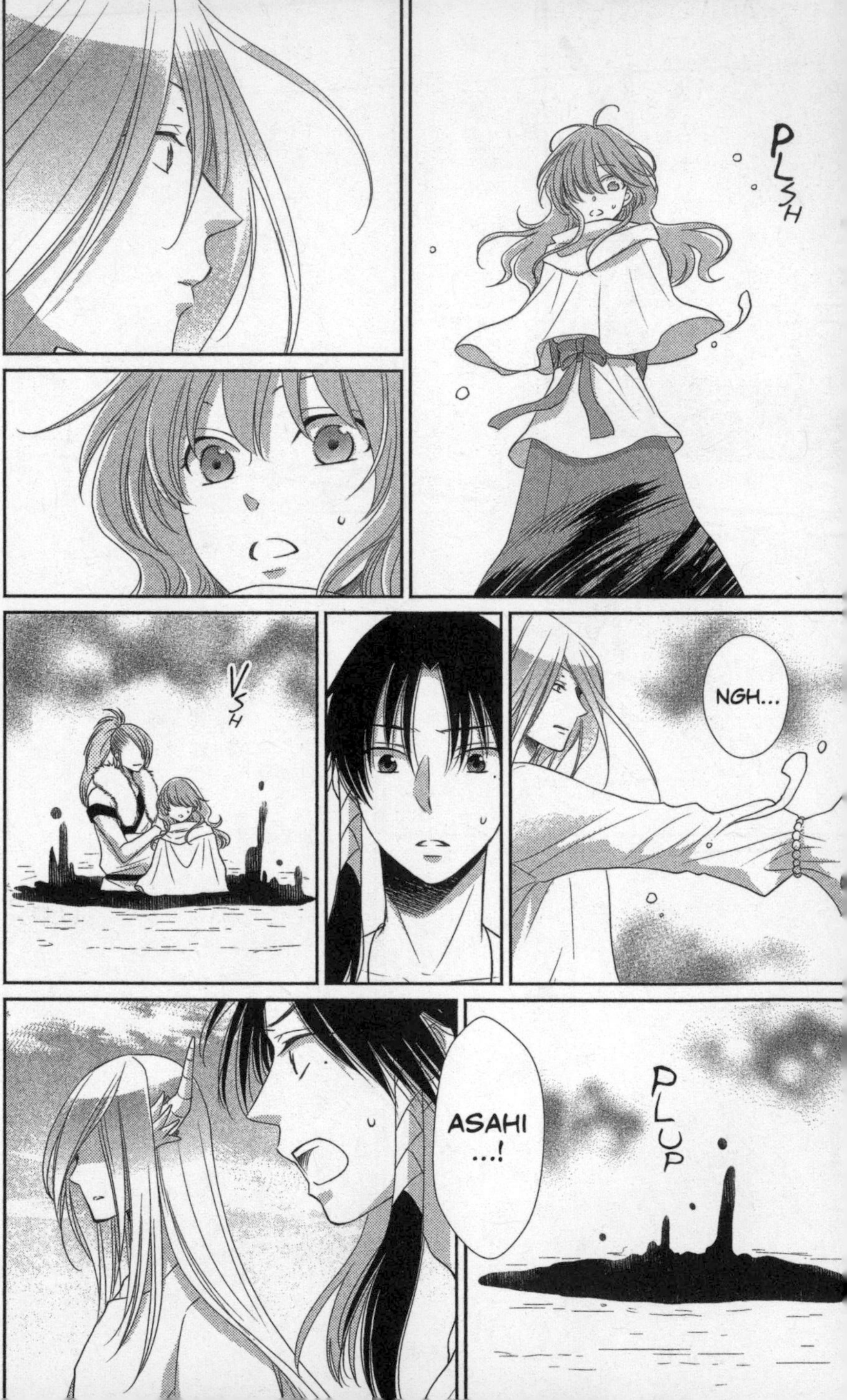
PLSH
VSH
NGH...
PLUP
ASAHI ...!

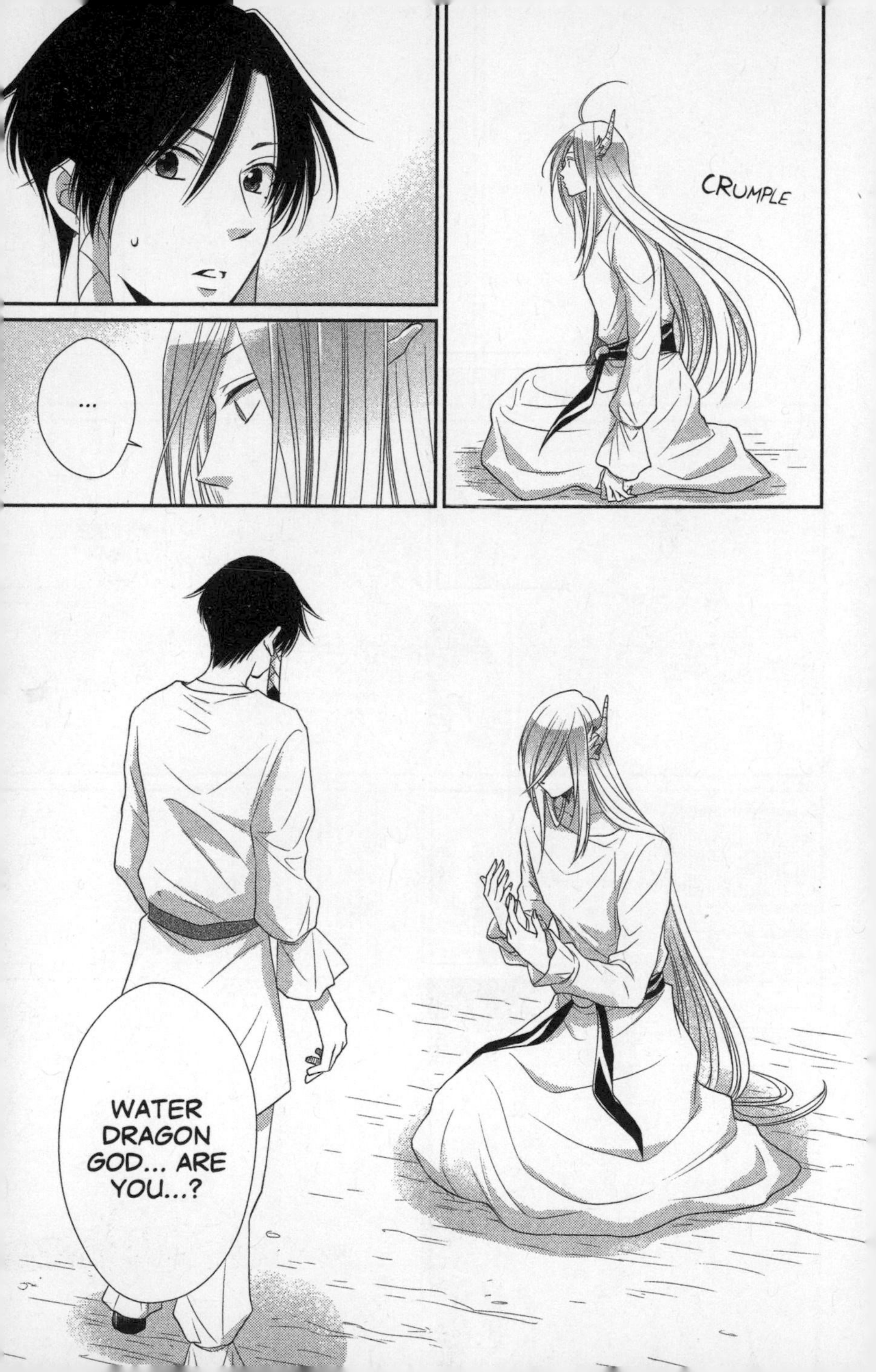
CRUMPLE
...
WATER DRAGON GOD... ARE YOU...?

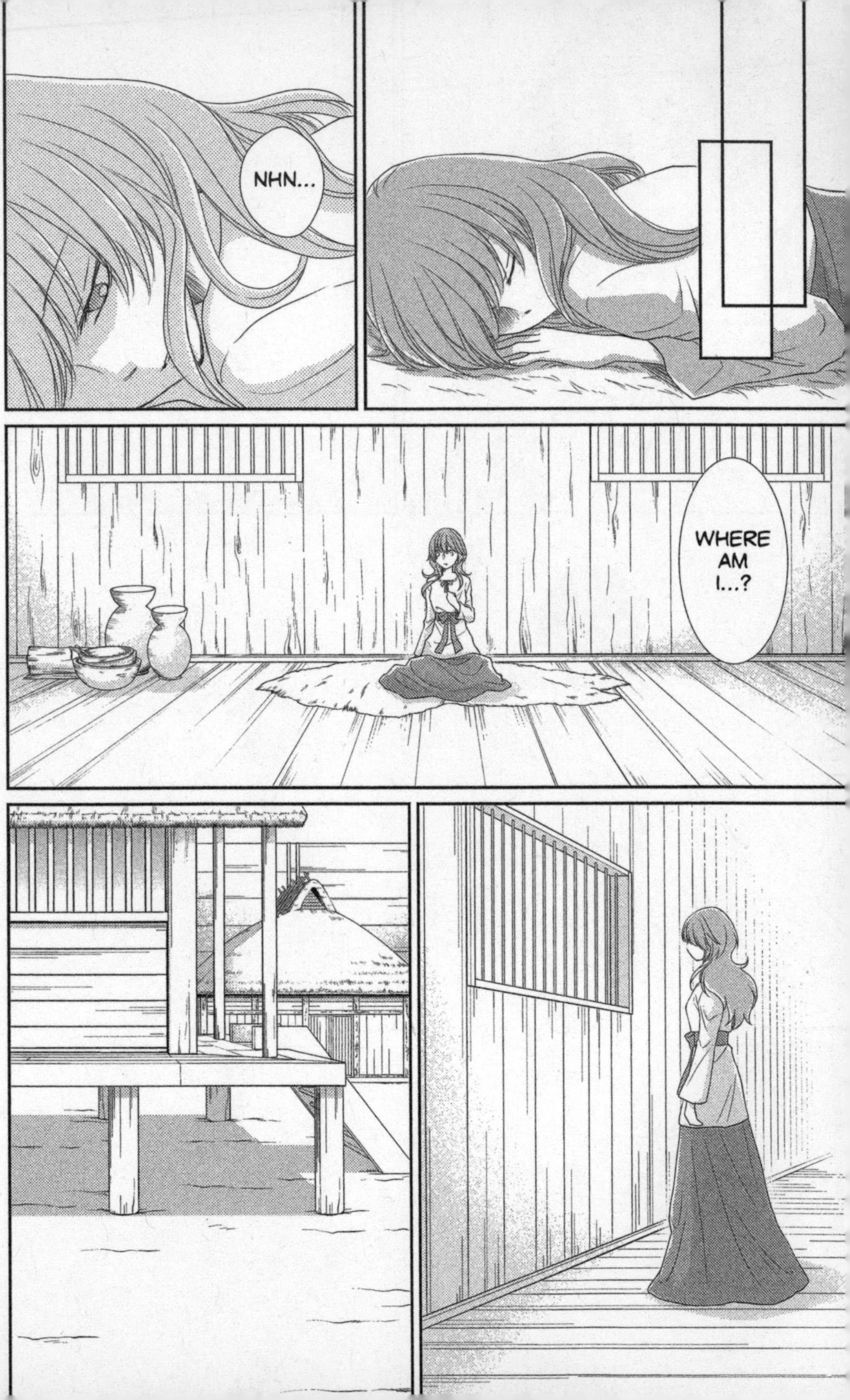
NHN...
WHERE AM I...?

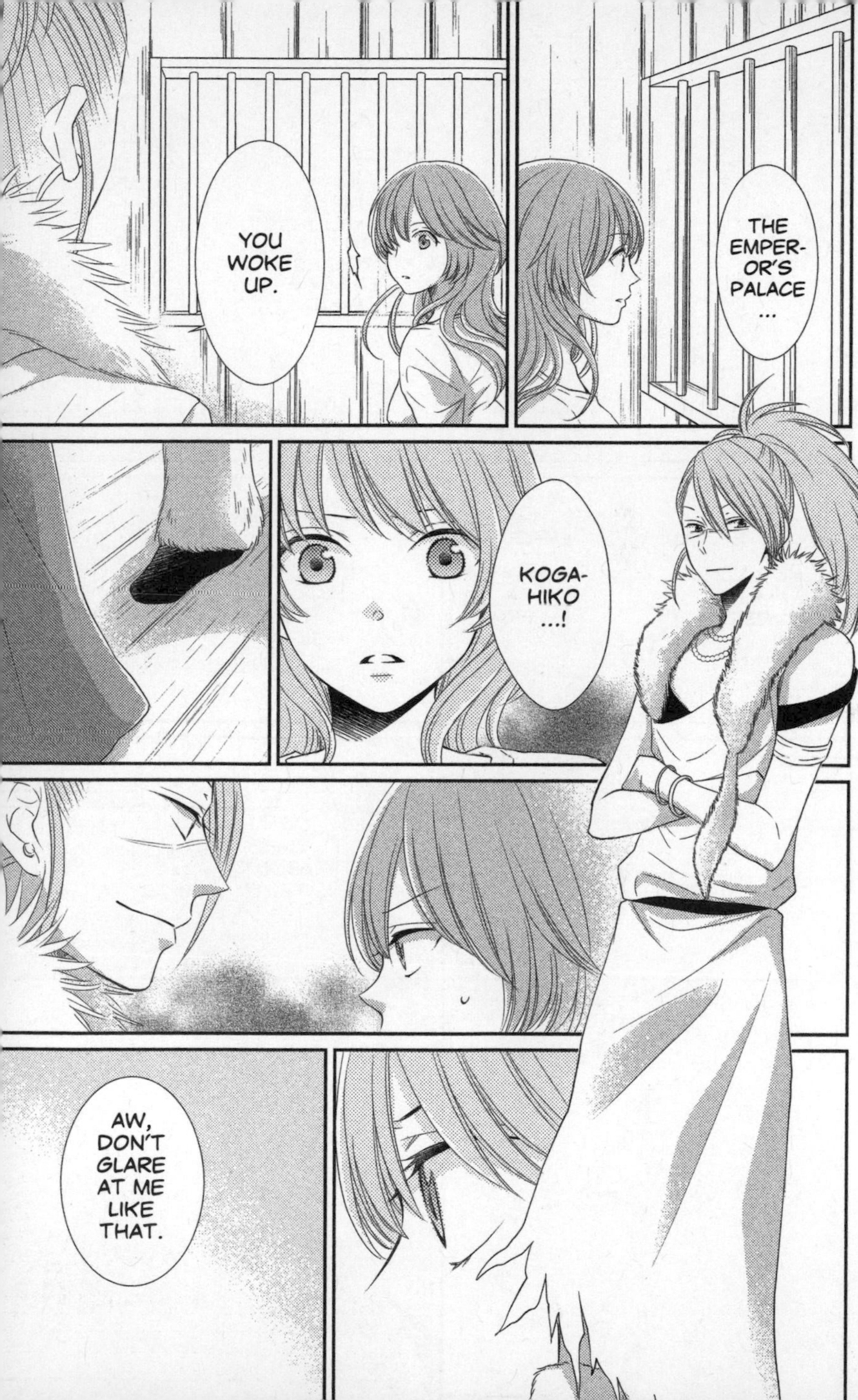
THE EMPEROR'S PALACE...
YOU WOKE UP.
KOGAHIKO...!
AW, DON'T GLARE AT ME LIKE THAT.

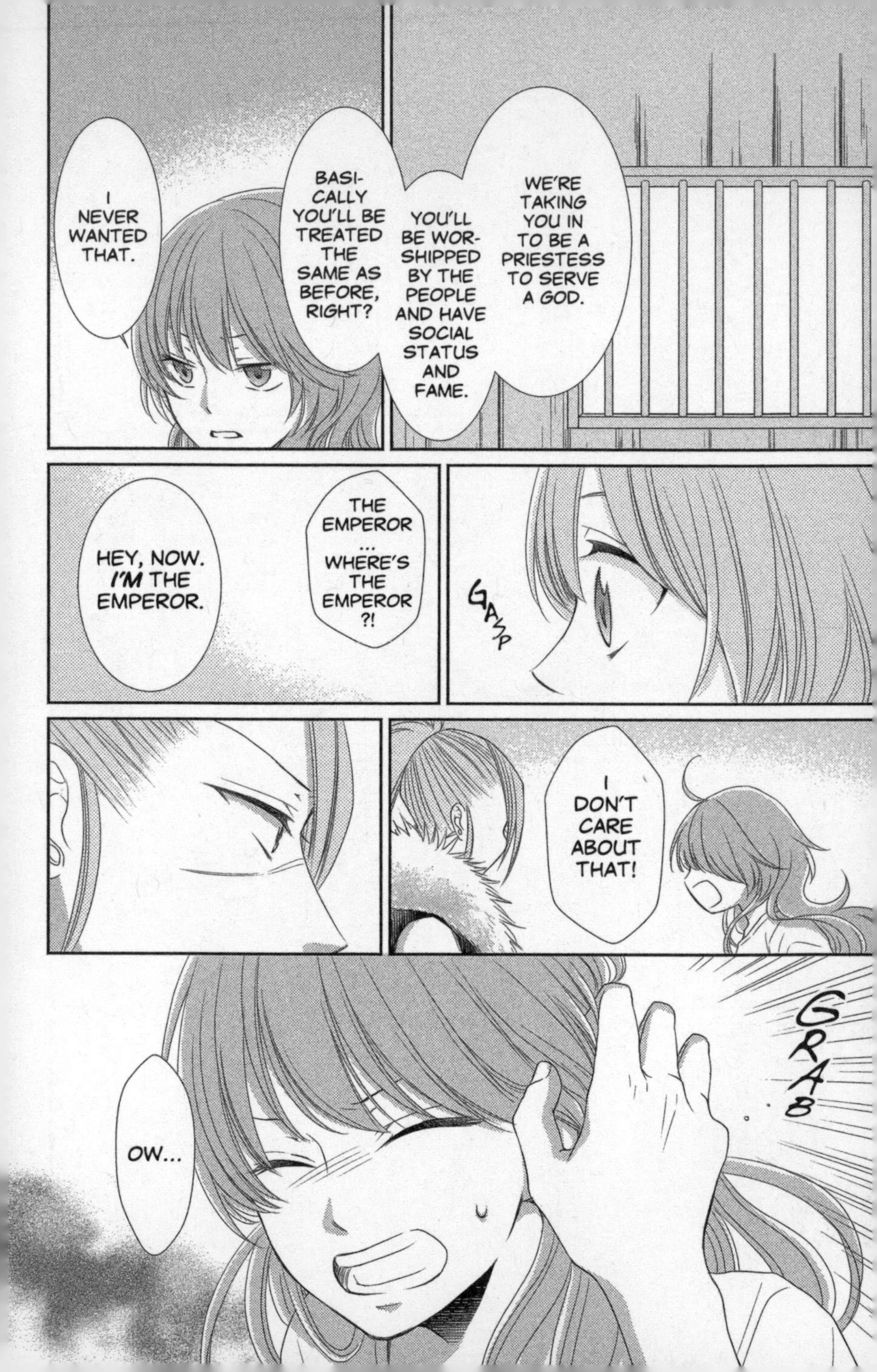
WE'RE TAKING YOU IN TO BE A PRIESTESS TO SERVE A GOD.
YOU'LL BE WORSHIPPED BY THE PEOPLE AND HAVE SOCIAL STATUS AND FAME.
BASICALLY YOU'LL BE TREATED THE SAME AS BEFORE, RIGHT?
I NEVER WANTED THAT.
GASP
THE EMPEROR ... WHERE'S THE EMPEROR?!
HEY, NOW. *I'M* THE EMPEROR.
I DON'T CARE ABOUT THAT!
GRAB
OW...

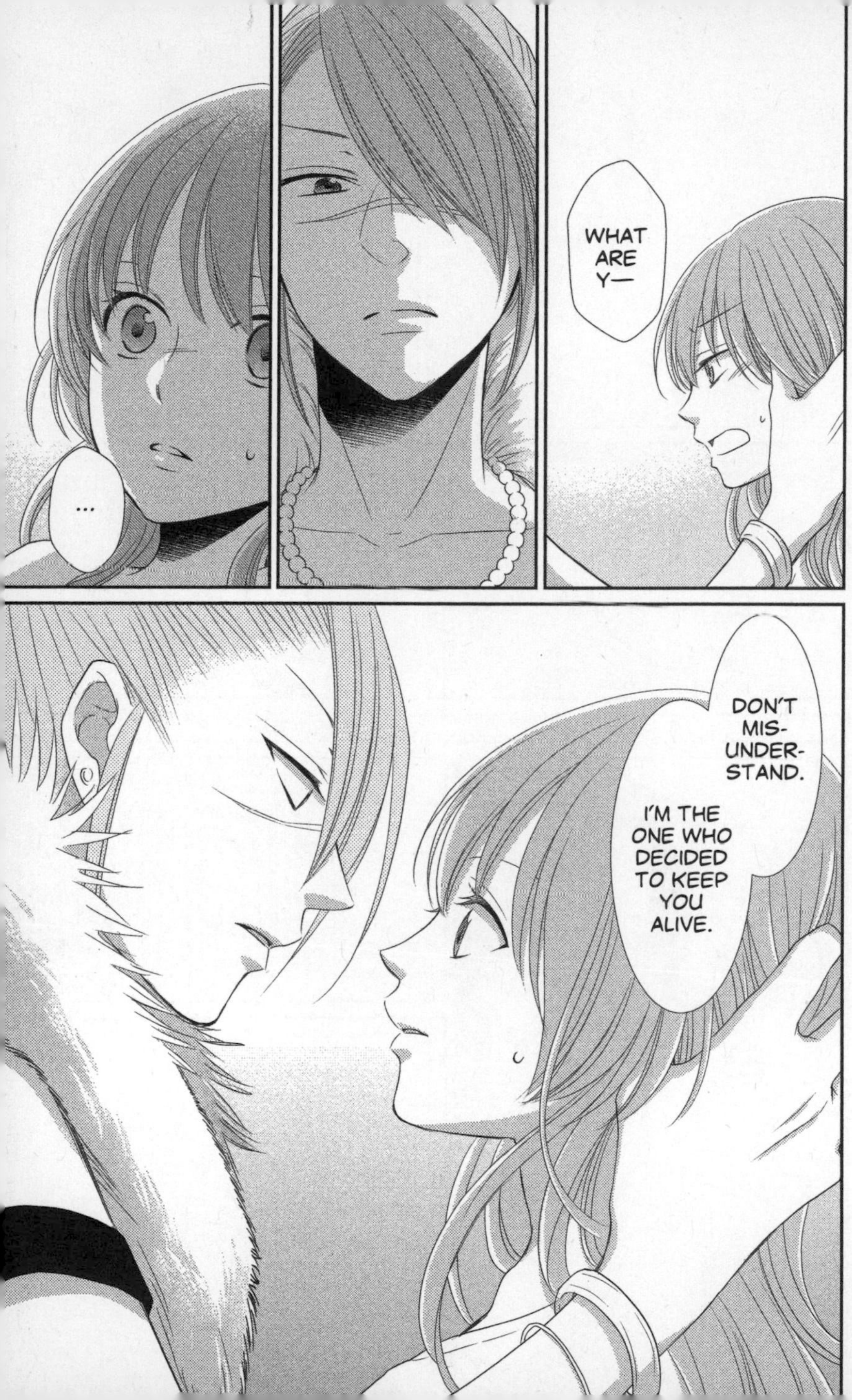
WHAT ARE Y—
...
DON'T MIS-UNDERSTAND.
I'M THE ONE WHO DECIDED TO KEEP YOU ALIVE.

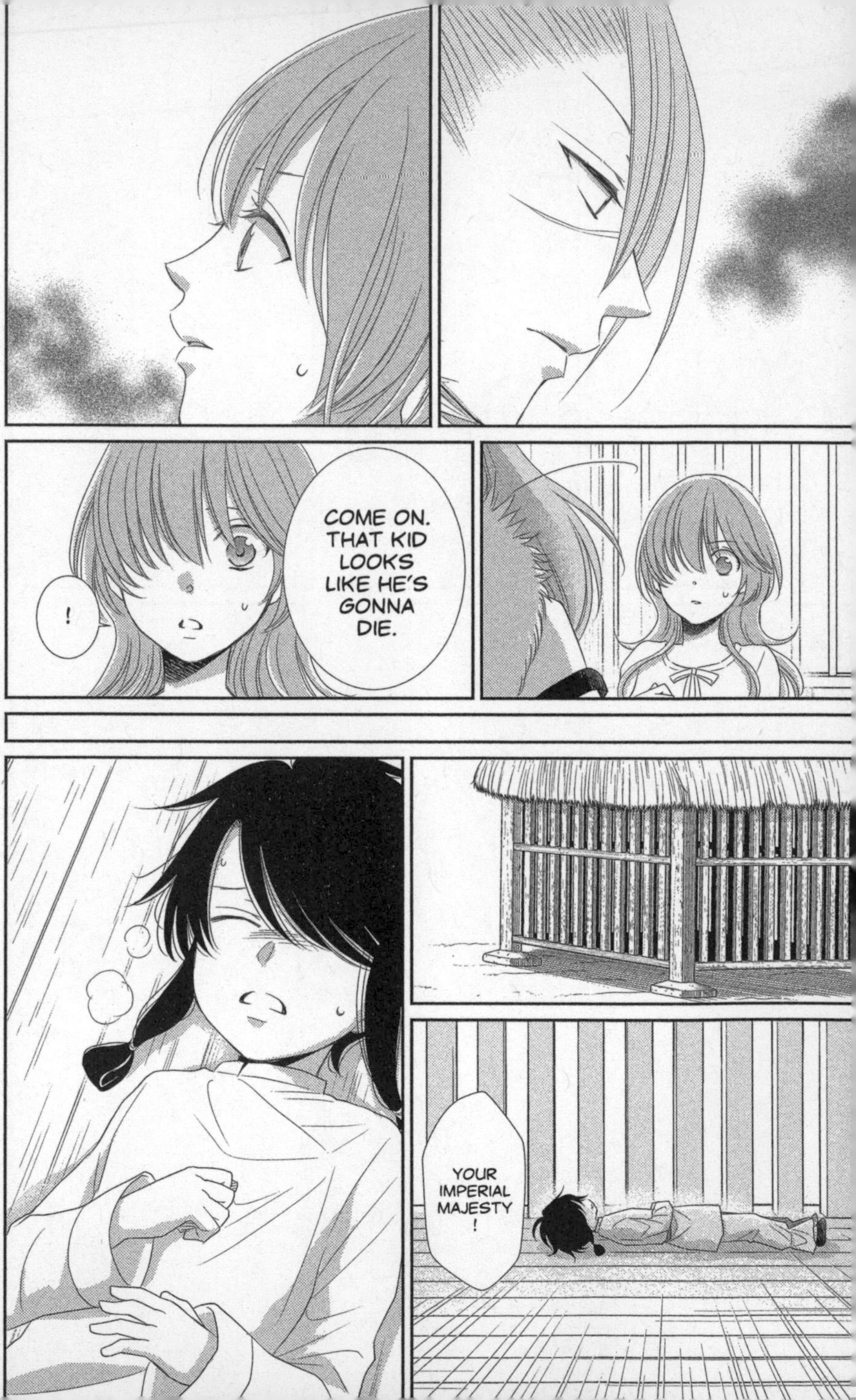
COME ON. THAT KID LOOKS LIKE HE'S GONNA DIE.
!
YOUR IMPERIAL MAJESTY!

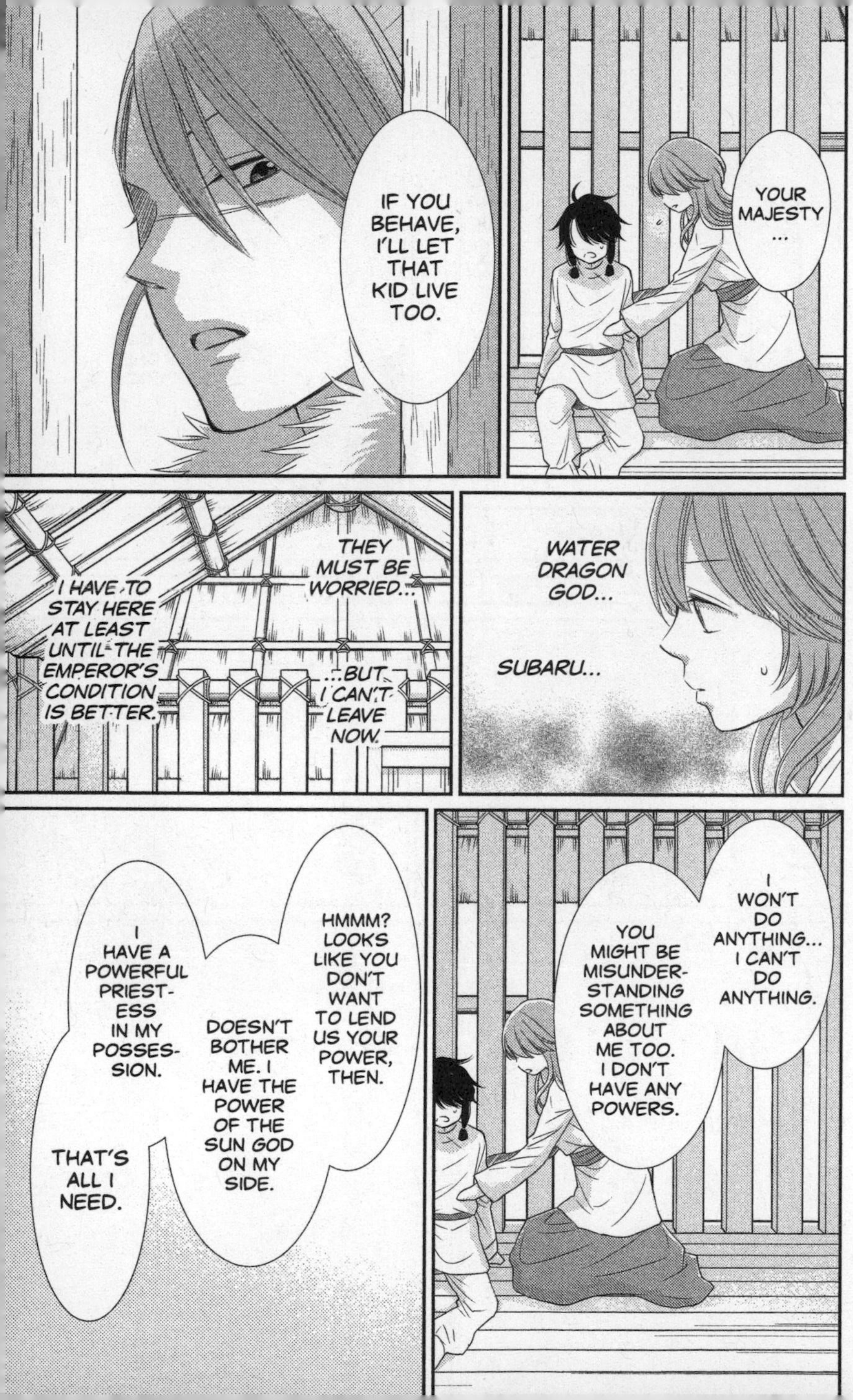
YOUR MAJESTY ...
IF YOU BEHAVE, I'LL LET THAT KID LIVE TOO.
WATER DRAGON GOD...
SUBARU...
THEY MUST BE WORRIED...
...BUT I CAN'T LEAVE NOW.
I HAVE TO STAY HERE AT LEAST UNTIL THE EMPEROR'S CONDITION IS BETTER.
I WON'T DO ANYTHING... I CAN'T DO ANYTHING.
YOU MIGHT BE MISUNDER-STANDING SOMETHING ABOUT ME TOO. I DON'T HAVE ANY POWERS.
HMMM? LOOKS LIKE YOU DON'T WANT TO LEND US YOUR POWER, THEN.
DOESN'T BOTHER ME. I HAVE THE POWER OF THE SUN GOD ON MY SIDE.
I HAVE A POWERFUL PRIEST-ESS IN MY POSSES-SION.
THAT'S ALL I NEED.

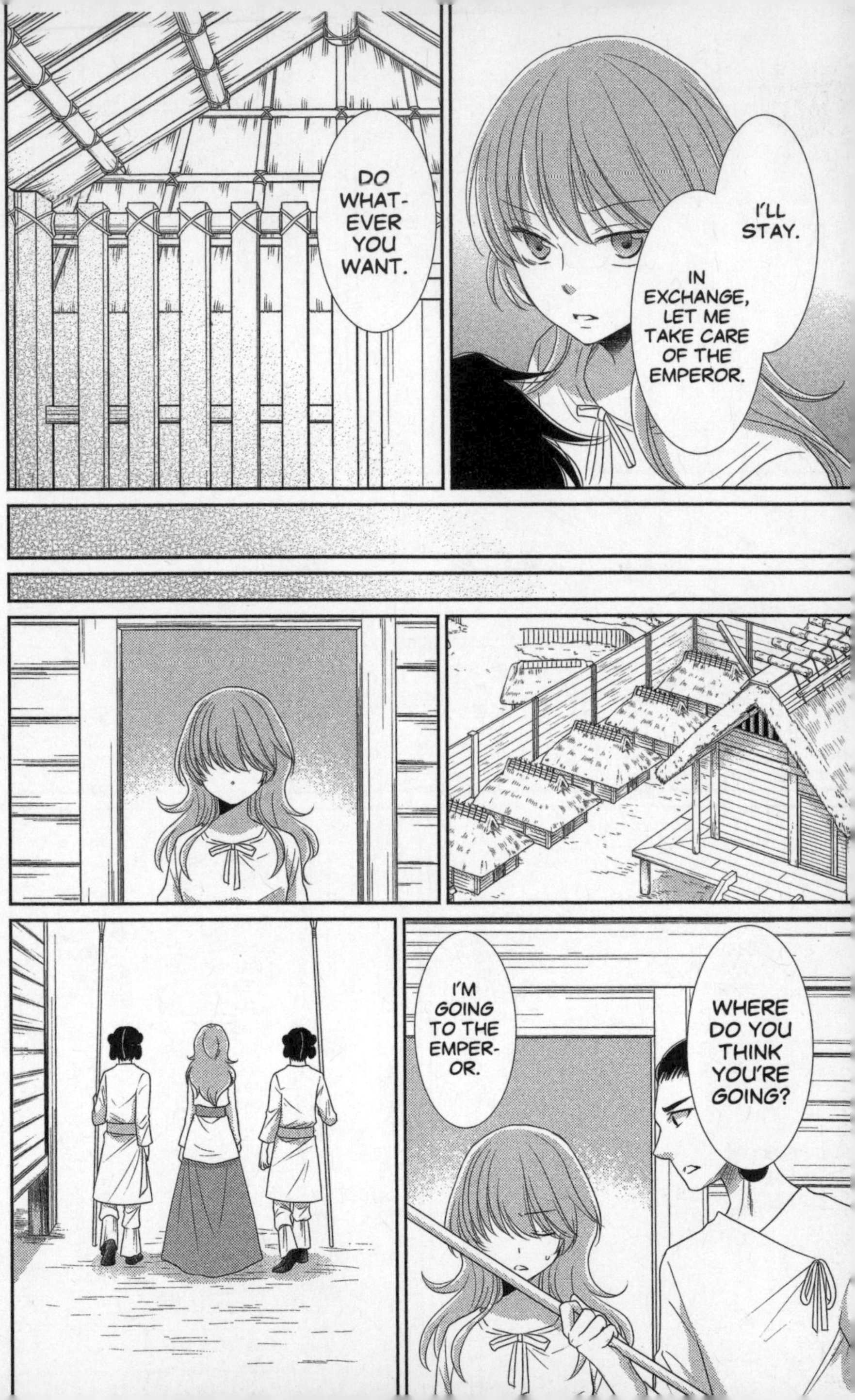
I'LL STAY.
IN EXCHANGE, LET ME TAKE CARE OF THE EMPEROR.
DO WHAT-EVER YOU WANT.
WHERE DO YOU THINK YOU'RE GOING?
I'M GOING TO THE EMPER-OR.

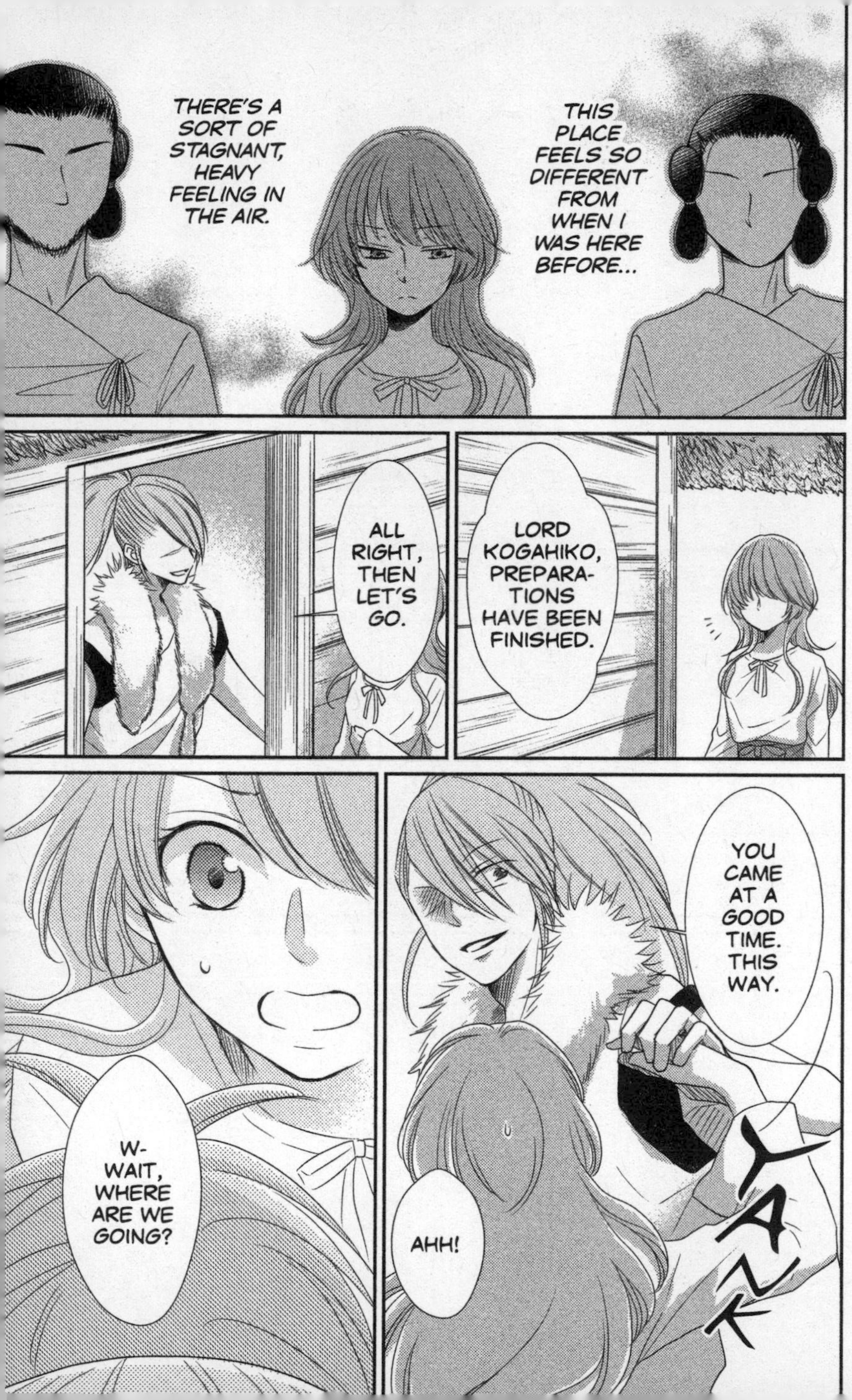
THIS PLACE FEELS SO DIFFERENT FROM WHEN I WAS HERE BEFORE...
THERE'S A SORT OF STAGNANT, HEAVY FEELING IN THE AIR.
LORD KOGAHIKO, PREPARATIONS HAVE BEEN FINISHED.
ALL RIGHT, THEN LET'S GO.
YOU CAME AT A GOOD TIME. THIS WAY.
YANK
AHH!
W-WAIT, WHERE ARE WE GOING?

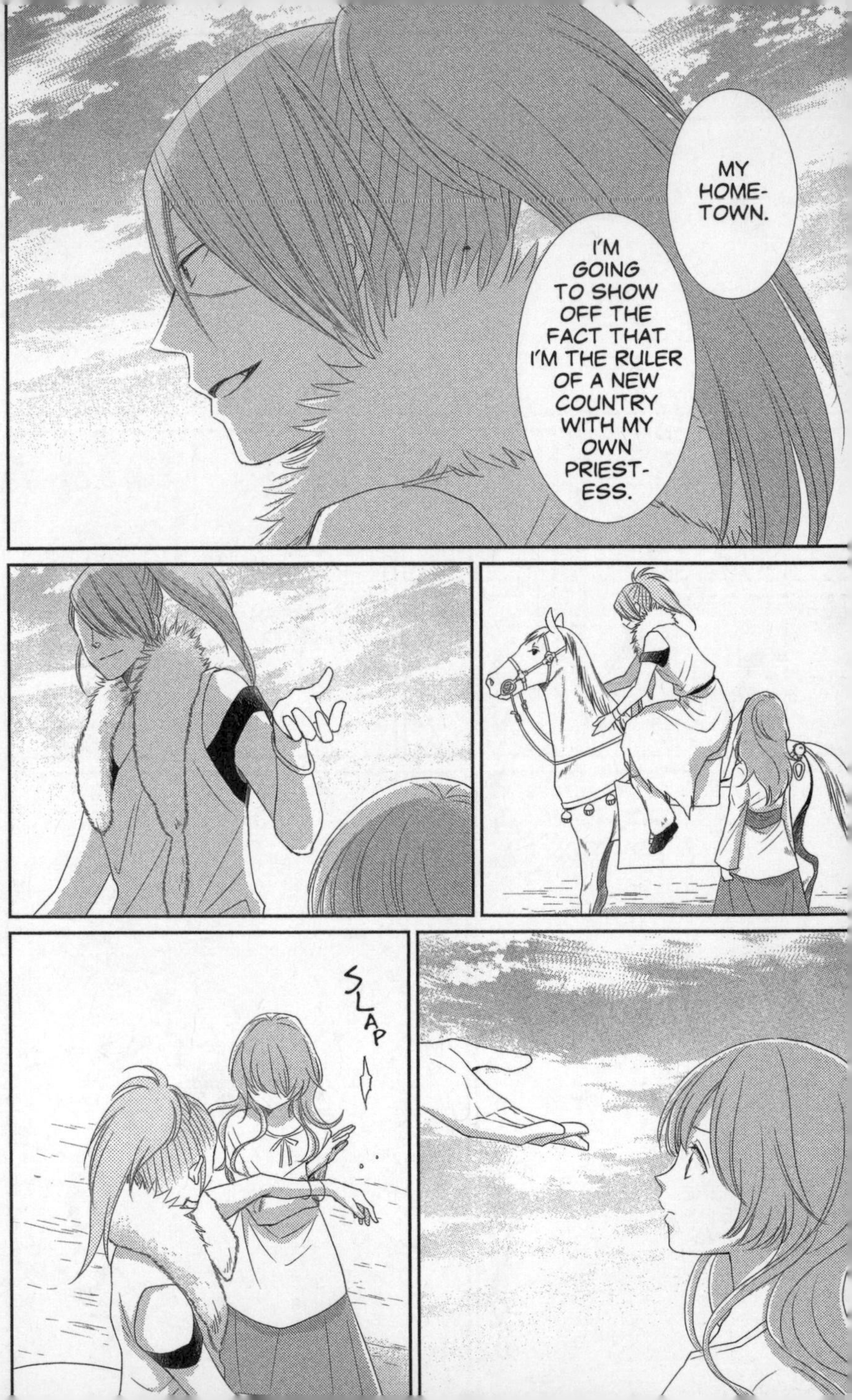
MY HOME-TOWN.
I'M GOING TO SHOW OFF THE FACT THAT I'M THE RULER OF A NEW COUNTRY WITH MY OWN PRIEST-ESS.
SLAP

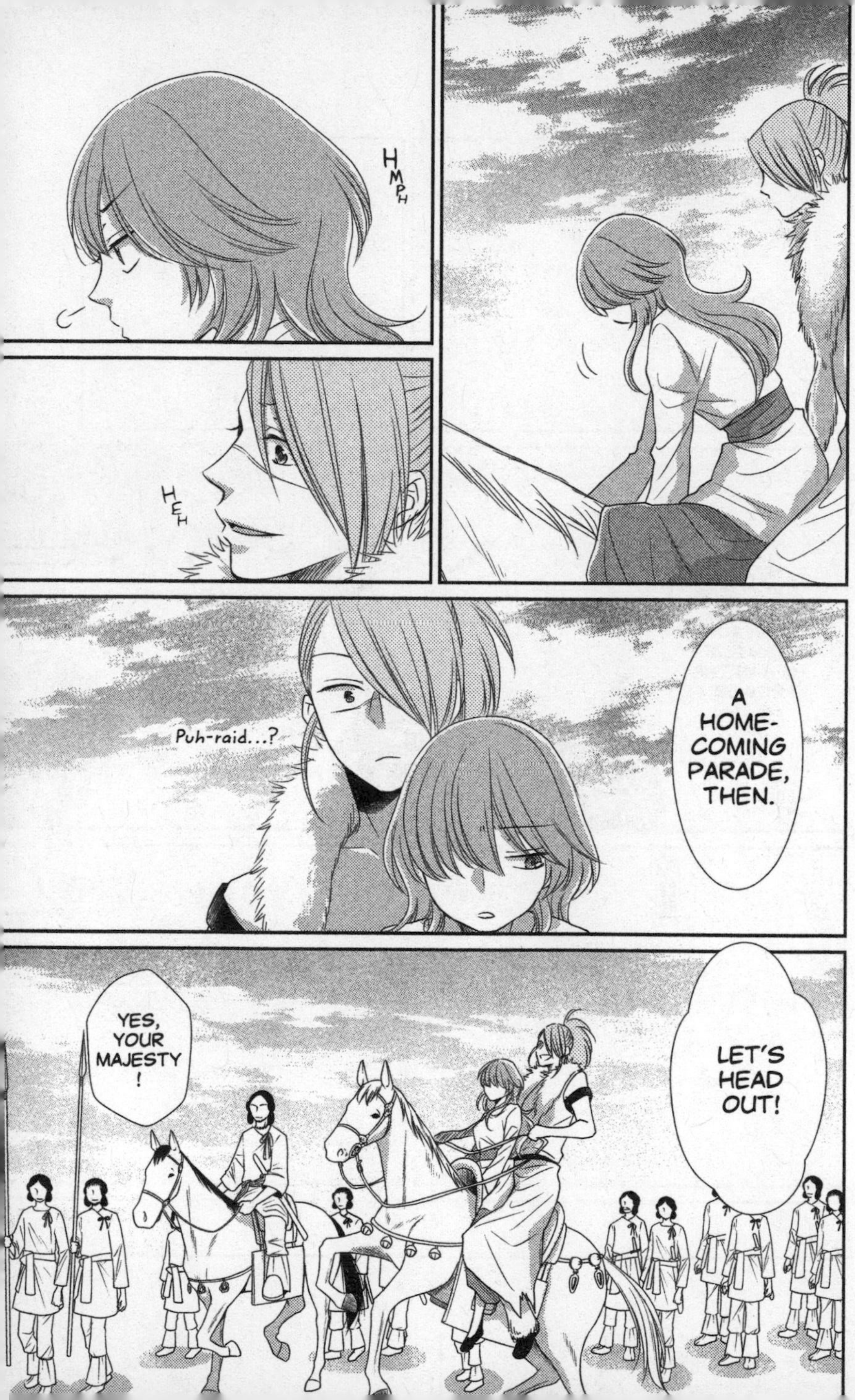
HMPH
HEH
A HOME-COMING PARADE, THEN.
Puh-raid...?
LET'S HEAD OUT!
YES, YOUR MAJESTY!

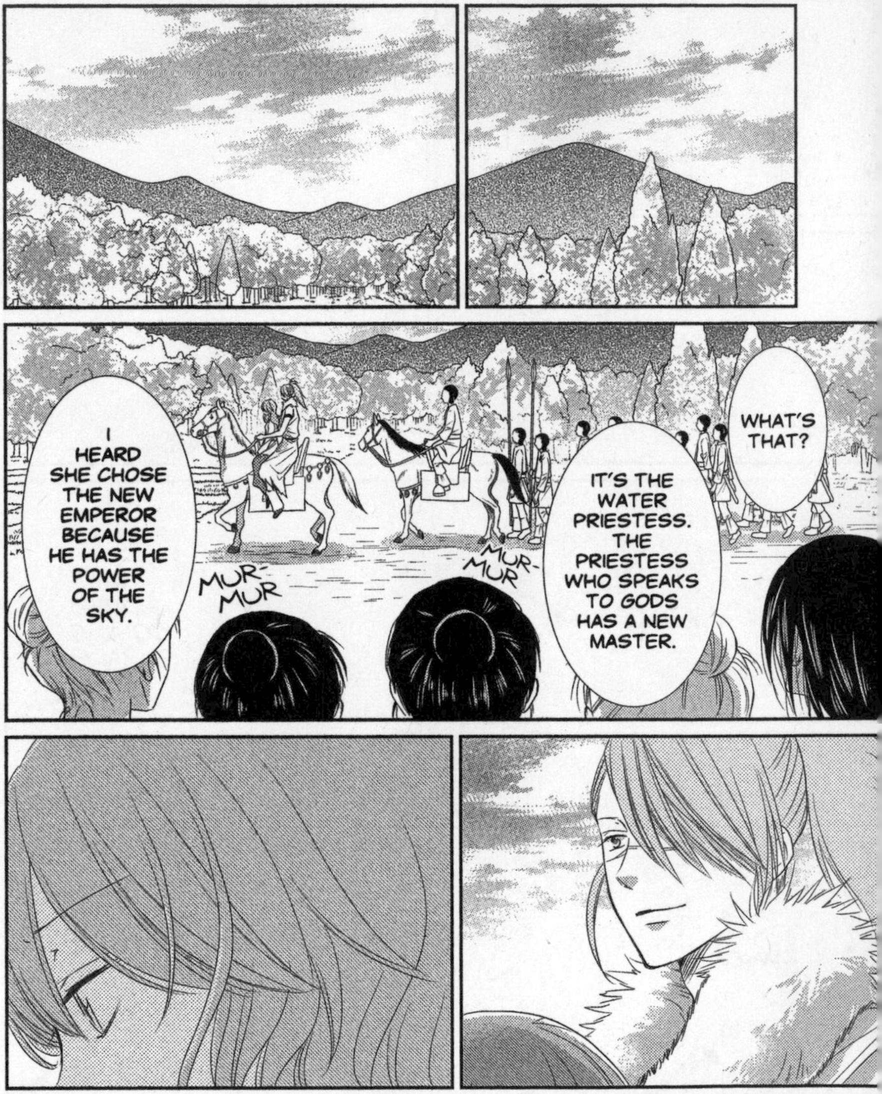
WHAT'S THAT?
IT'S THE WATER PRIESTESS. THE PRIESTESS WHO SPEAKS TO GODS HAS A NEW MASTER.
MUR-MUR
MUR-MUR
I HEARD SHE CHOSE THE NEW EMPEROR BECAUSE HE HAS THE POWER OF THE SKY.

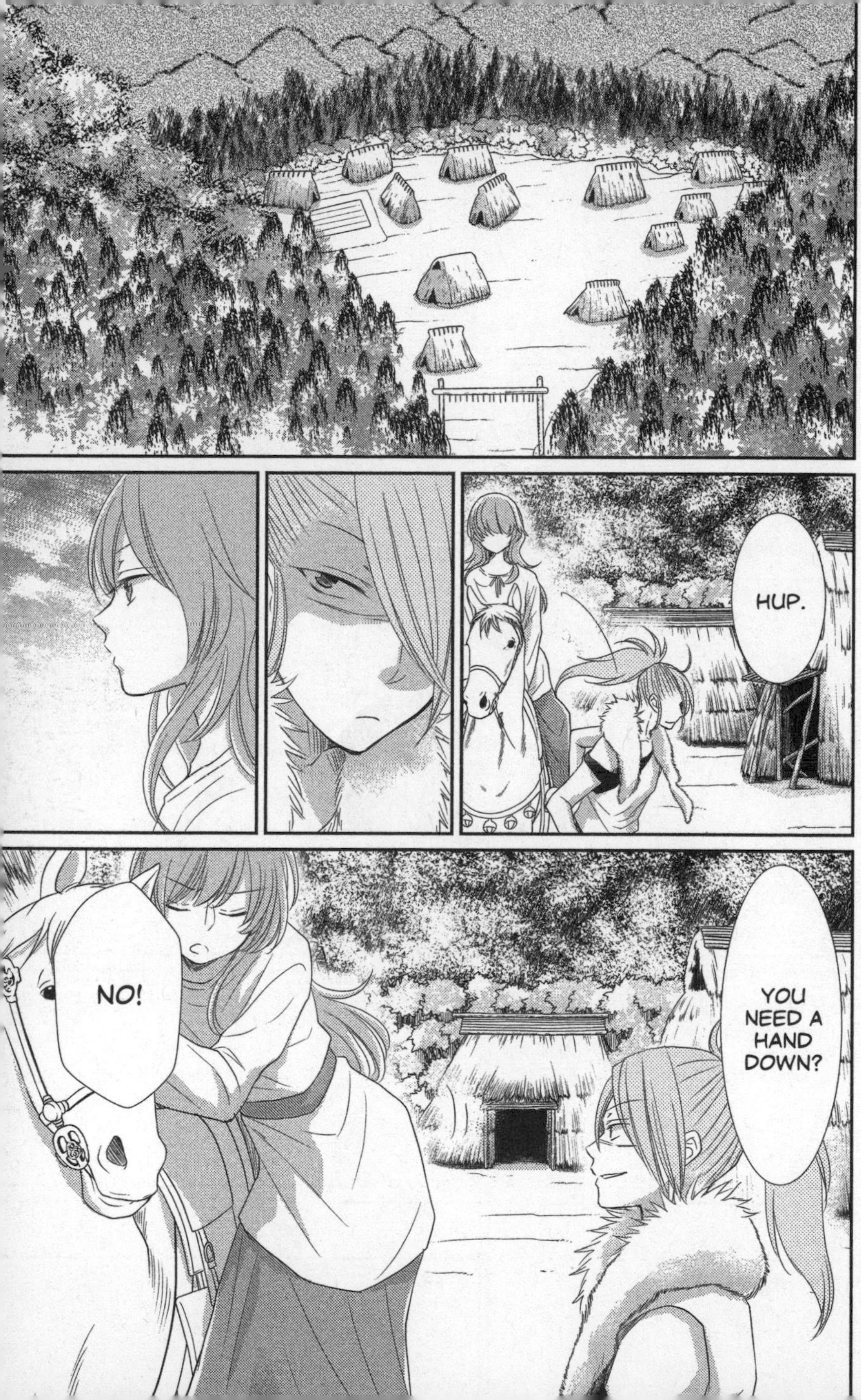
HUP.
YOU NEED A HAND DOWN?
NO!

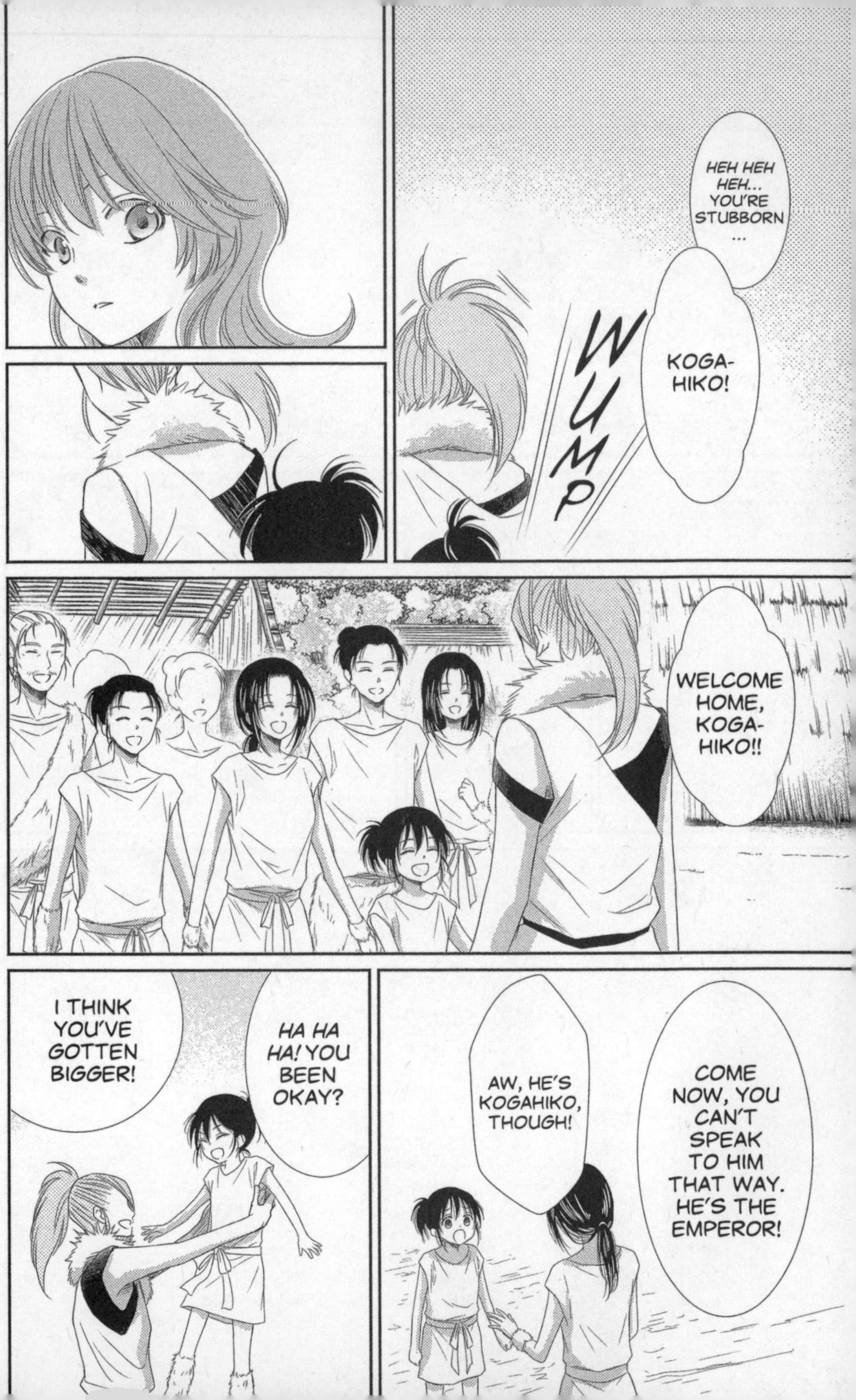
HEH HEH HEH... YOU'RE STUBBORN ...
KOGA-HIKO!
WUMP
WELCOME HOME, KOGA-HIKO!!
COME NOW, YOU CAN'T SPEAK TO HIM THAT WAY. HE'S THE EMPEROR!
AW, HE'S KOGAHIKO, THOUGH!
HA HA HA! YOU BEEN OKAY?
I THINK YOU'VE GOTTEN BIGGER!

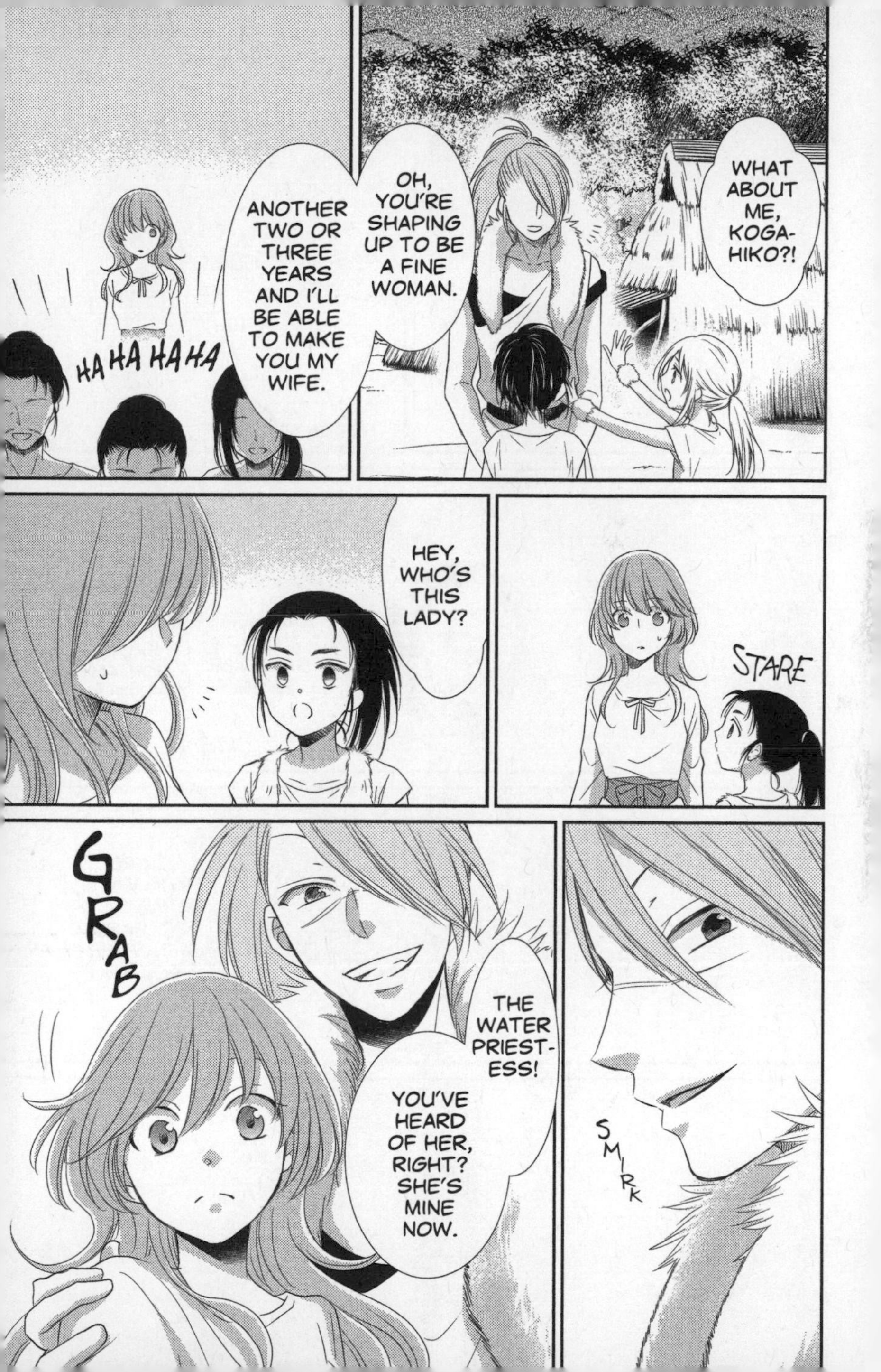
WHAT ABOUT ME, KOGA-HIKO?!
OH, YOU'RE SHAPING UP TO BE A FINE WOMAN.
ANOTHER TWO OR THREE YEARS AND I'LL BE ABLE TO MAKE YOU MY WIFE.
HA HA HA HA
STARE
HEY, WHO'S THIS LADY?
SMIRK
GRAB
THE WATER PRIEST-ESS!
YOU'VE HEARD OF HER, RIGHT? SHE'S MINE NOW.

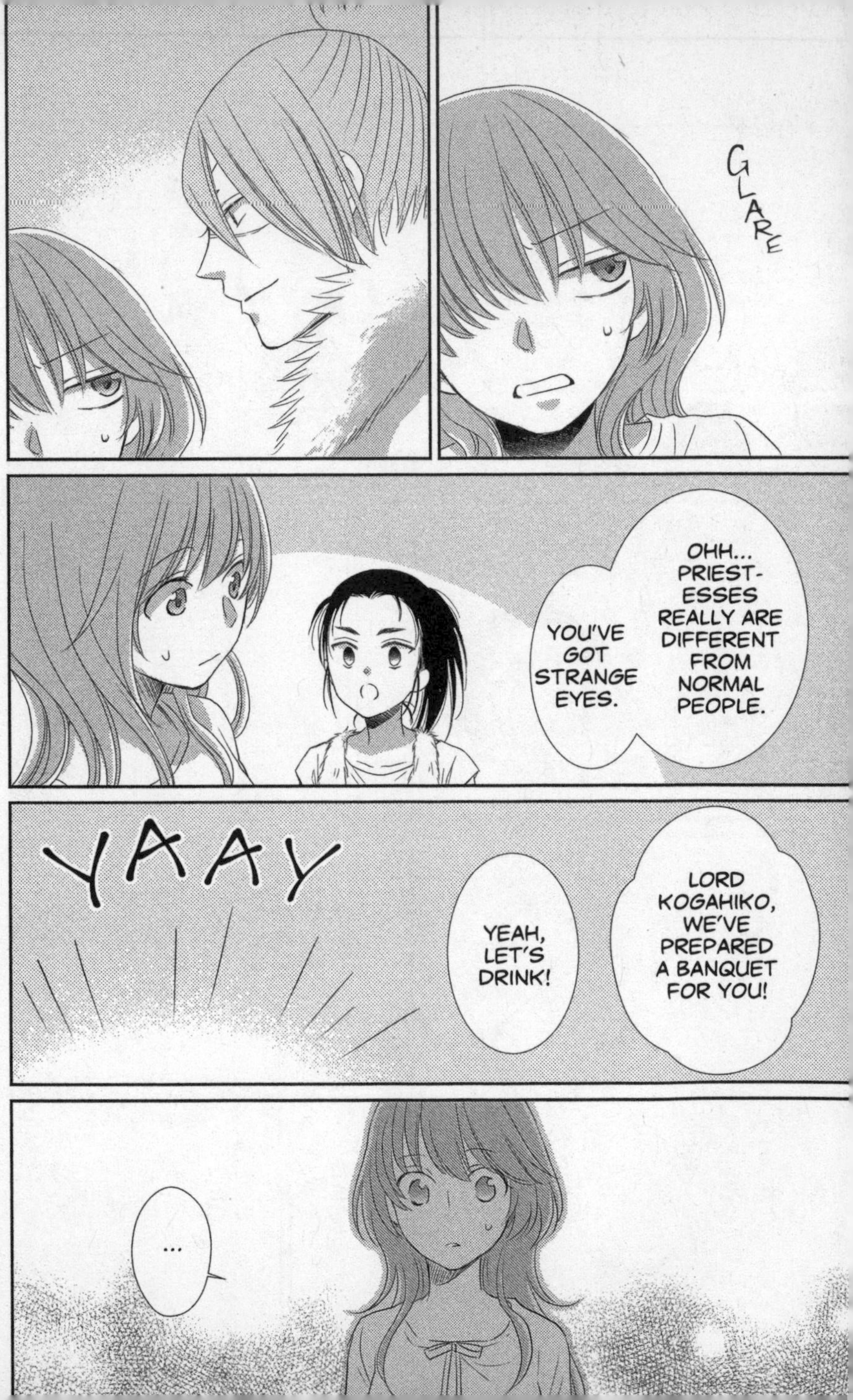
GLARE
OHH... PRIEST-ESSES REALLY ARE DIFFERENT FROM NORMAL PEOPLE.
YOU'VE GOT STRANGE EYES.
LORD KOGAHIKO, WE'VE PREPARED A BANQUET FOR YOU!
YEAH, LET'S DRINK!
YAAY
...

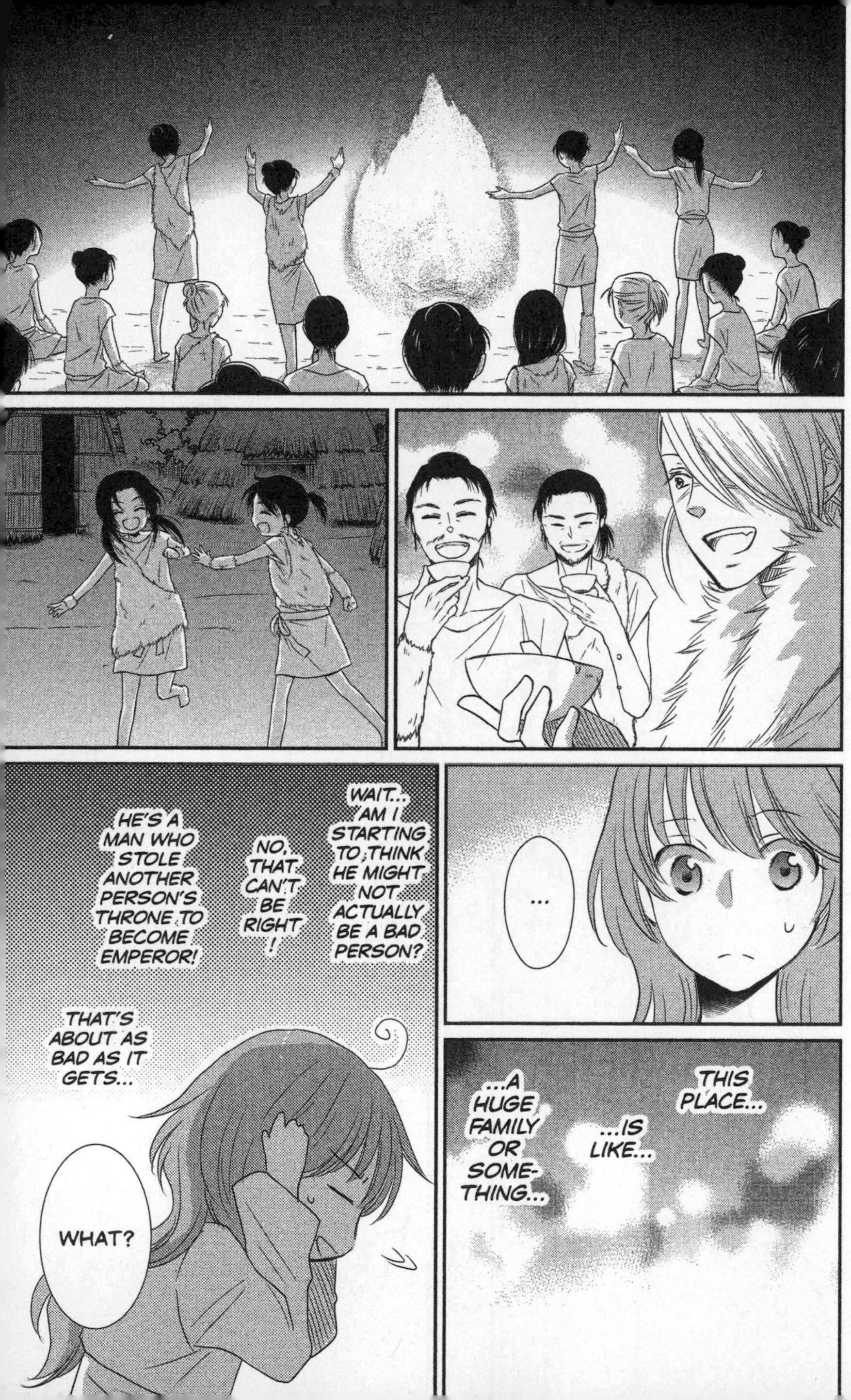
...
THIS PLACE...
...IS LIKE...
...A HUGE FAMILY OR SOMETHING...
WAIT... AM I STARTING TO THINK HE MIGHT NOT ACTUALLY BE A BAD PERSON?
NO, THAT CAN'T BE RIGHT!
HE'S A MAN WHO STOLE ANOTHER PERSON'S THRONE TO BECOME EMPEROR!
THAT'S ABOUT AS BAD AS IT GETS...
WHAT?

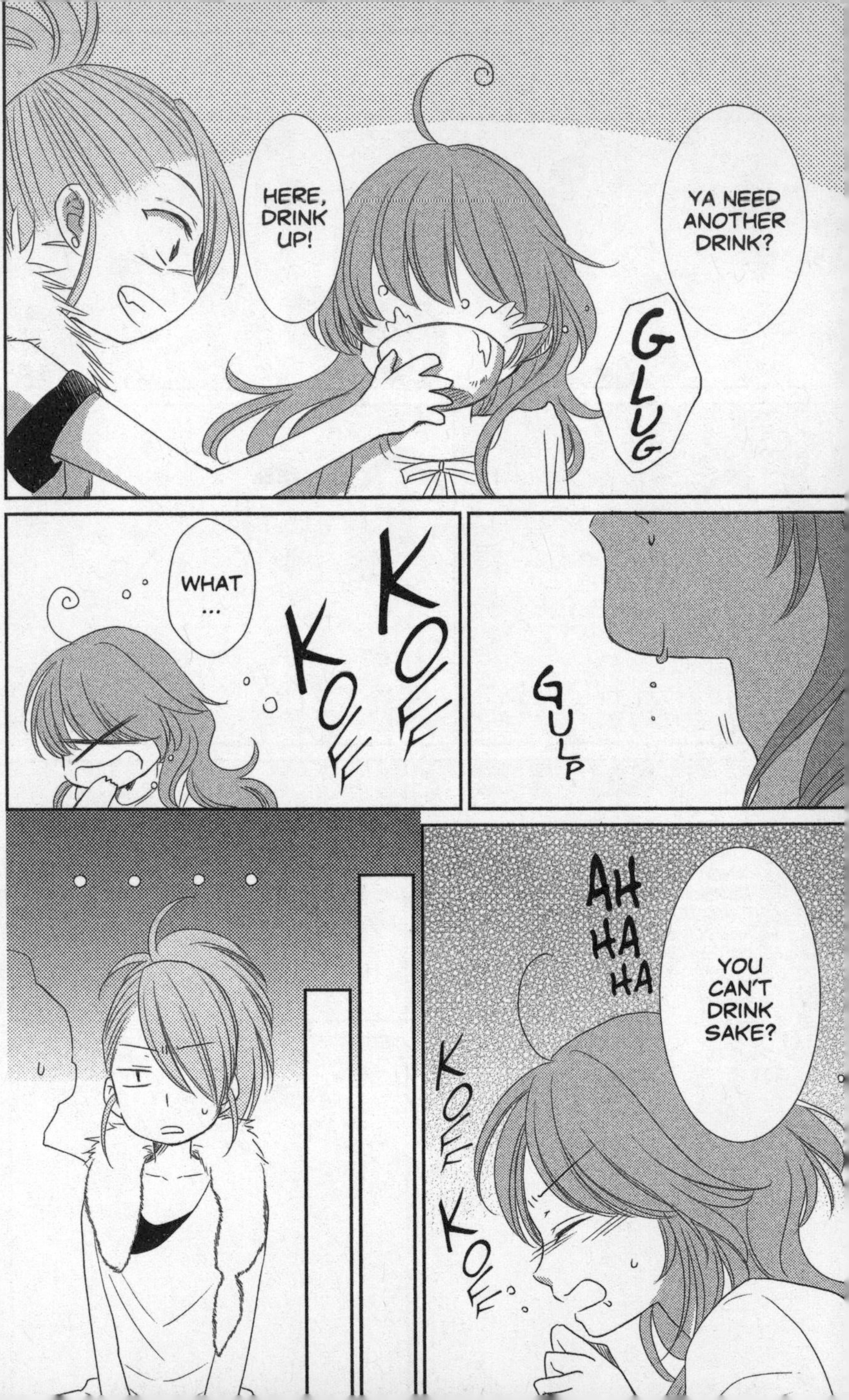
YA NEED ANOTHER DRINK?
GLUG
HERE, DRINK UP!
GULP
KOFF KOFF
WHAT...
YOU CAN'T DRINK SAKE?
AH HA HA
KOFF KOFF
....

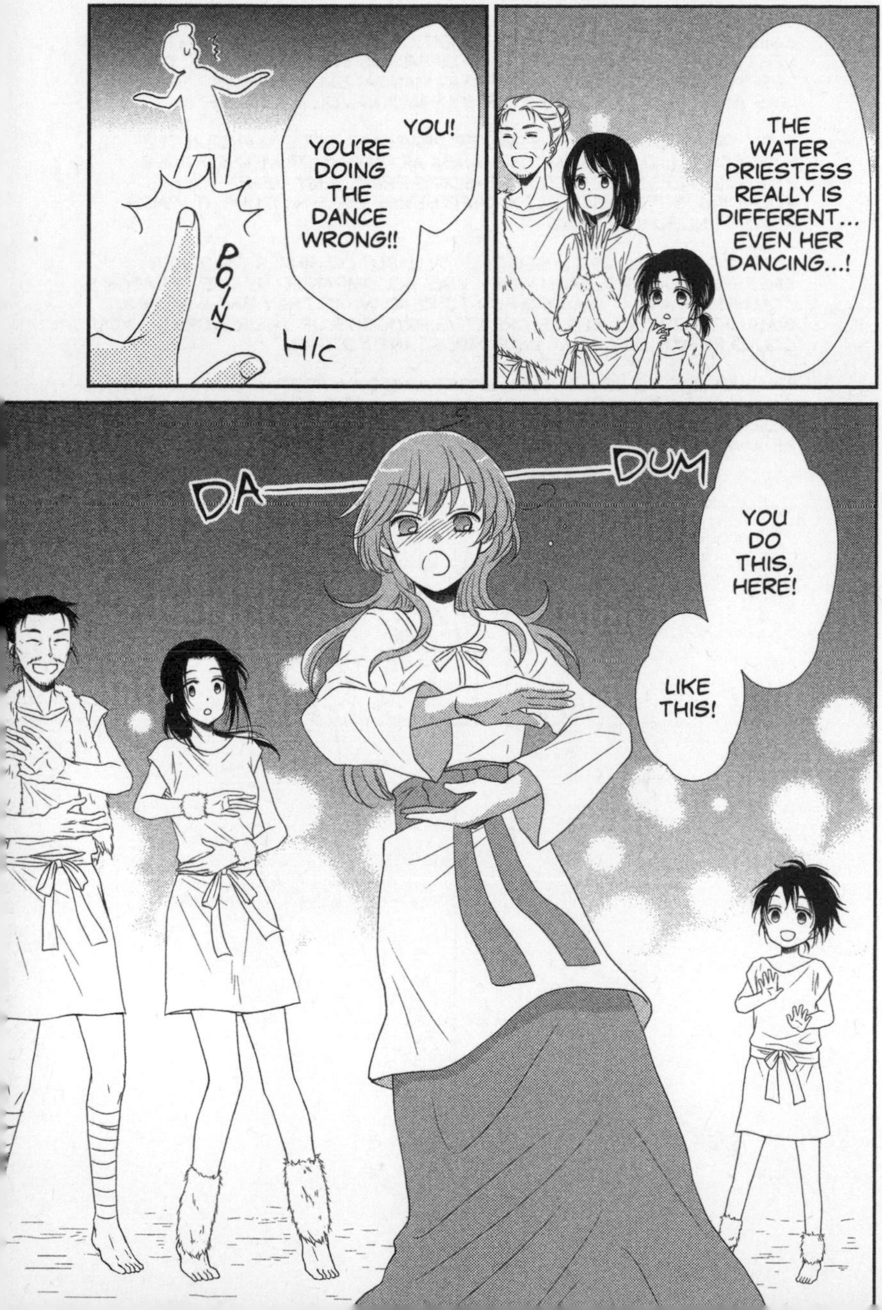
THE WATER PRIESTESS REALLY IS DIFFERENT... EVEN HER DANCING...!
YOU!
YOU'RE DOING THE DANCE WRONG!!
POINT
HIC
DA—DUM
YOU DO THIS, HERE!
LIKE THIS!

I WENT TO AN EXHIBITION OF ORIGINAL ART.

CHEESE! HAS AN ORIGINAL ART EXHIBITION GOING ON, SO WHEN I FINISHED MEETING WITH MY EDITOR, I WENT OVER AND CHECKED IT OUT. IT WAS THE "HOT MEN'S VOICES AND SHOJO MANGA" EXHIBITION AND THERE WAS AN AUDIO GUIDE NARRATED BY FAMOUS VOICE ACTORS.

THEY GRACIOUSLY LET *THE WATER DRAGON'S BRIDE* IN AMONG THE WORK OF ALL THESE FAMOUS MANGA ARTISTS. HOT MEN'S VOICES...! INTRODUCING...! *THE WATER DRAGON'S BRIDE*...! MY HEART WAS POUNDING, BUT I ALSO FELT A DEEP SENSE OF GRATITUDE. IT WAS A REALLY UNUSUAL FEELING.

IT WAS SO THRILLING TO SEE THE VALUABLE ORIGINALS OF OTHER *CHEESE!* CREATORS. EACH WORK WAS ACCOMPANIED BY THE CREATOR'S COMMENTS, AND IT WAS SO FUN TO READ WHAT THEY HAD WRITTEN. IT WAS LIKE LOOKING AT THE CREATIVE PROCESS OF THEIR WORKS—YOU COULD REALLY SEE WHAT WAS IMPORTANT TO THEM.

IF YOU'D LIKE TO BE A MANGA ARTIST ONE DAY, I DEFINITELY RECOMMEND TAKING ADVANTAGE OF AN OPPORTUNITY LIKE THIS TO GO SEE ORIGINAL WORK IN REAL LIFE. IT'LL REALLY ENCOURAGE YOU, AND ABOVE ALL, IT'LL BE A VALUABLE LEARNING EXPERIENCE!

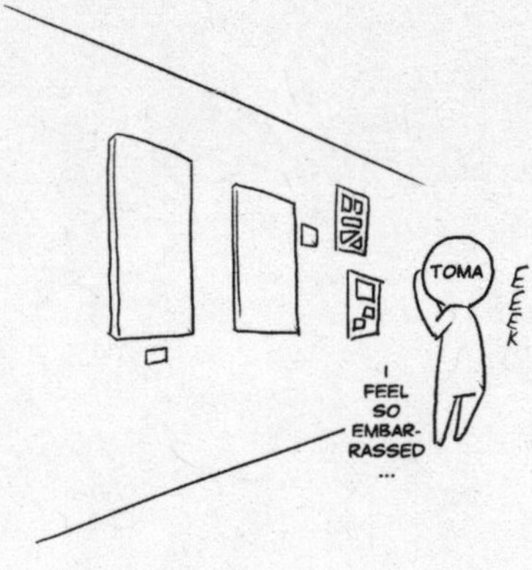

TOMA
EEEK
I FEEL SO EMBARRASSED...

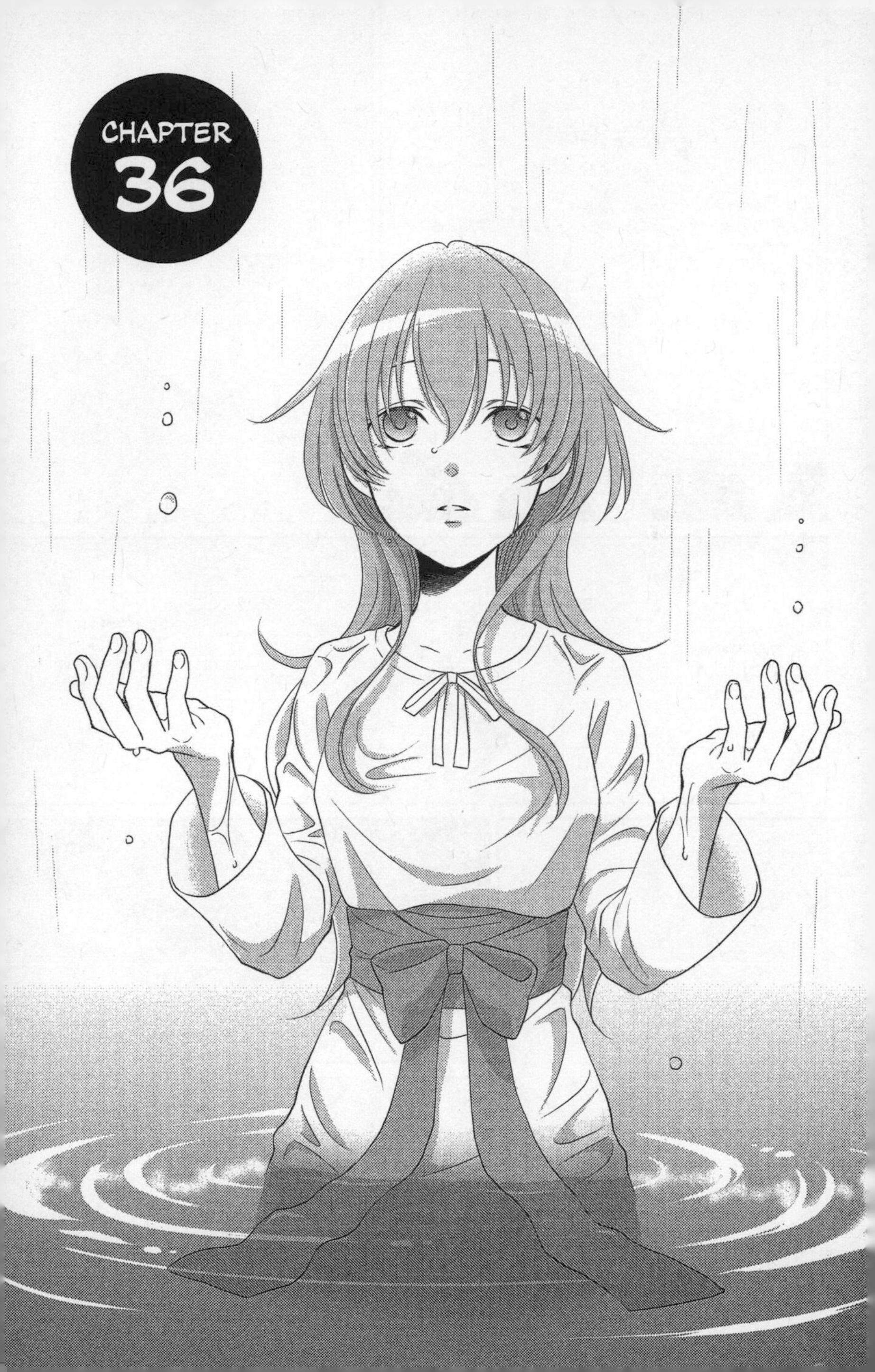
CHAPTER
36

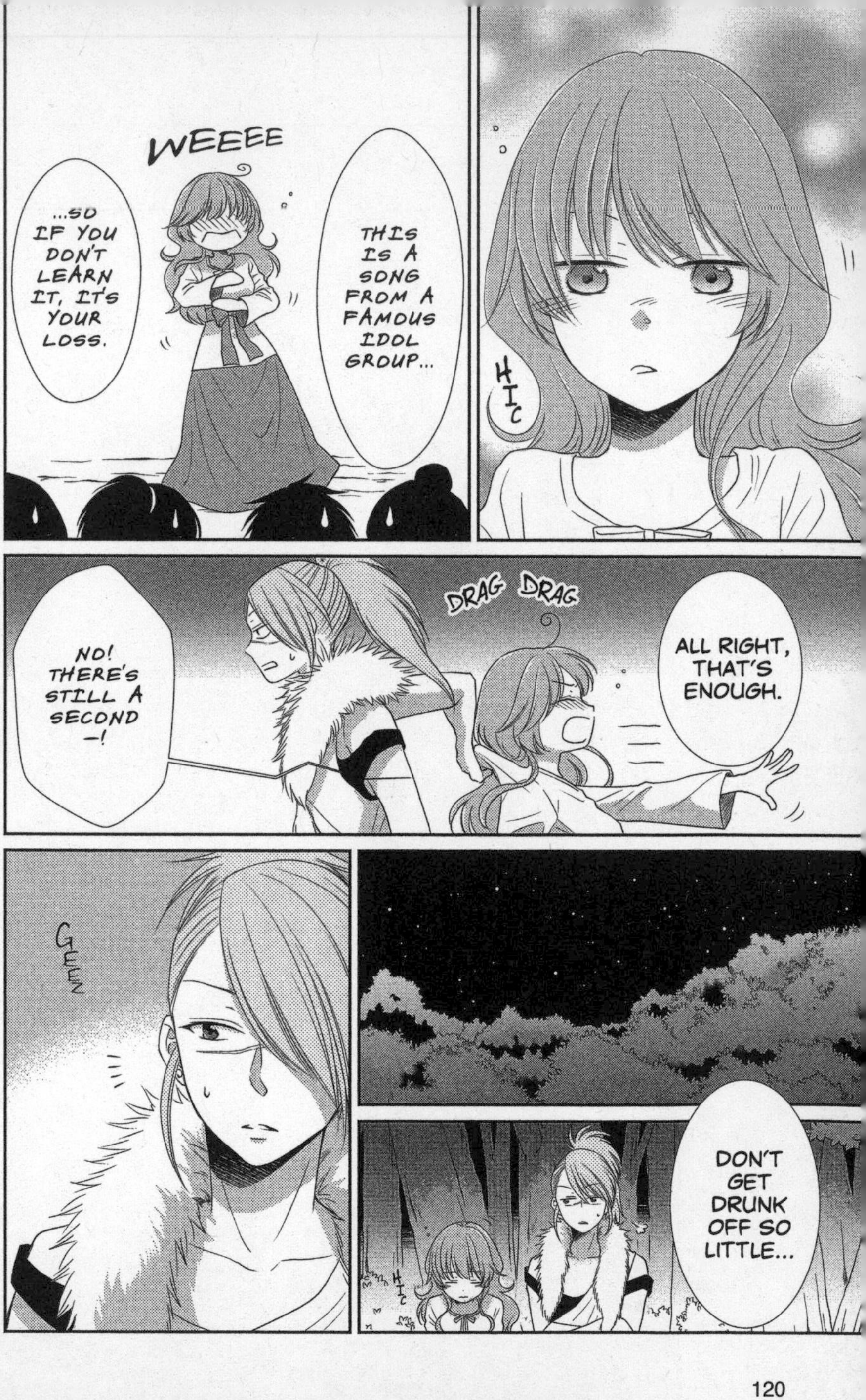
HIC
THIS IS A SONG FROM A FAMOUS IDOL GROUP...
WEEEE
...SO IF YOU DON'T LEARN IT, IT'S YOUR LOSS.
ALL RIGHT, THAT'S ENOUGH.
DRAG DRAG
NO! THERE'S STILL A SECOND—!
DON'T GET DRUNK OFF SO LITTLE...
HIC
GEEZ

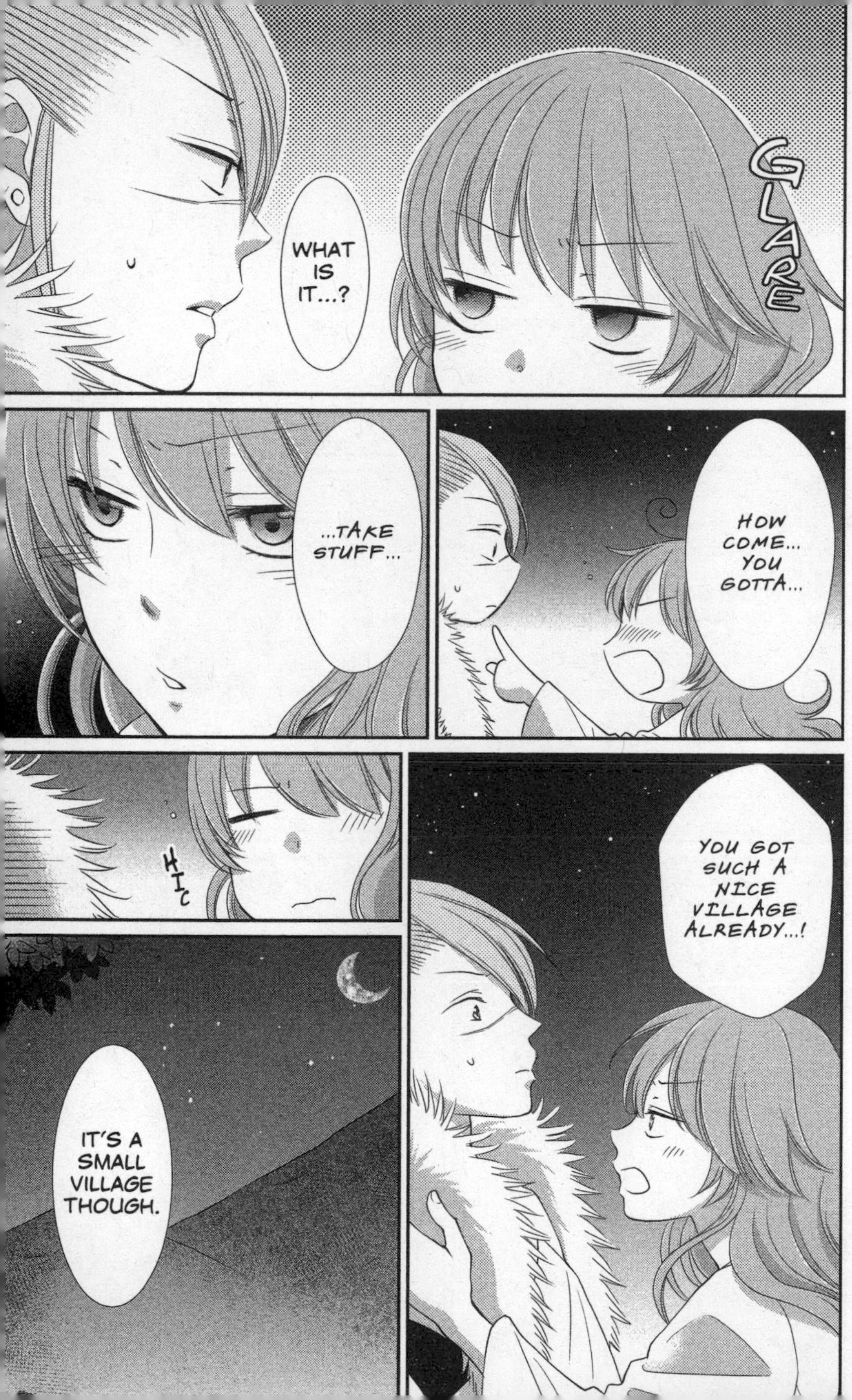
GLARE
WHAT IS IT...?
HOW COME... YOU GOTTA...
...TAKE STUFF...
YOU GOT SUCH A NICE VILLAGE ALREADY...!
HIC
IT'S A SMALL VILLAGE THOUGH.

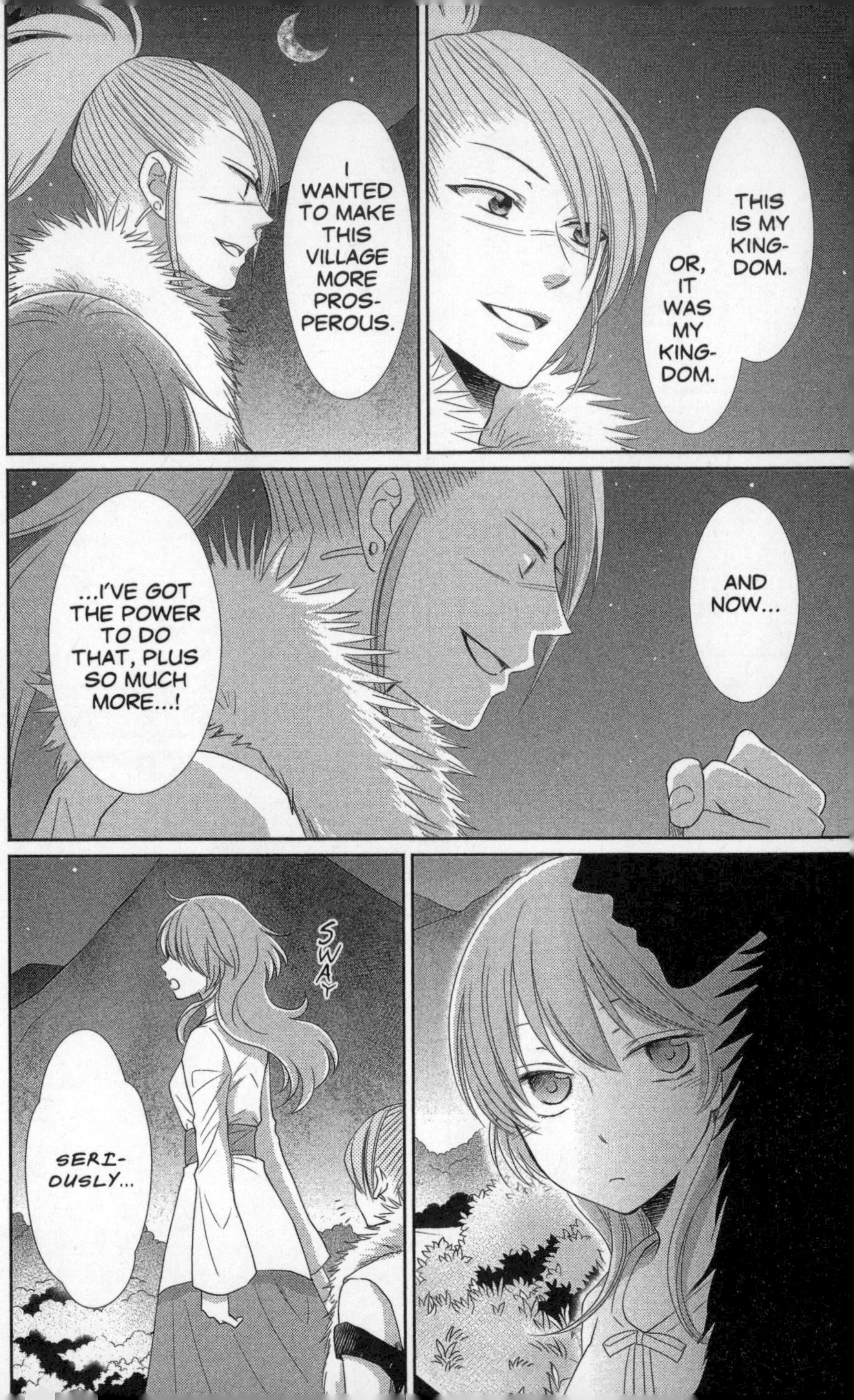
THIS IS MY KINGDOM.
OR, IT WAS MY KINGDOM.
I WANTED TO MAKE THIS VILLAGE MORE PROSPEROUS.
AND NOW...
...I'VE GOT THE POWER TO DO THAT, PLUS SO MUCH MORE...!
SWAY
SERIOUSLY...

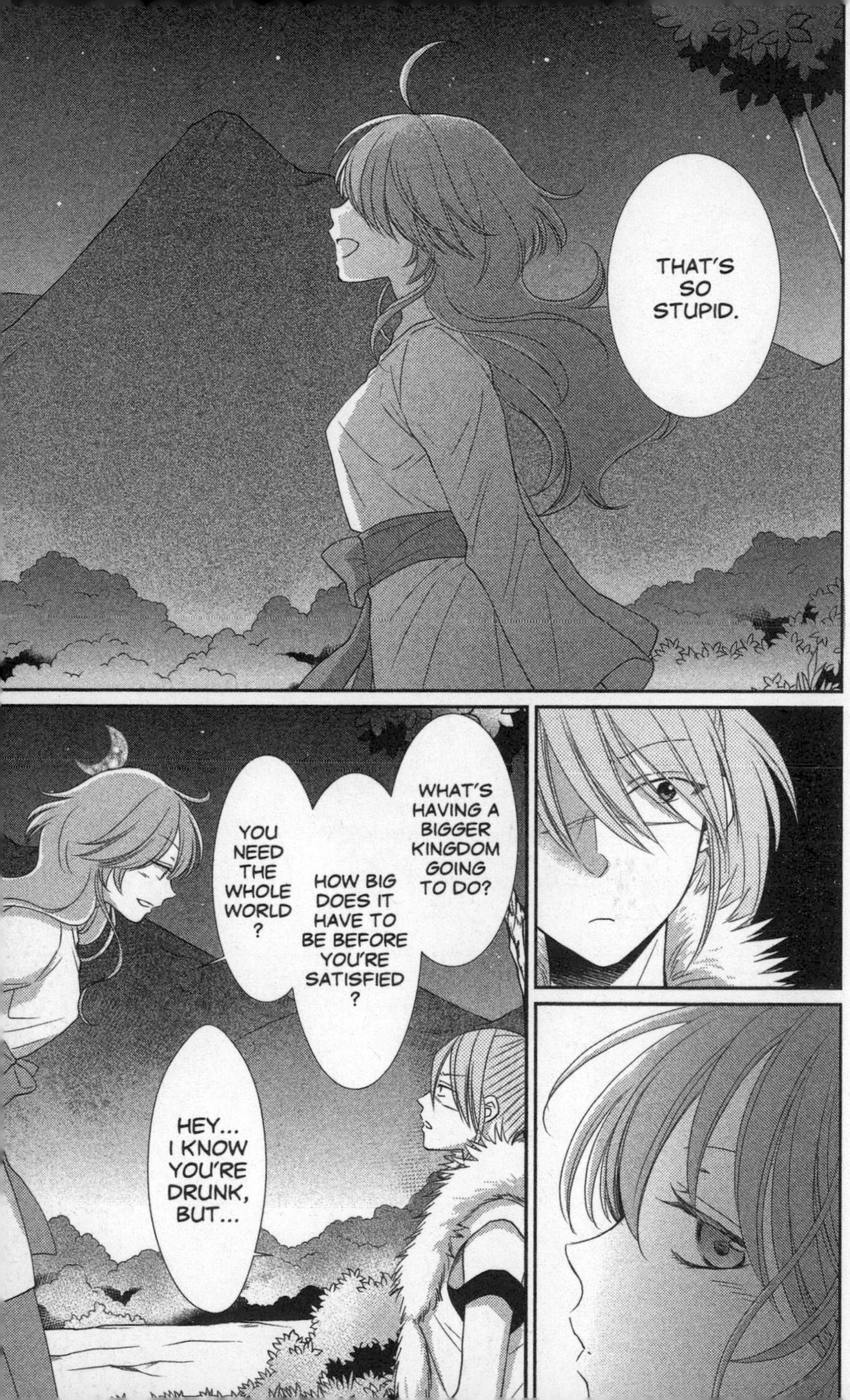
THAT'S SO STUPID.
WHAT'S HAVING A BIGGER KINGDOM GOING TO DO?
HOW BIG DOES IT HAVE TO BE BEFORE YOU'RE SATISFIED?
YOU NEED THE WHOLE WORLD?
HEY... I KNOW YOU'RE DRUNK, BUT...

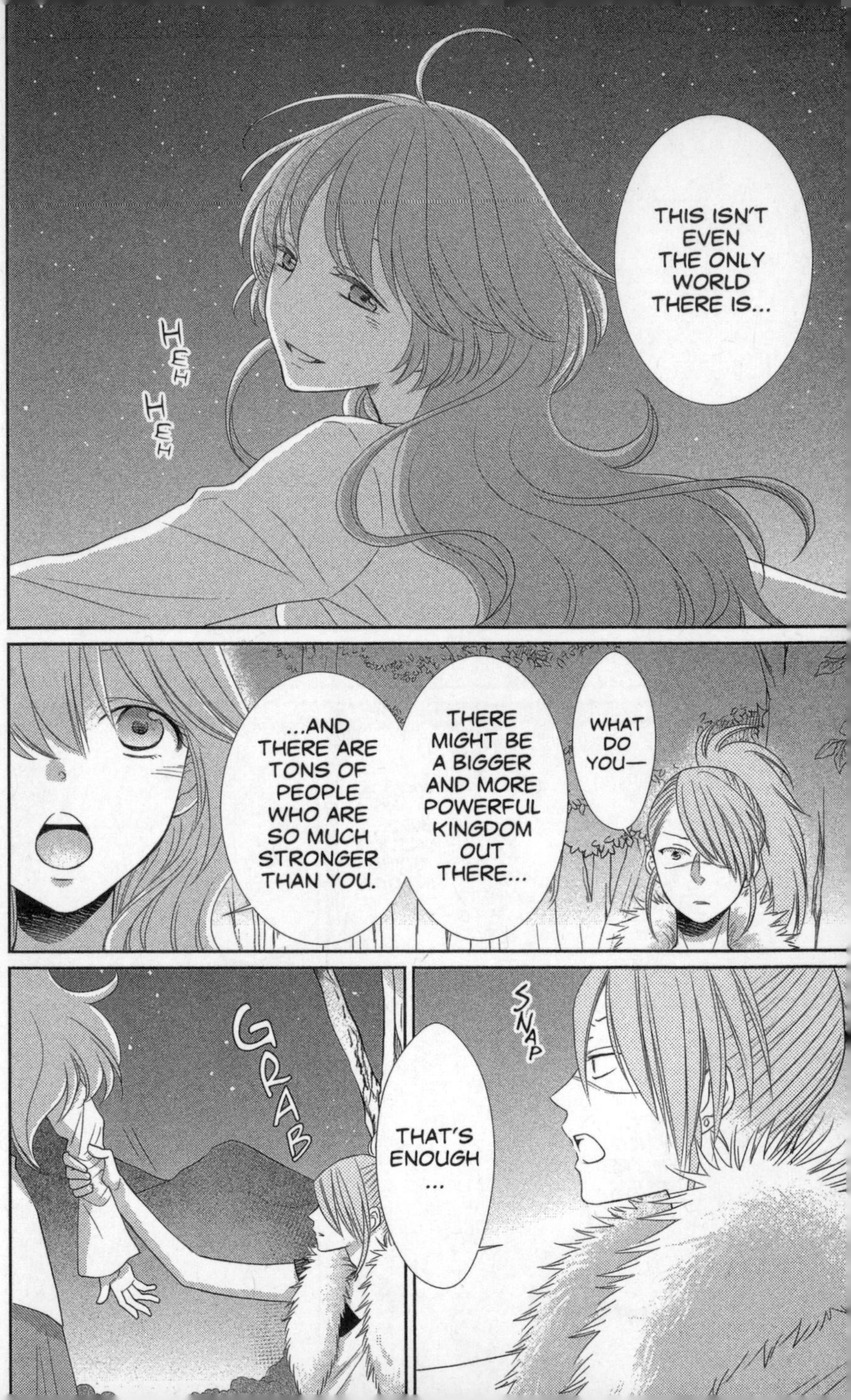
THIS ISN'T EVEN THE ONLY WORLD THERE IS...
HEH HEH
WHAT DO YOU—
THERE MIGHT BE A BIGGER AND MORE POWERFUL KINGDOM OUT THERE...
...AND THERE ARE TONS OF PEOPLE WHO ARE SO MUCH STRONGER THAN YOU.
SNAP
THAT'S ENOUGH ...
GRAB

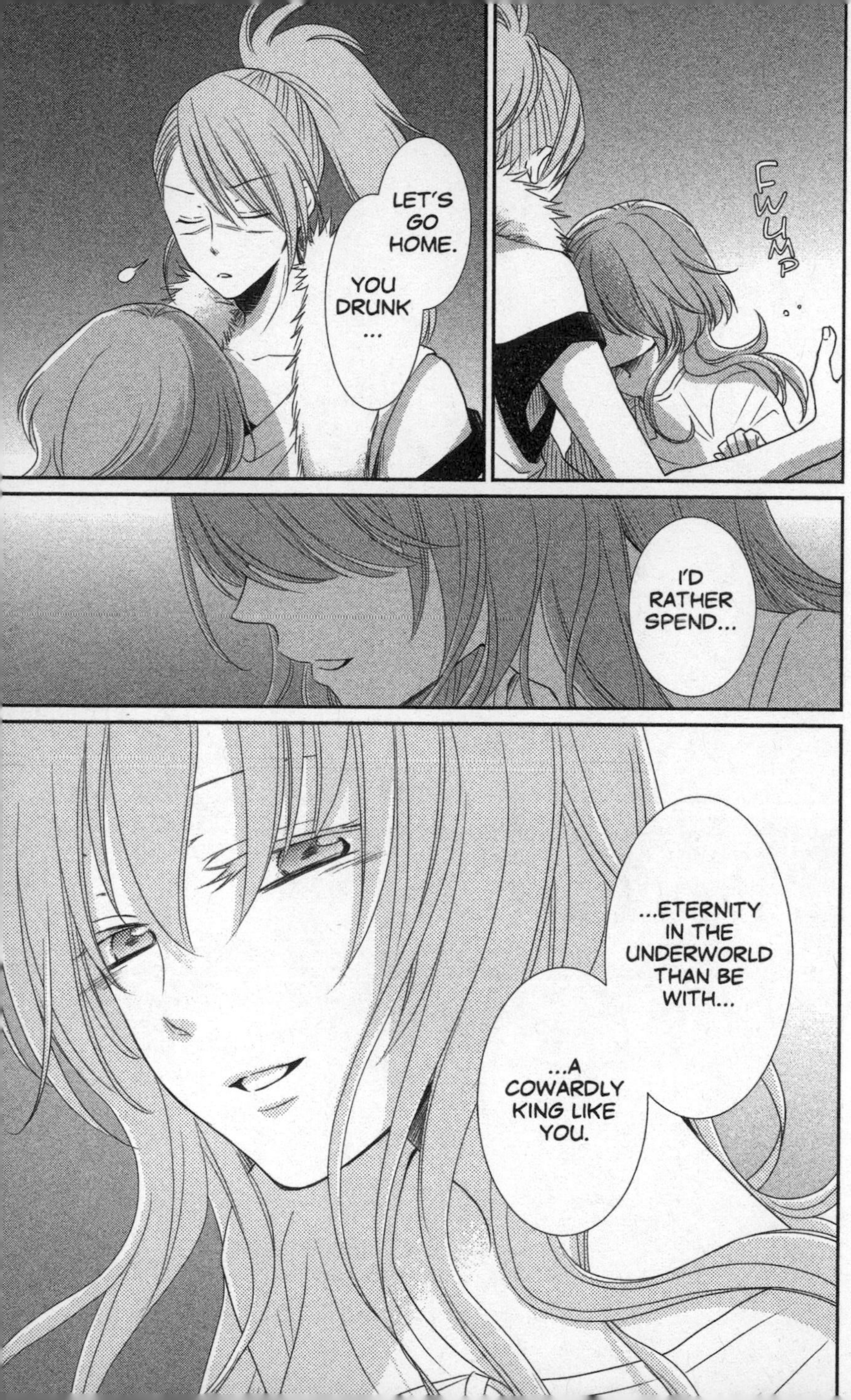
FWUMP
LET'S GO HOME.
YOU DRUNK ...
I'D RATHER SPEND...
...ETERNITY IN THE UNDERWORLD THAN BE WITH...
...A COWARDLY KING LIKE YOU.

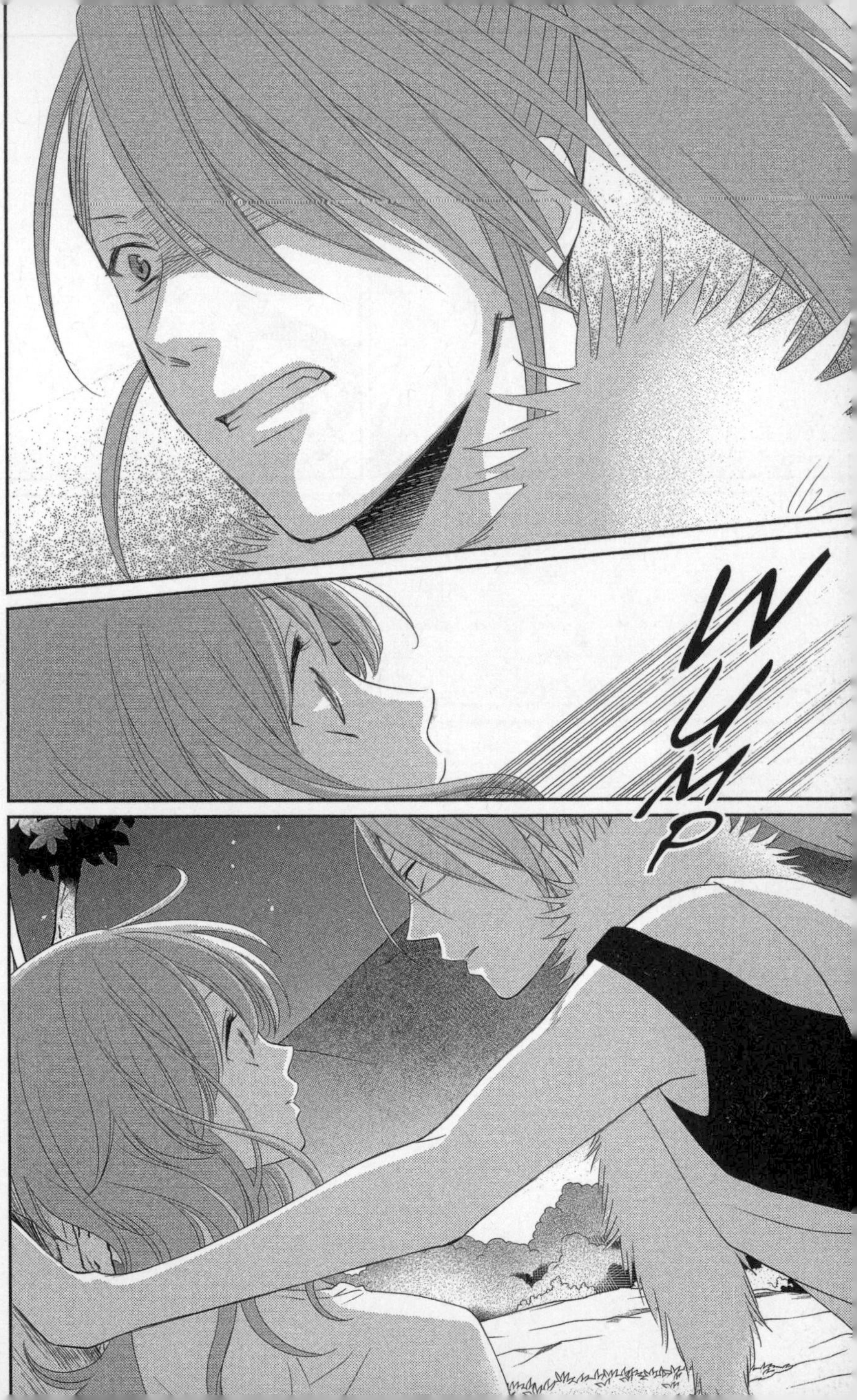
WUMP

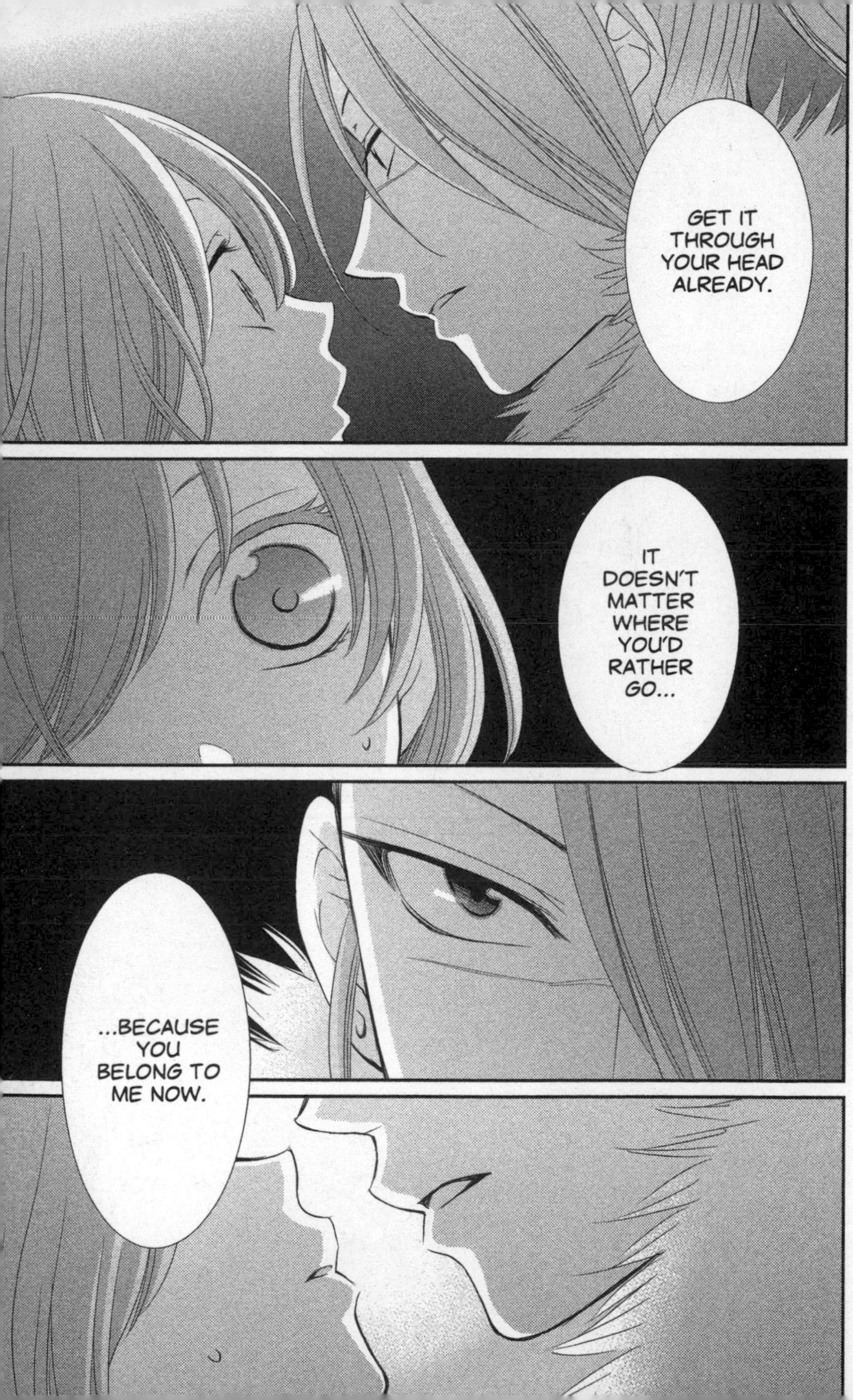
GET IT THROUGH YOUR HEAD ALREADY.
IT DOESN'T MATTER WHERE YOU'D RATHER GO...
...BECAUSE YOU BELONG TO ME NOW.

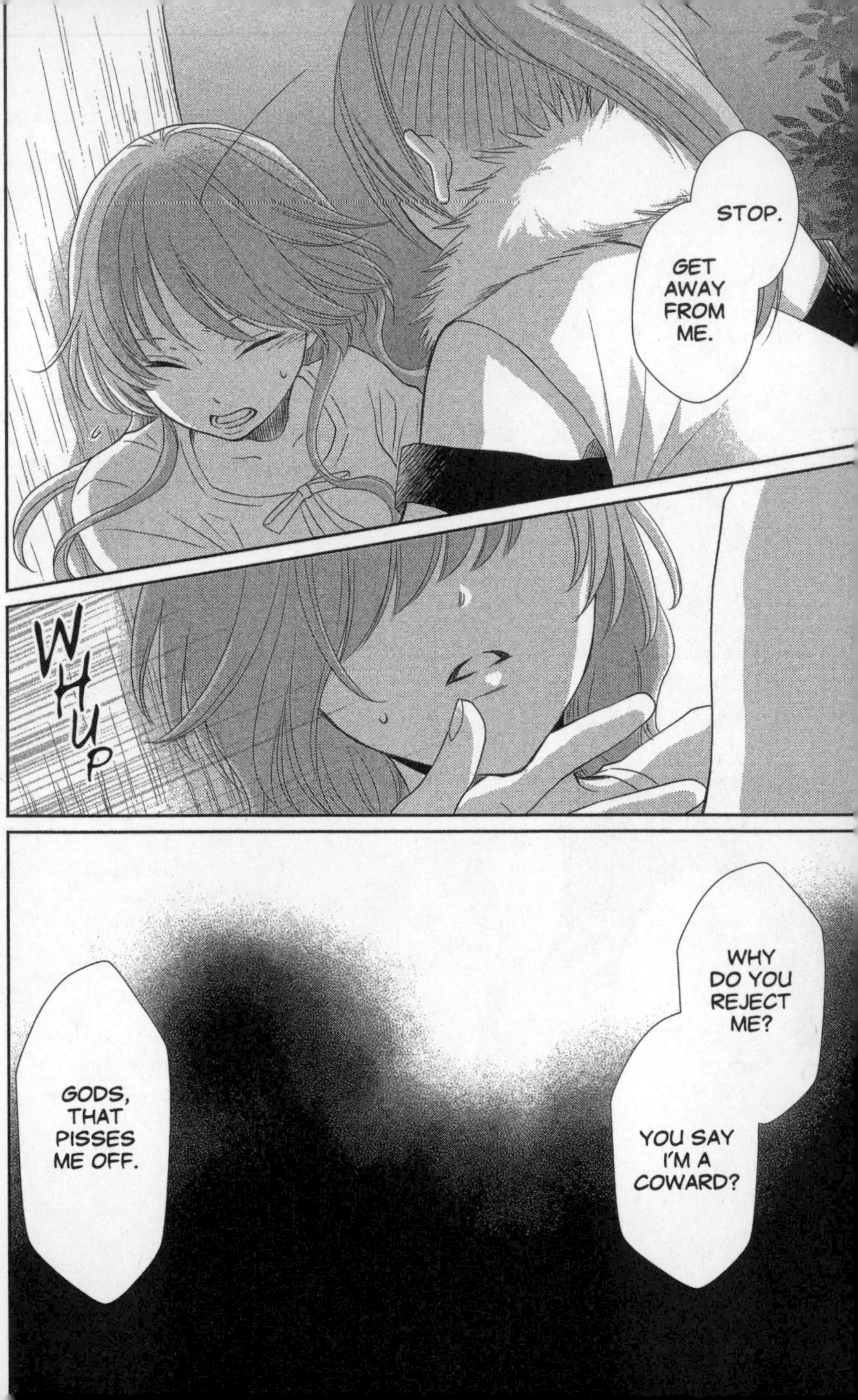
STOP.
GET AWAY FROM ME.
WHUP
WHY DO YOU REJECT ME?
YOU SAY I'M A COWARD?
GODS, THAT PISSES ME OFF.

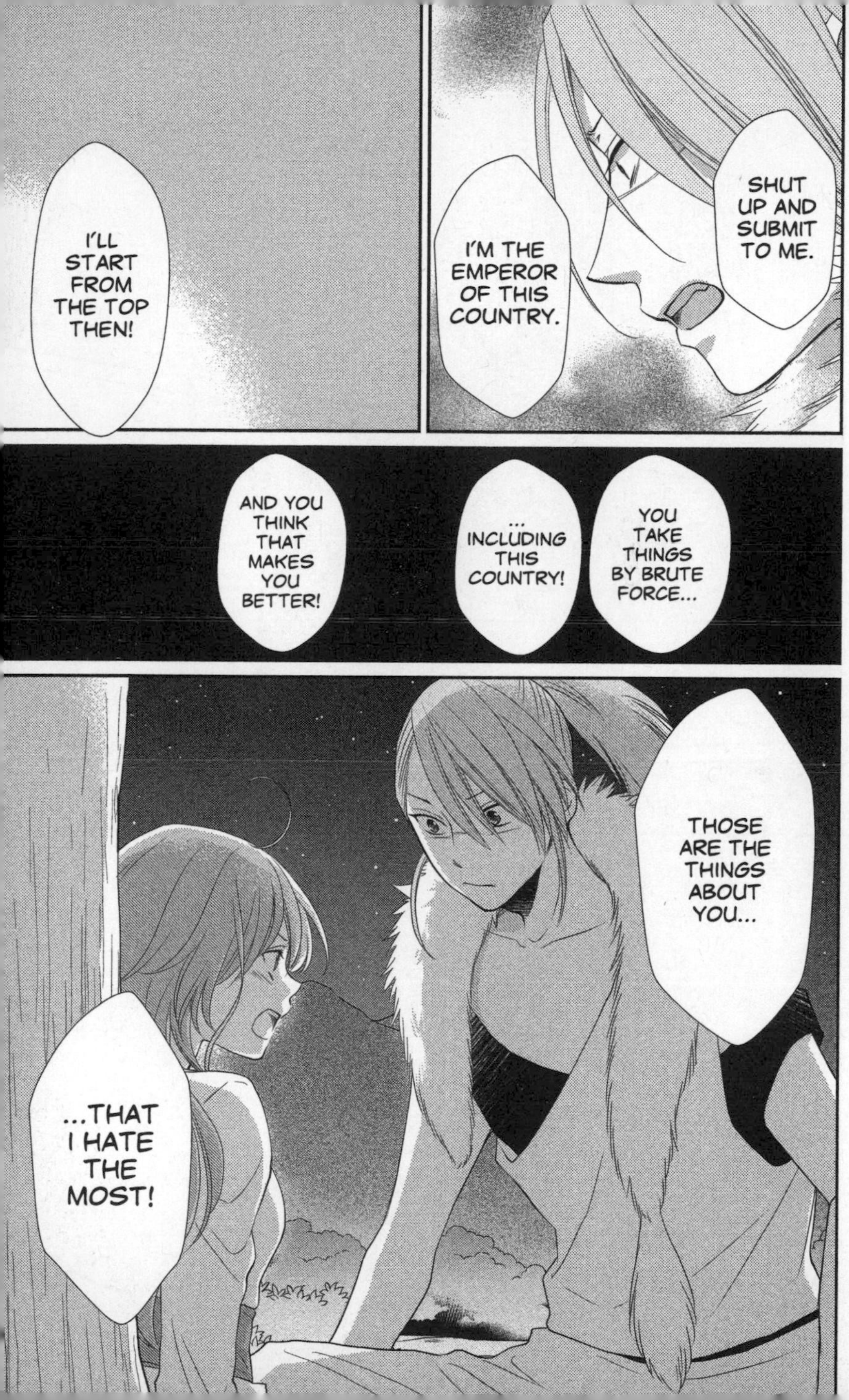
SHUT UP AND SUBMIT TO ME.
I'M THE EMPEROR OF THIS COUNTRY.
I'LL START FROM THE TOP THEN!
YOU TAKE THINGS BY BRUTE FORCE...
...INCLUDING THIS COUNTRY!
AND YOU THINK THAT MAKES YOU BETTER!
THOSE ARE THE THINGS ABOUT YOU...
...THAT I HATE THE MOST!

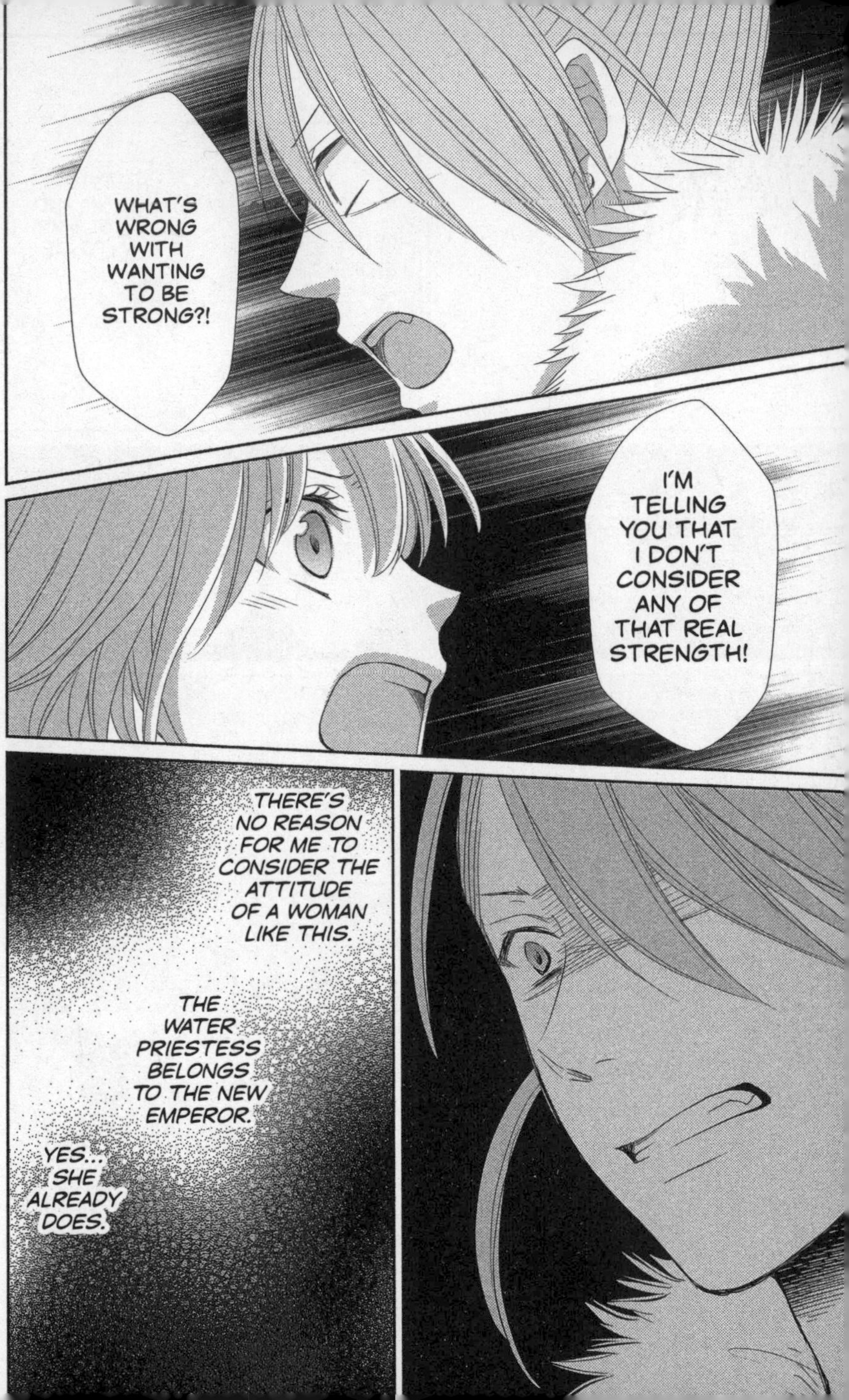
WHAT'S WRONG WITH WANTING TO BE STRONG?!
I'M TELLING YOU THAT I DON'T CONSIDER ANY OF THAT REAL STRENGTH!
THERE'S NO REASON FOR ME TO CONSIDER THE ATTITUDE OF A WOMAN LIKE THIS.
THE WATER PRIESTESS BELONGS TO THE NEW EMPEROR.
YES... SHE ALREADY DOES.

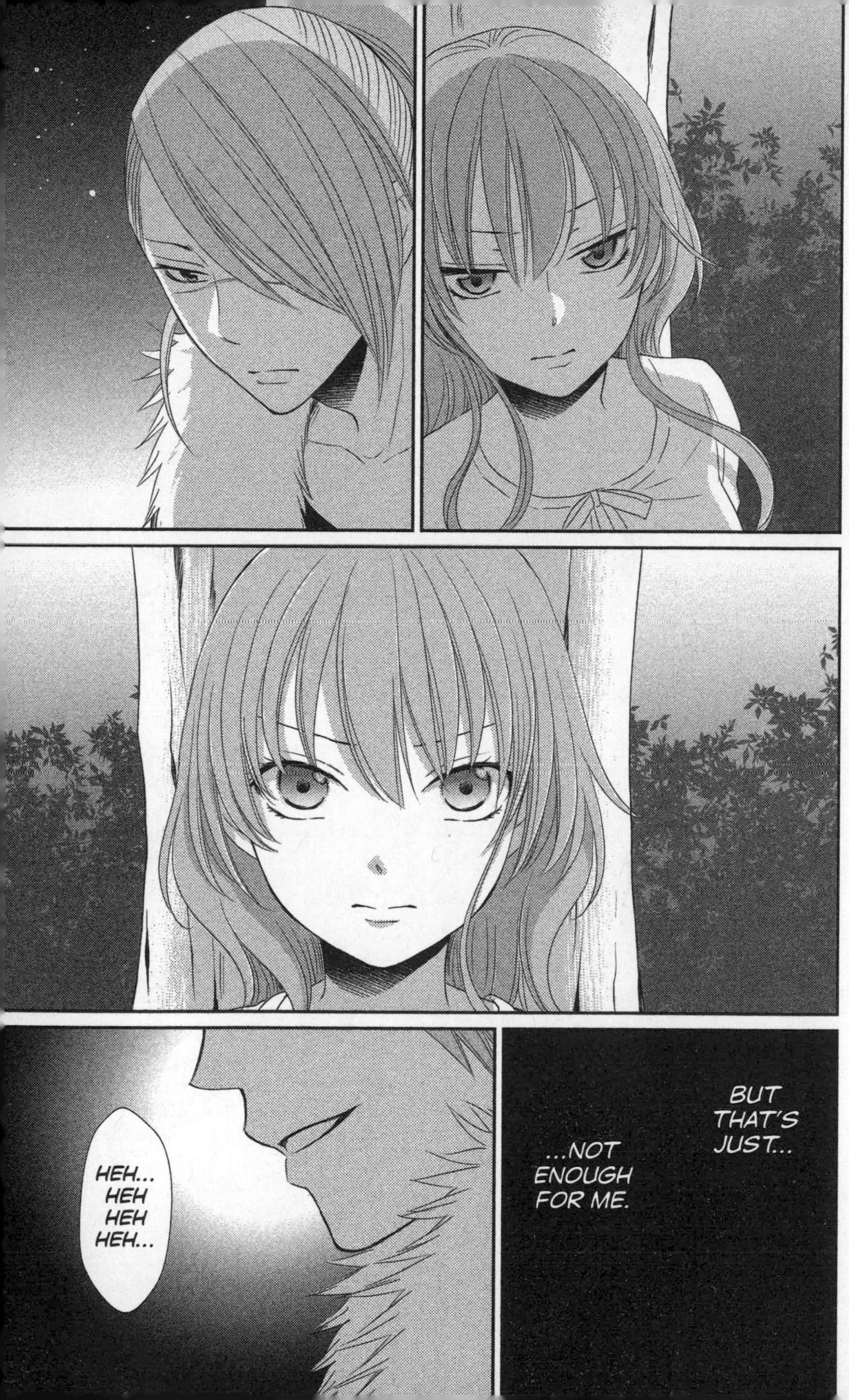
BUT THAT'S JUST...
...NOT ENOUGH FOR ME.
HEH... HEH HEH HEH...

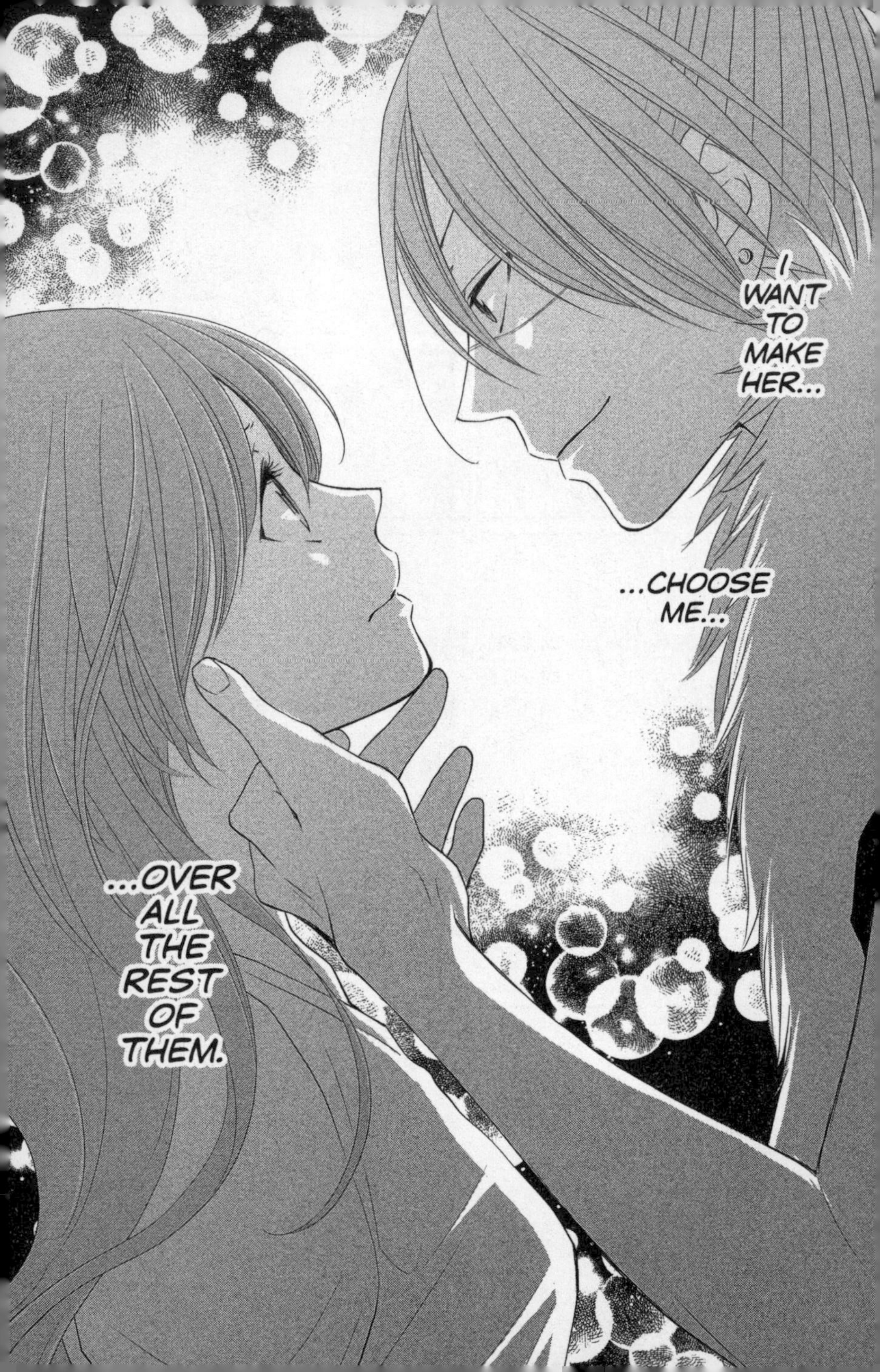
I WANT TO MAKE HER...
...CHOOSE ME...
...OVER ALL THE REST OF THEM.

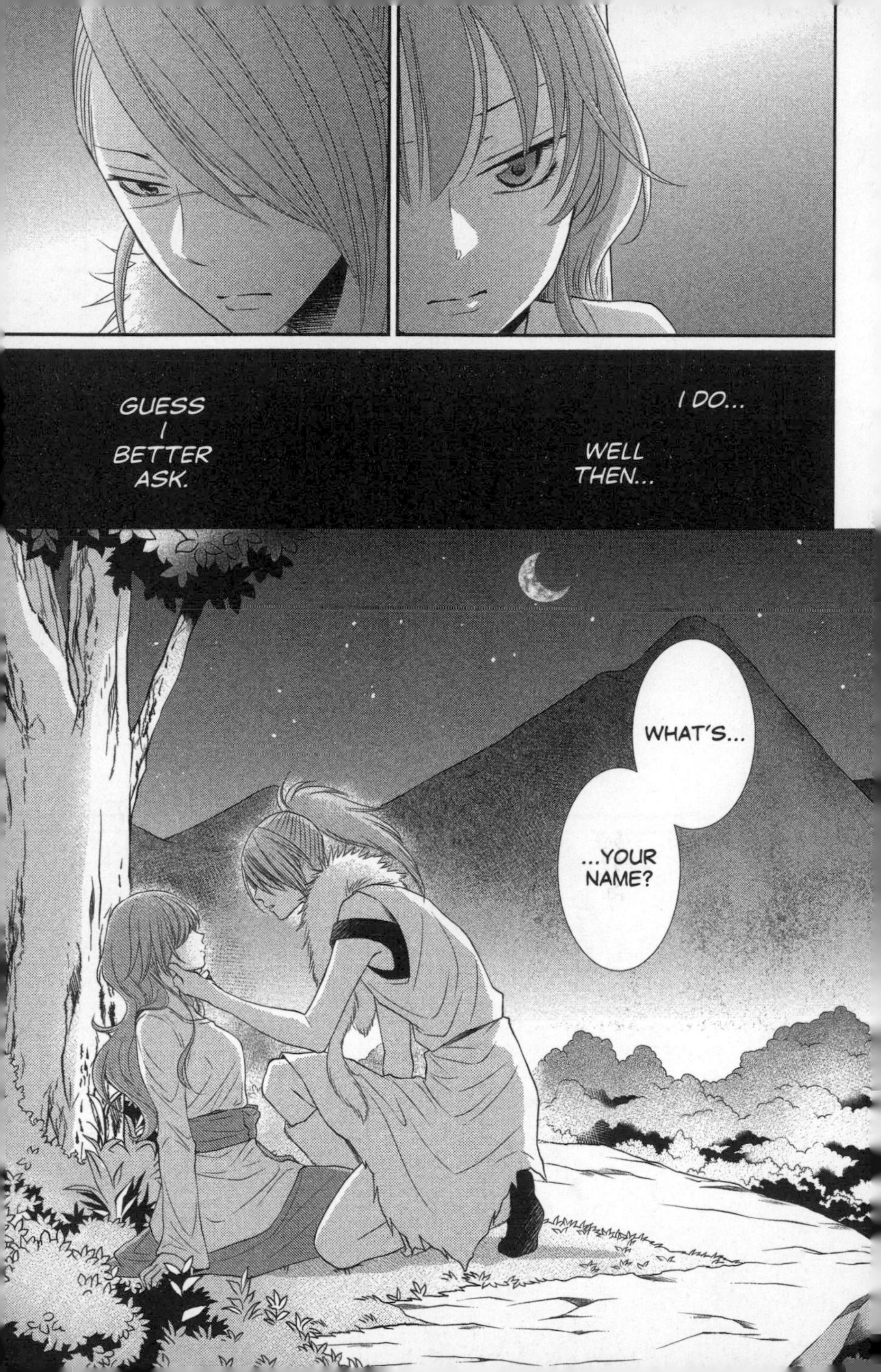
I DO...
WELL THEN...
GUESS I BETTER ASK.
WHAT'S...
...YOUR NAME?

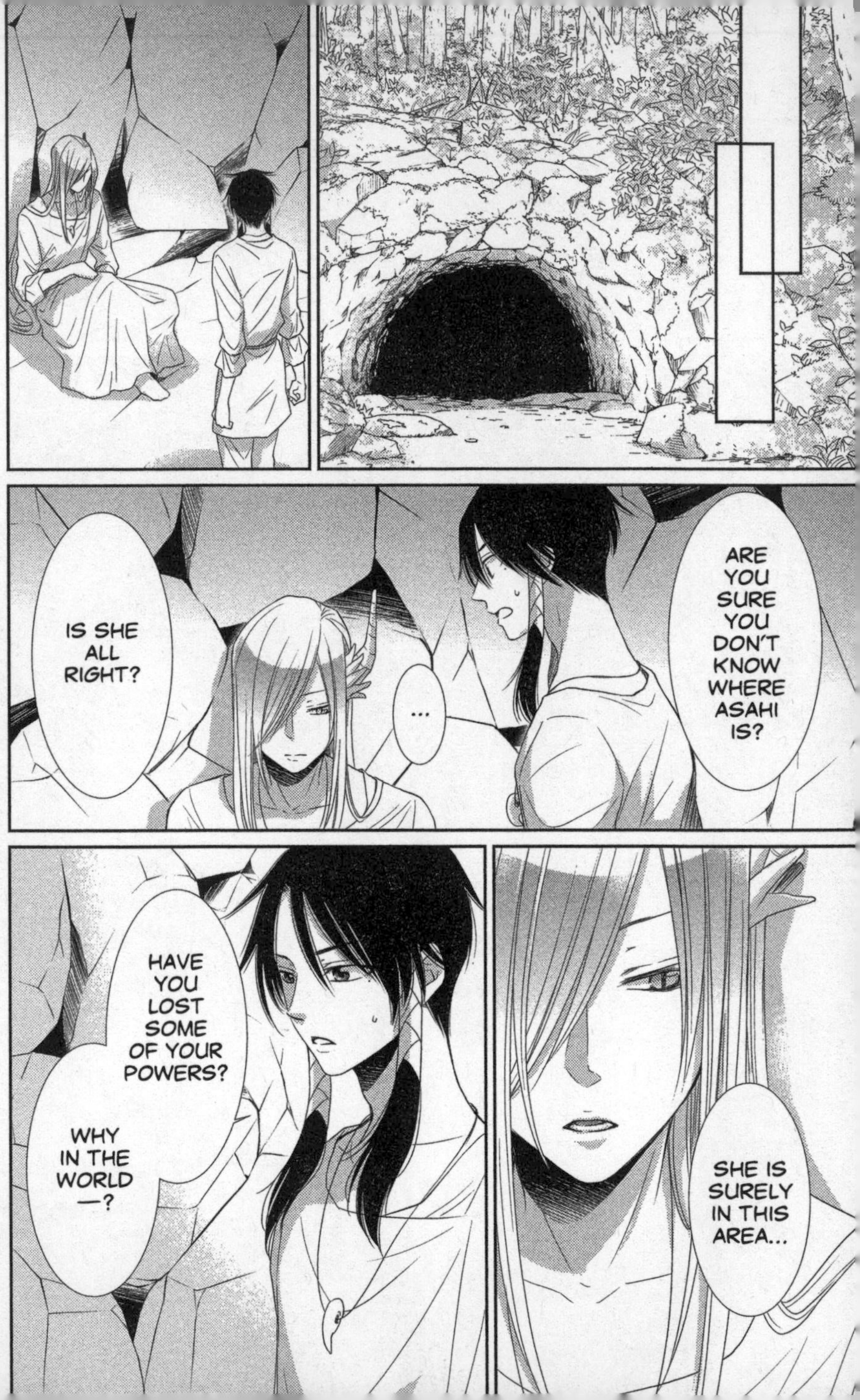
ARE YOU SURE YOU DON'T KNOW WHERE ASAHI IS?
...
IS SHE ALL RIGHT?
SHE IS SURELY IN THIS AREA...
HAVE YOU LOST SOME OF YOUR POWERS?
WHY IN THE WORLD —?

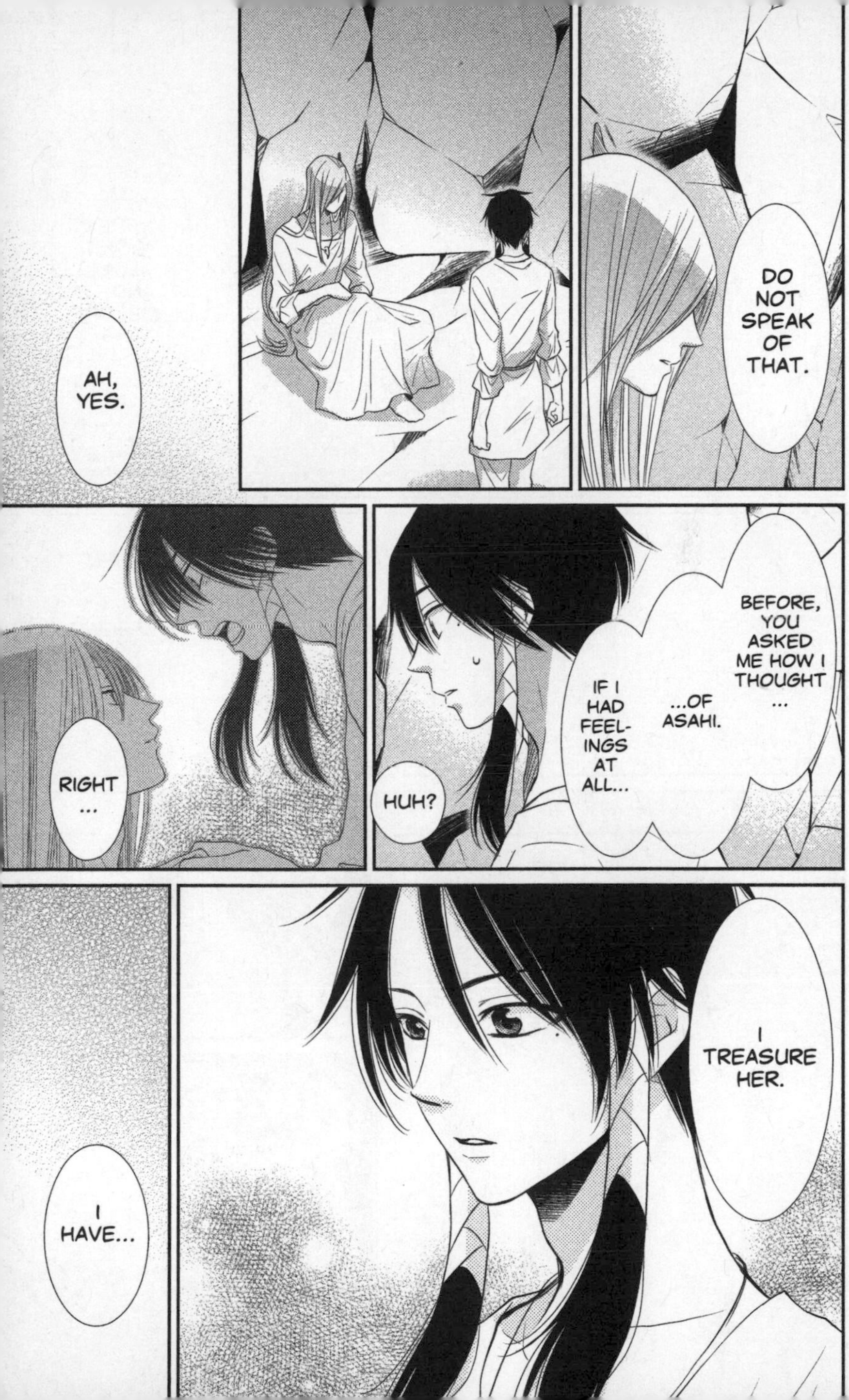
DO NOT SPEAK OF THAT.
AH, YES.
BEFORE, YOU ASKED ME HOW I THOUGHT...
...OF ASAHI.
IF I HAD FEELINGS AT ALL...
HUH?
RIGHT...
I TREASURE HER.
I HAVE...

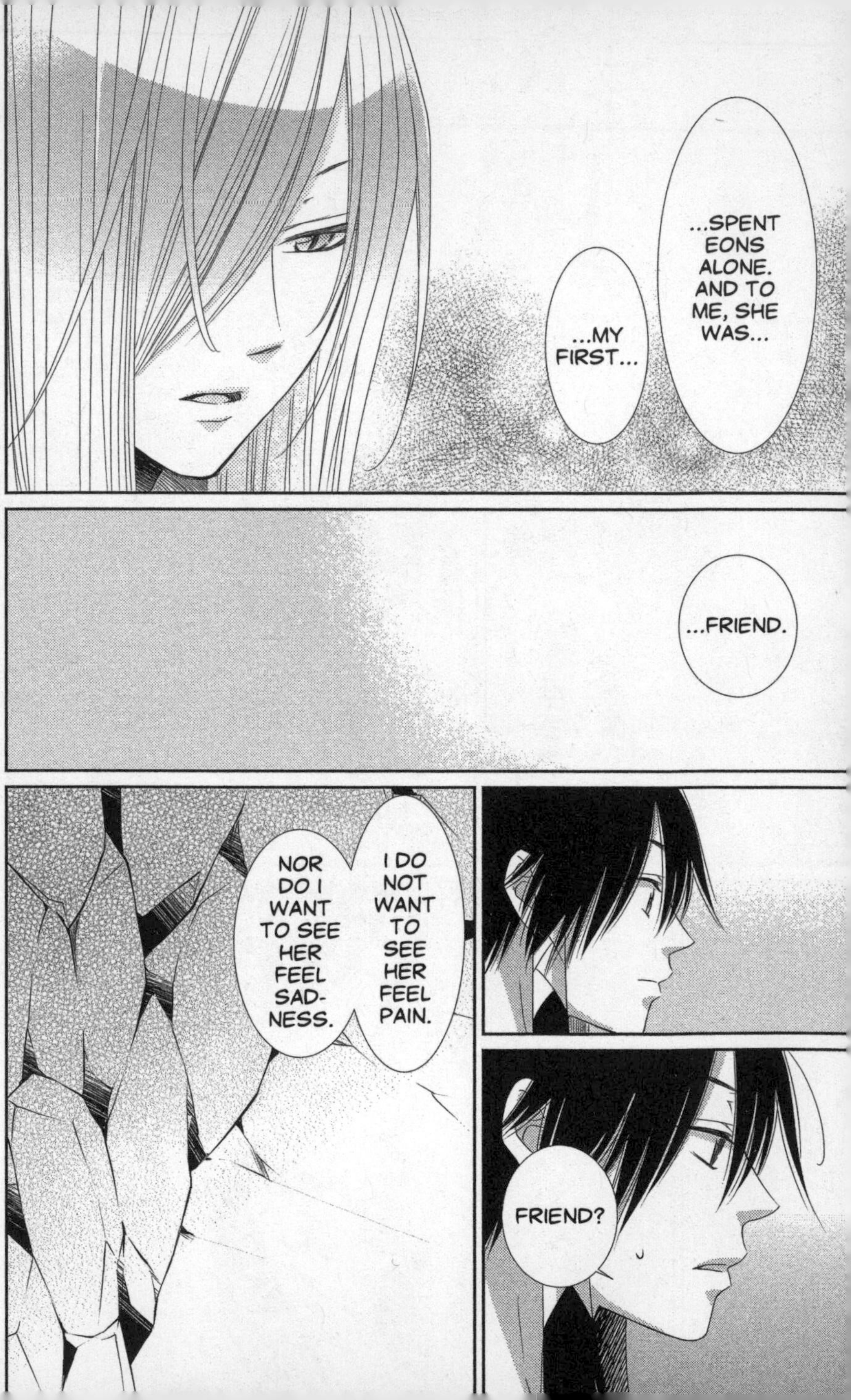
...SPENT EONS ALONE. AND TO ME, SHE WAS...
...MY FIRST...
...FRIEND.
FRIEND?
I DO NOT WANT TO SEE HER FEEL PAIN.
NOR DO I WANT TO SEE HER FEEL SAD-NESS.

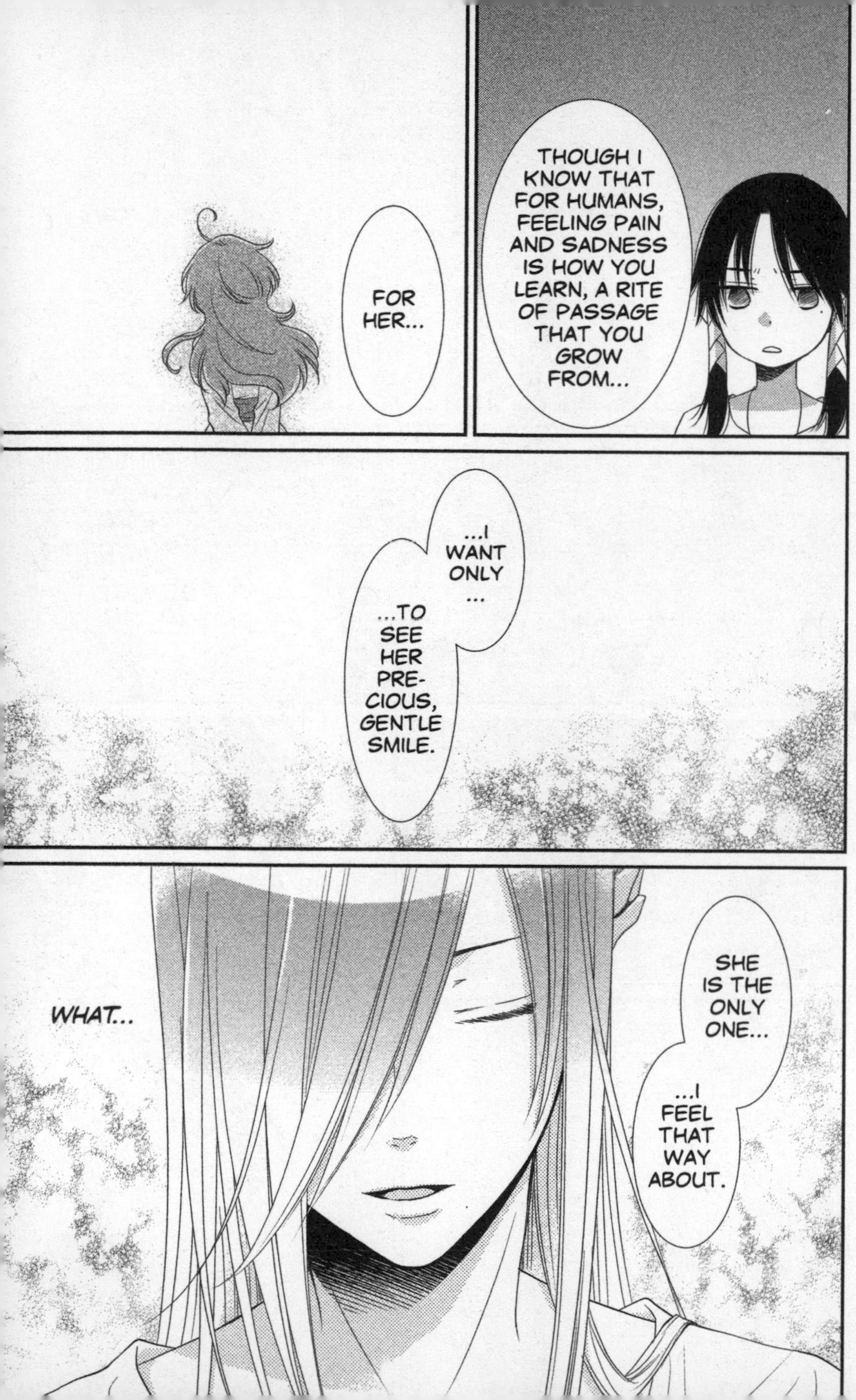
THOUGH I KNOW THAT FOR HUMANS, FEELING PAIN AND SADNESS IS HOW YOU LEARN, A RITE OF PASSAGE THAT YOU GROW FROM...
FOR HER...
...I WANT ONLY ...
...TO SEE HER PRE-CIOUS, GENTLE SMILE.
SHE IS THE ONLY ONE...
...I FEEL THAT WAY ABOUT.
WHAT...

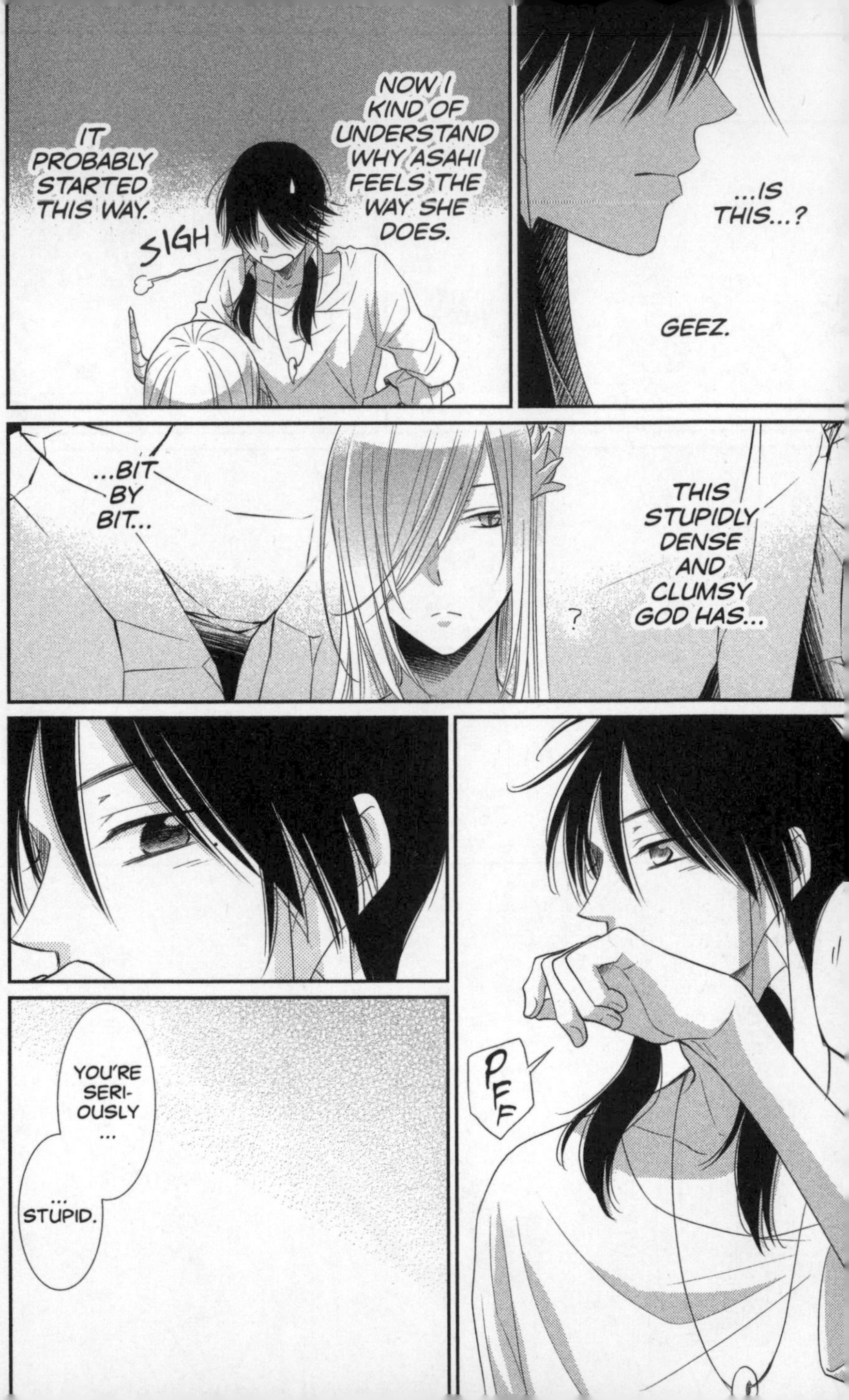
...IS THIS...?
GEEZ.
NOW I KIND OF UNDERSTAND WHY ASAHI FEELS THE WAY SHE DOES.
IT PROBABLY STARTED THIS WAY.
SIGH
THIS STUPIDLY DENSE AND CLUMSY GOD HAS...
?
...BIT BY BIT...
PFF
YOU'RE SERI-OUSLY ...
... STUPID.

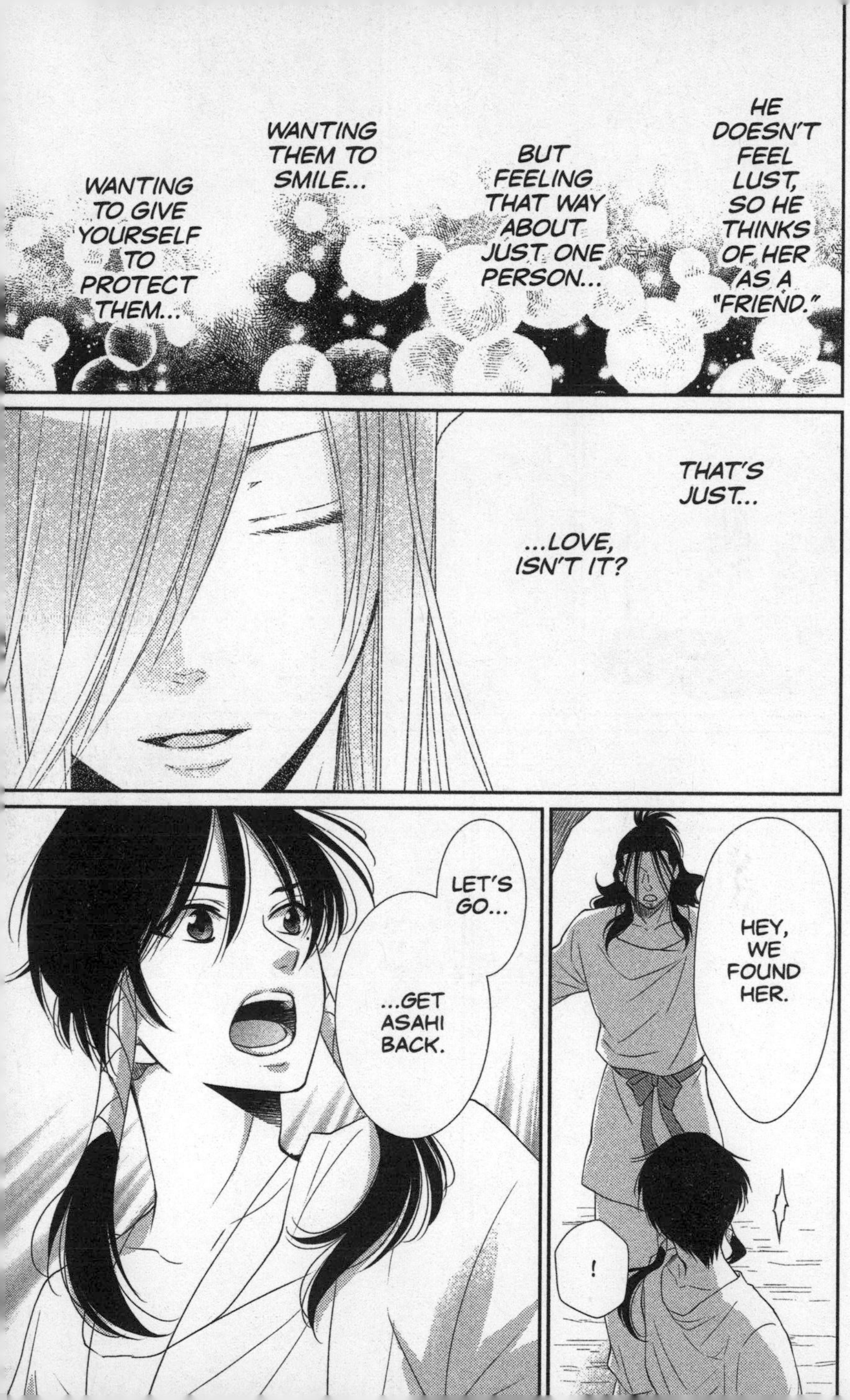
HE DOESN'T FEEL LUST, SO HE THINKS OF HER AS A "FRIEND."
BUT FEELING THAT WAY ABOUT JUST ONE PERSON...
WANTING THEM TO SMILE...
WANTING TO GIVE YOURSELF TO PROTECT THEM...
THAT'S JUST...
...LOVE, ISN'T IT?
HEY, WE FOUND HER.
!
LET'S GO...
...GET ASAHI BACK.

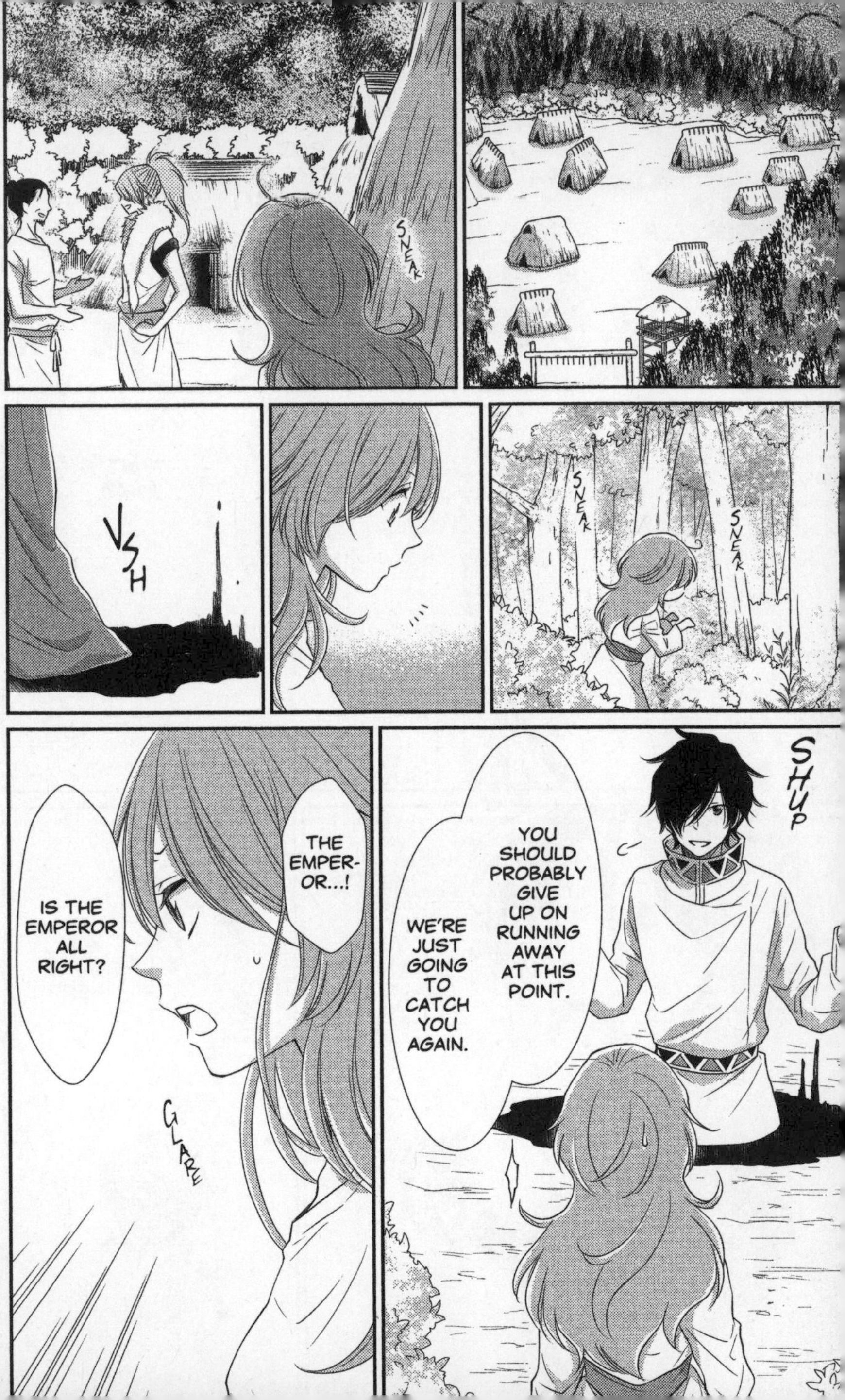
SNEAK
SNEAK
SNEAK
VSH
SHUP
YOU SHOULD PROBABLY GIVE UP ON RUNNING AWAY AT THIS POINT.
WE'RE JUST GOING TO CATCH YOU AGAIN.
THE EMPER-OR...!
IS THE EMPEROR ALL RIGHT?
GLARE

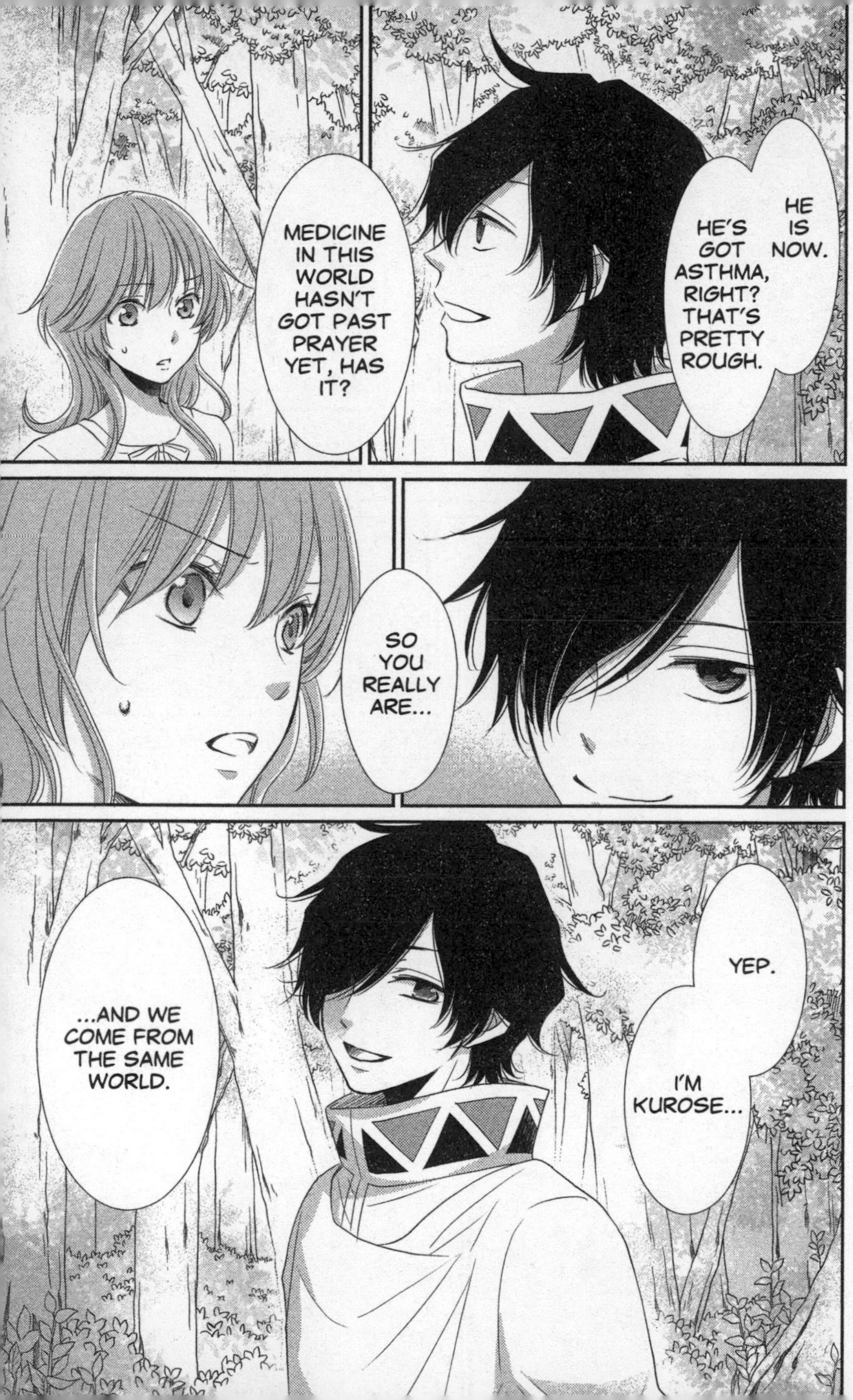
HE IS NOW.
HE'S GOT ASTHMA, RIGHT? THAT'S PRETTY ROUGH.
MEDICINE IN THIS WORLD HASN'T GOT PAST PRAYER YET, HAS IT?
SO YOU REALLY ARE...
YEP.
I'M KUROSE...
...AND WE COME FROM THE SAME WORLD.

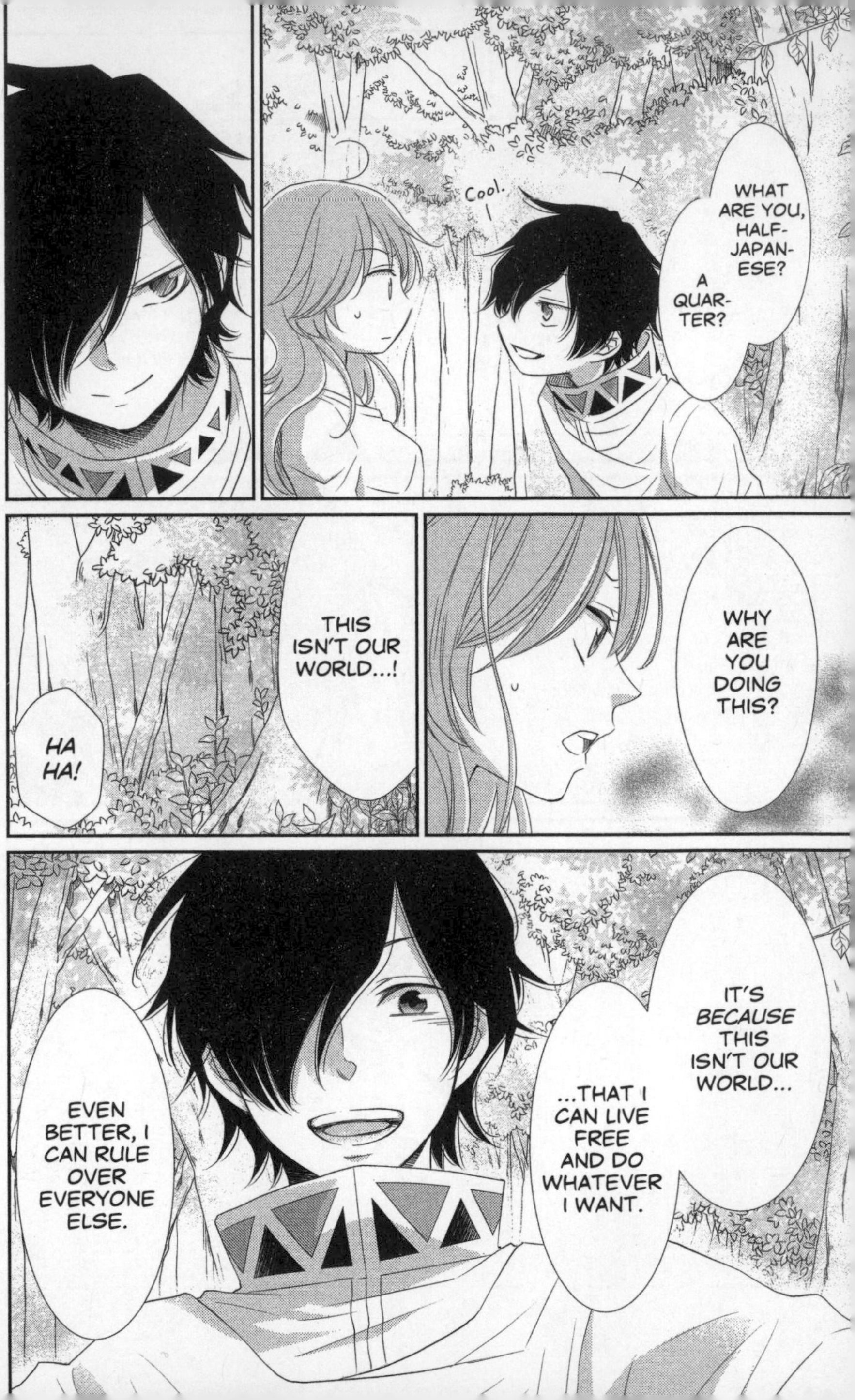
WHAT ARE YOU, HALF-JAPANESE?
A QUARTER?
Cool.
WHY ARE YOU DOING THIS?
THIS ISN'T OUR WORLD...!
HA HA!
IT'S *BECAUSE* THIS ISN'T OUR WORLD...
...THAT I CAN LIVE FREE AND DO WHATEVER I WANT.
EVEN BETTER, I CAN RULE OVER EVERYONE ELSE.

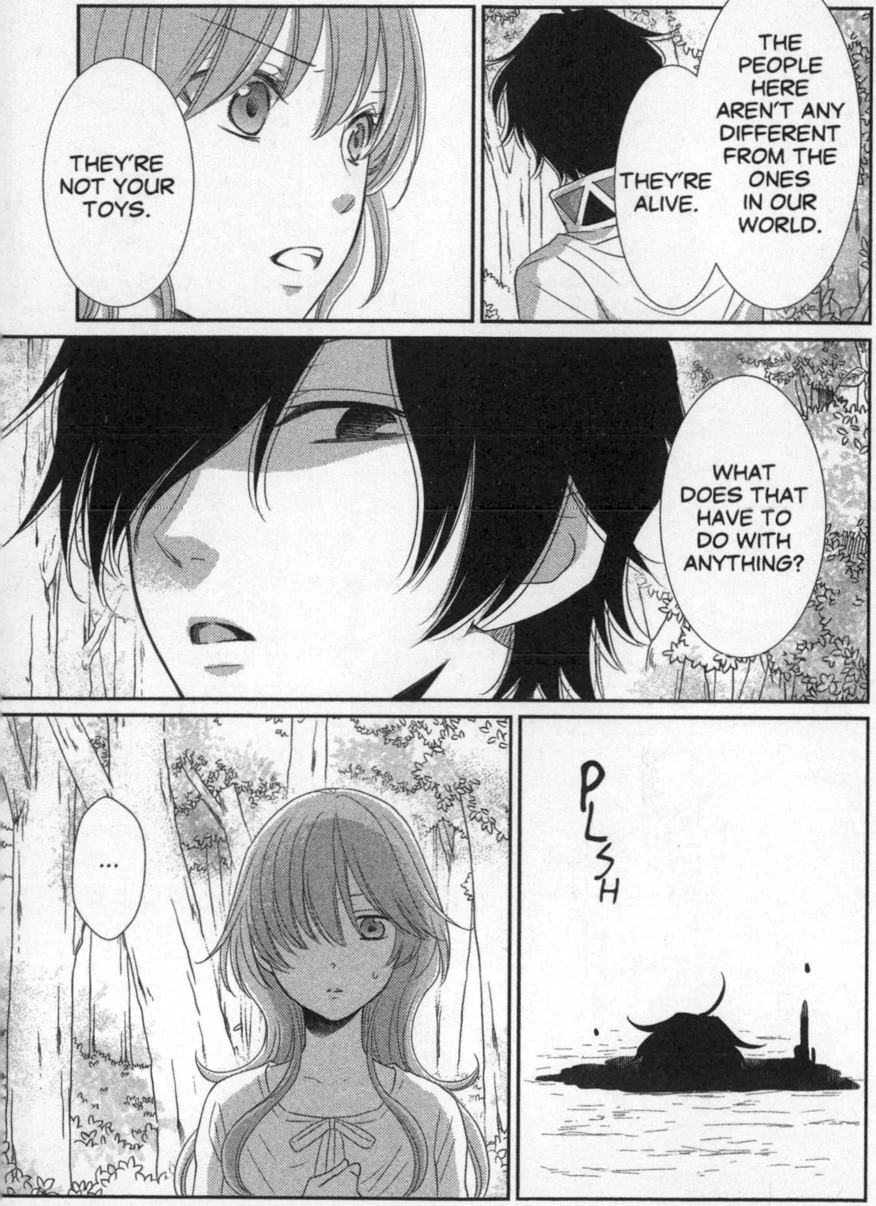
THE PEOPLE HERE AREN'T ANY DIFFERENT FROM THE ONES IN OUR WORLD.
THEY'RE ALIVE.
THEY'RE NOT YOUR TOYS.
WHAT DOES THAT HAVE TO DO WITH ANYTHING?
PLSH
...

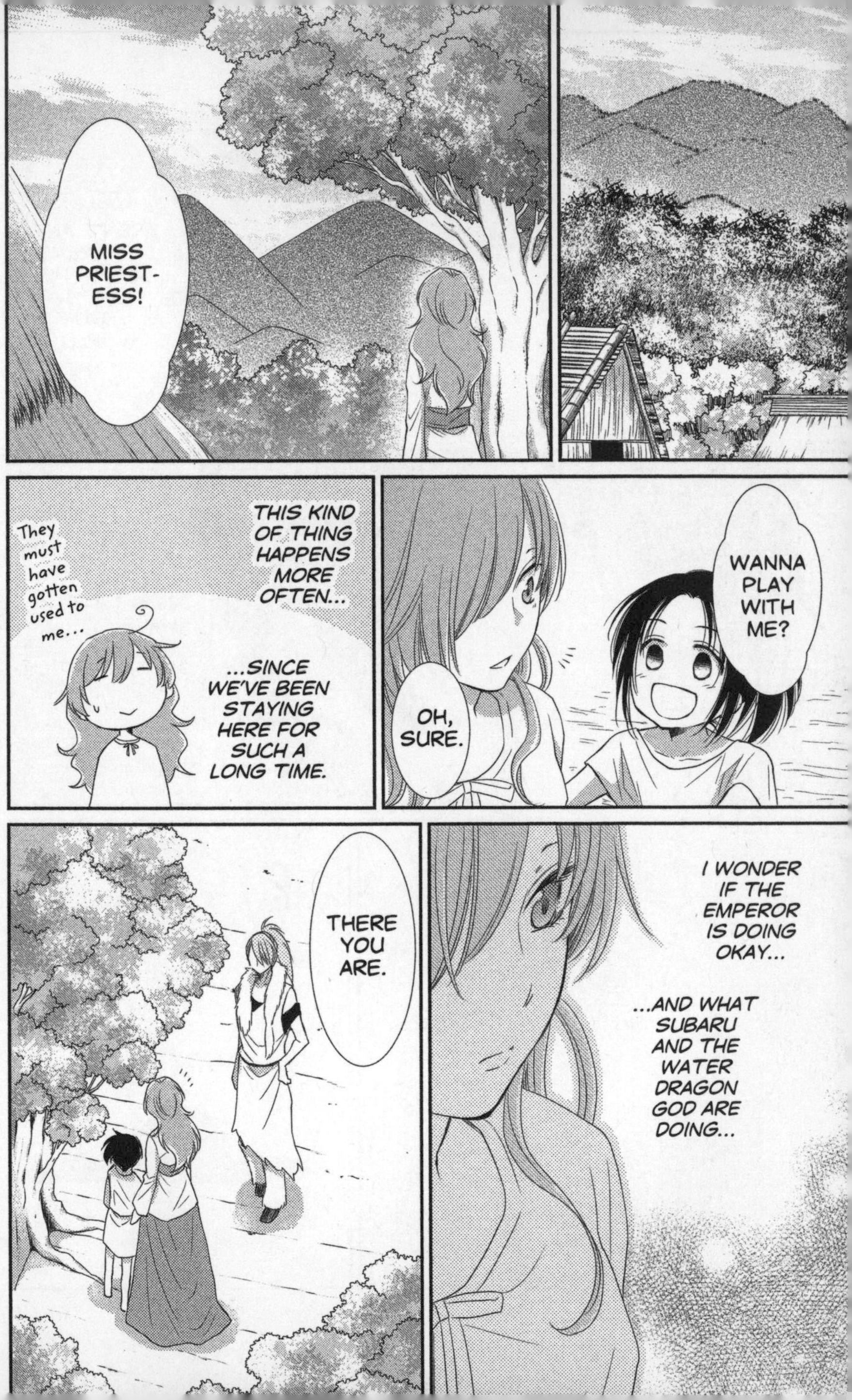
MISS PRIEST-ESS!
WANNA PLAY WITH ME?
OH, SURE.
THIS KIND OF THING HAPPENS MORE OFTEN...
They must have gotten used to me...
...SINCE WE'VE BEEN STAYING HERE FOR SUCH A LONG TIME.
I WONDER IF THE EMPEROR IS DOING OKAY...
...AND WHAT SUBARU AND THE WATER DRAGON GOD ARE DOING...
THERE YOU ARE.

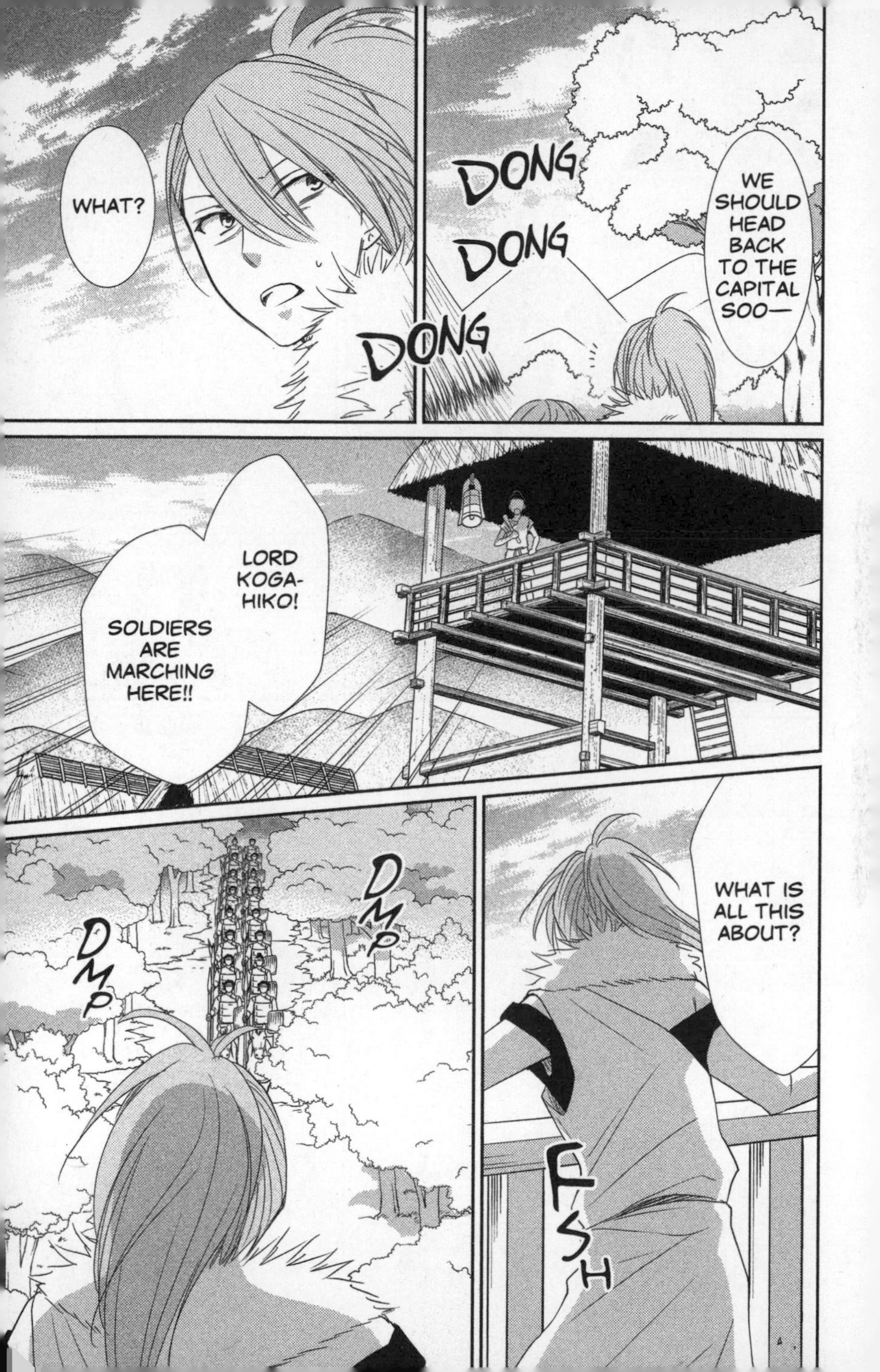
WE SHOULD HEAD BACK TO THE CAPITAL SOO—
DONG
DONG
DONG
WHAT?
LORD KOGA-HIKO!
SOLDIERS ARE MARCHING HERE!!
WHAT IS ALL THIS ABOUT?
FSH
DMP
DMP

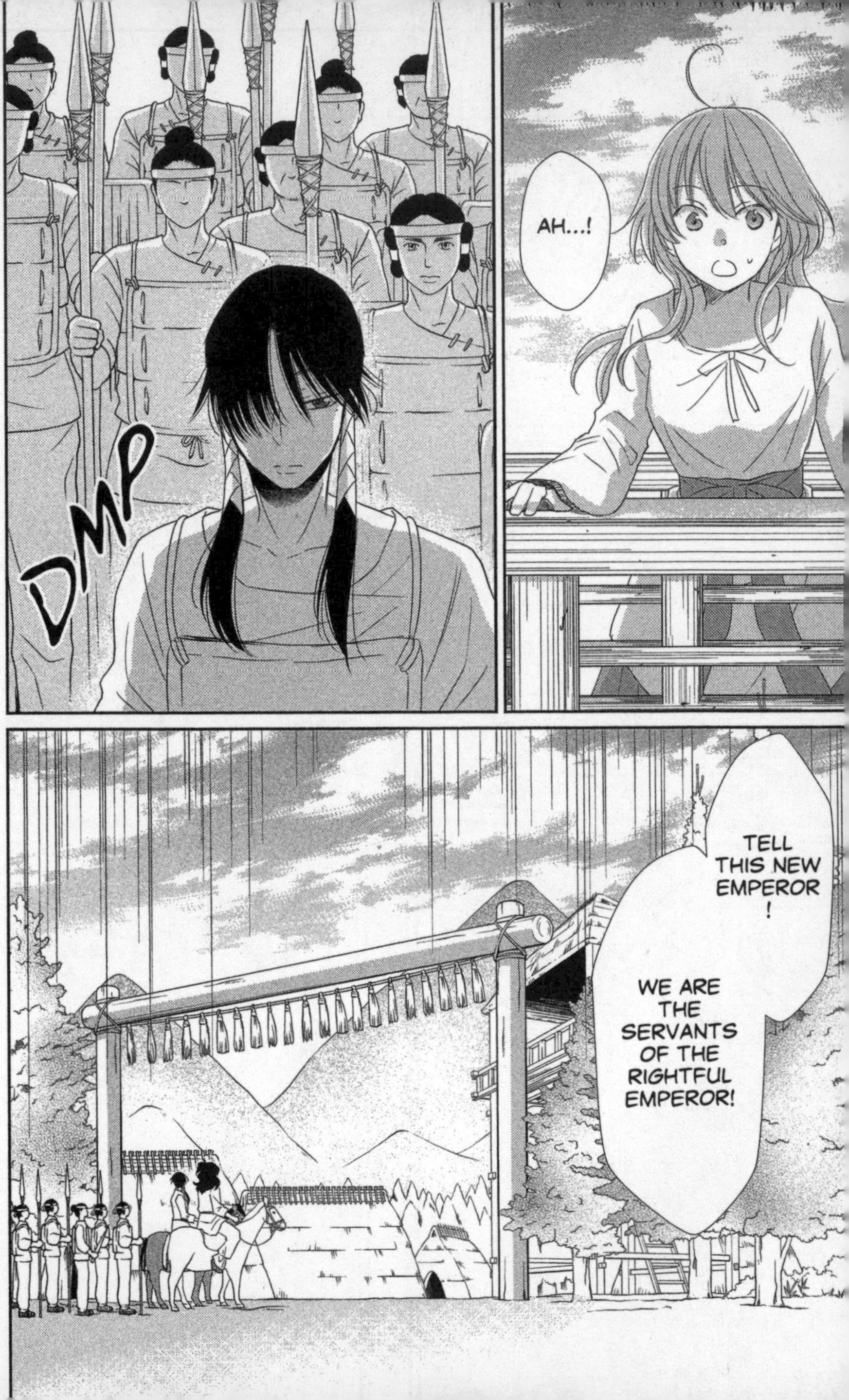
AH...!
DMP
TELL THIS NEW EMPEROR !
WE ARE THE SERVANTS OF THE RIGHTFUL EMPEROR!

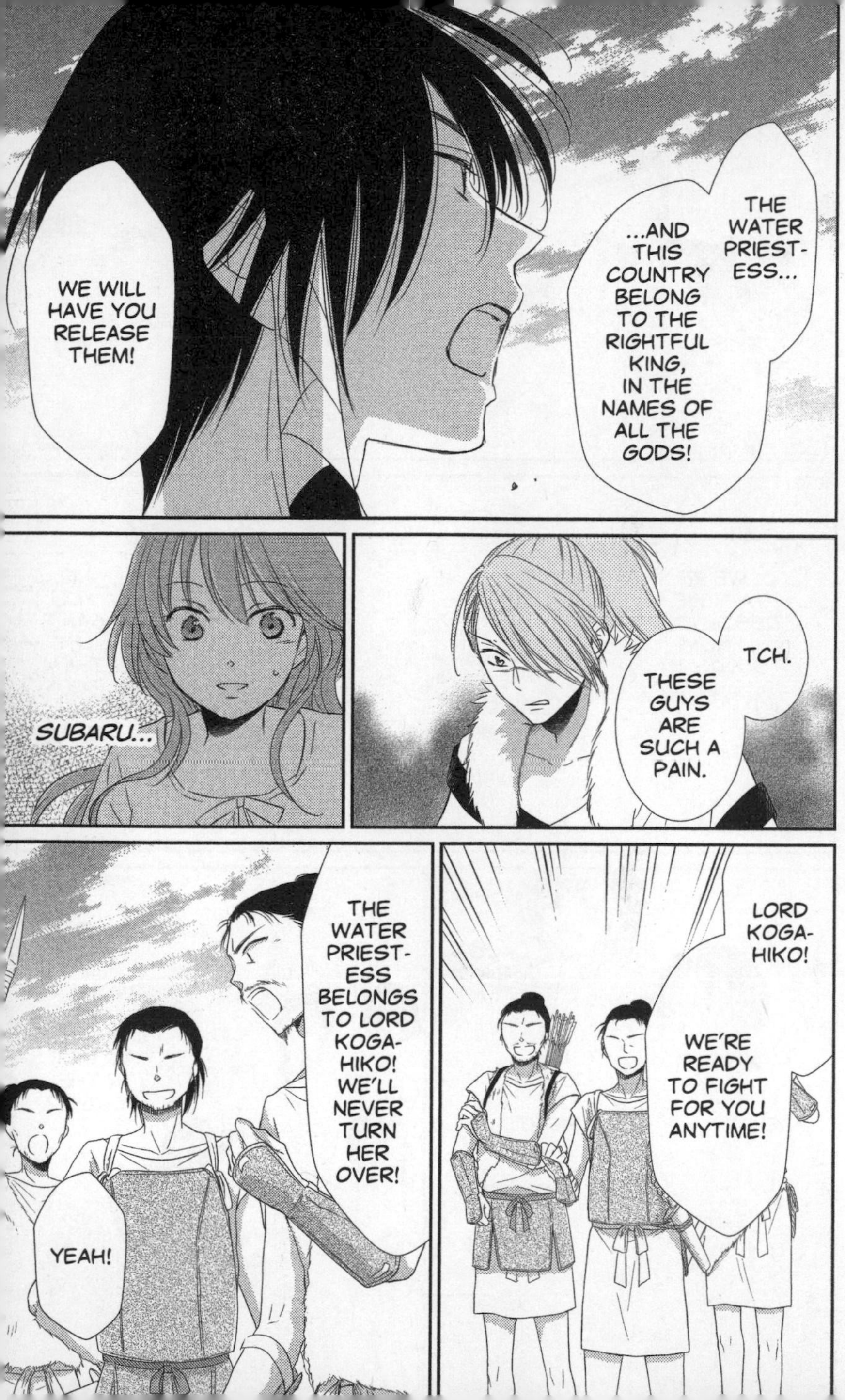
THE WATER PRIEST-ESS...
...AND THIS COUNTRY BELONG TO THE RIGHTFUL KING, IN THE NAMES OF ALL THE GODS!
WE WILL HAVE YOU RELEASE THEM!
TCH.
THESE GUYS ARE SUCH A PAIN.
SUBARU...
LORD KOGA-HIKO!
WE'RE READY TO FIGHT FOR YOU ANYTIME!
THE WATER PRIEST-ESS BELONGS TO LORD KOGA-HIKO! WE'LL NEVER TURN HER OVER!
YEAH!

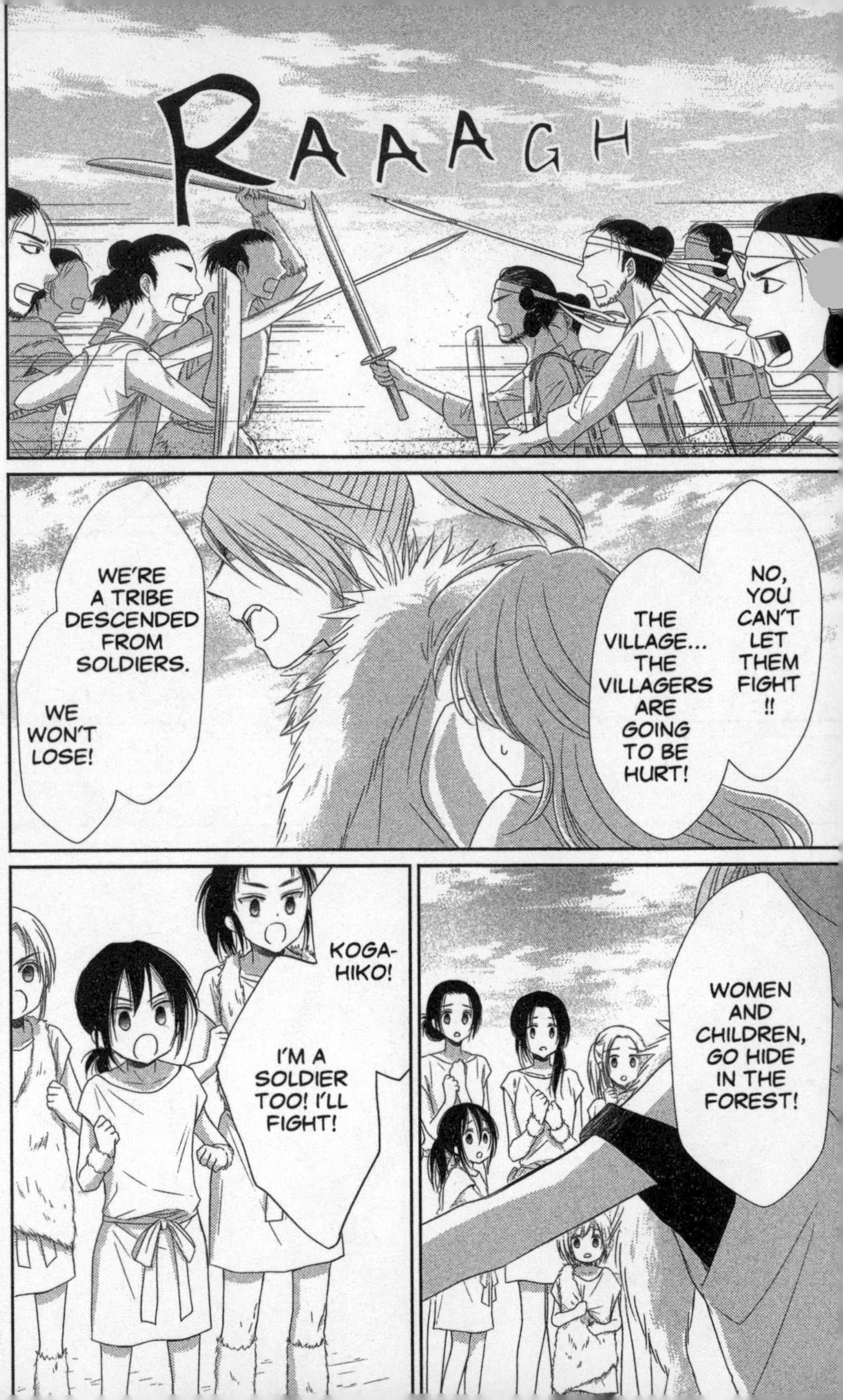
RAAAGH
NO, YOU CAN'T LET THEM FIGHT!!
THE VILLAGE... THE VILLAGERS ARE GOING TO BE HURT!
WE'RE A TRIBE DESCENDED FROM SOLDIERS.
WE WON'T LOSE!
WOMEN AND CHILDREN, GO HIDE IN THE FOREST!
KOGA-HIKO!
I'M A SOLDIER TOO! I'LL FIGHT!

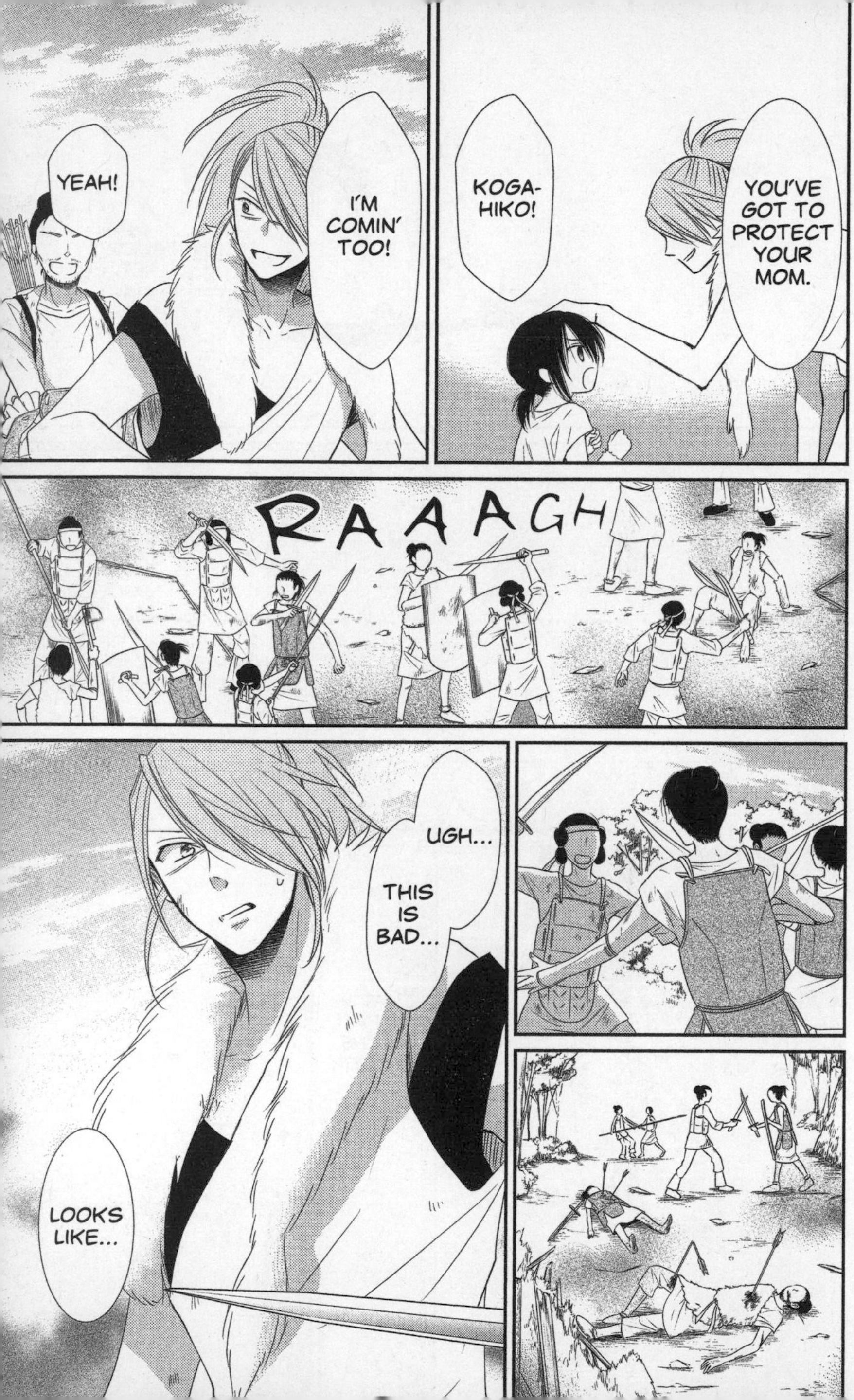
YOU'VE GOT TO PROTECT YOUR MOM.
KOGA-HIKO!
I'M COMIN' TOO!
YEAH!
RAAAGH
UGH...
THIS IS BAD...
LOOKS LIKE...

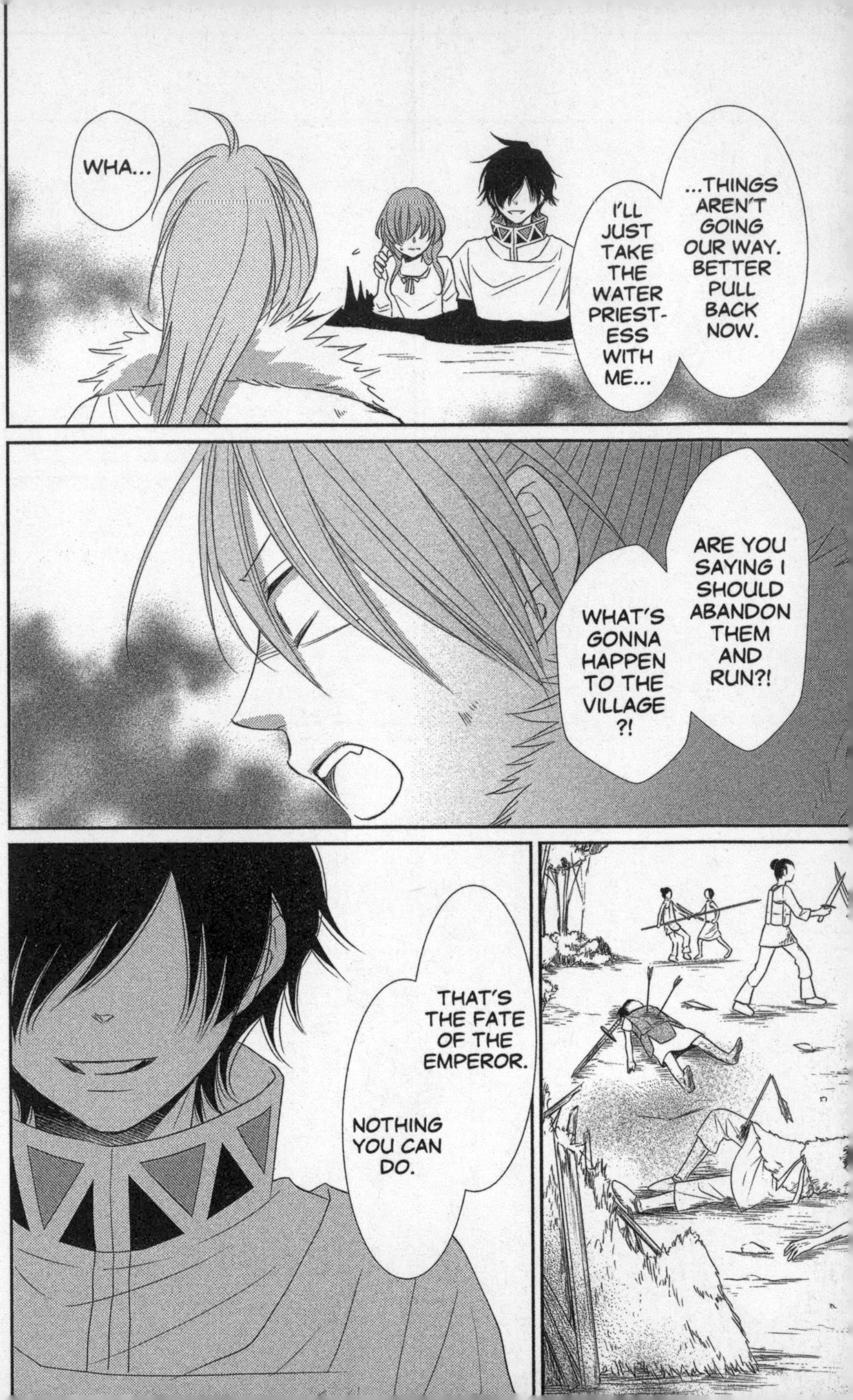
...THINGS AREN'T GOING OUR WAY. BETTER PULL BACK NOW.
I'LL JUST TAKE THE WATER PRIEST-ESS WITH ME...
WHA...
ARE YOU SAYING I SHOULD ABANDON THEM AND RUN?!
WHAT'S GONNA HAPPEN TO THE VILLAGE?!
THAT'S THE FATE OF THE EMPEROR.
NOTHING YOU CAN DO.

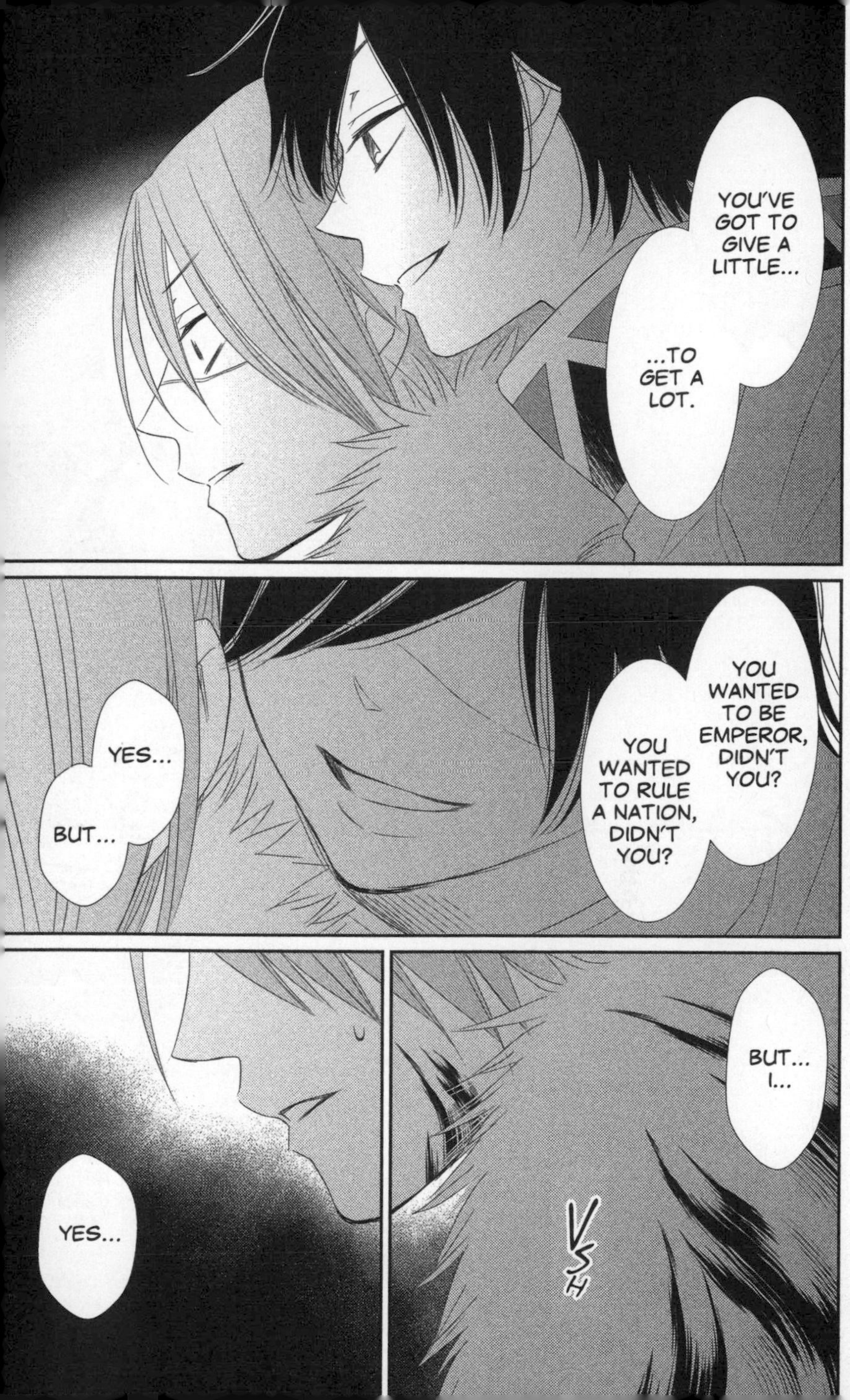
YOU'VE GOT TO GIVE A LITTLE...
...TO GET A LOT.
YOU WANTED TO BE EMPEROR, DIDN'T YOU?
YOU WANTED TO RULE A NATION, DIDN'T YOU?
YES...
BUT...
BUT... I...
VSH
YES...

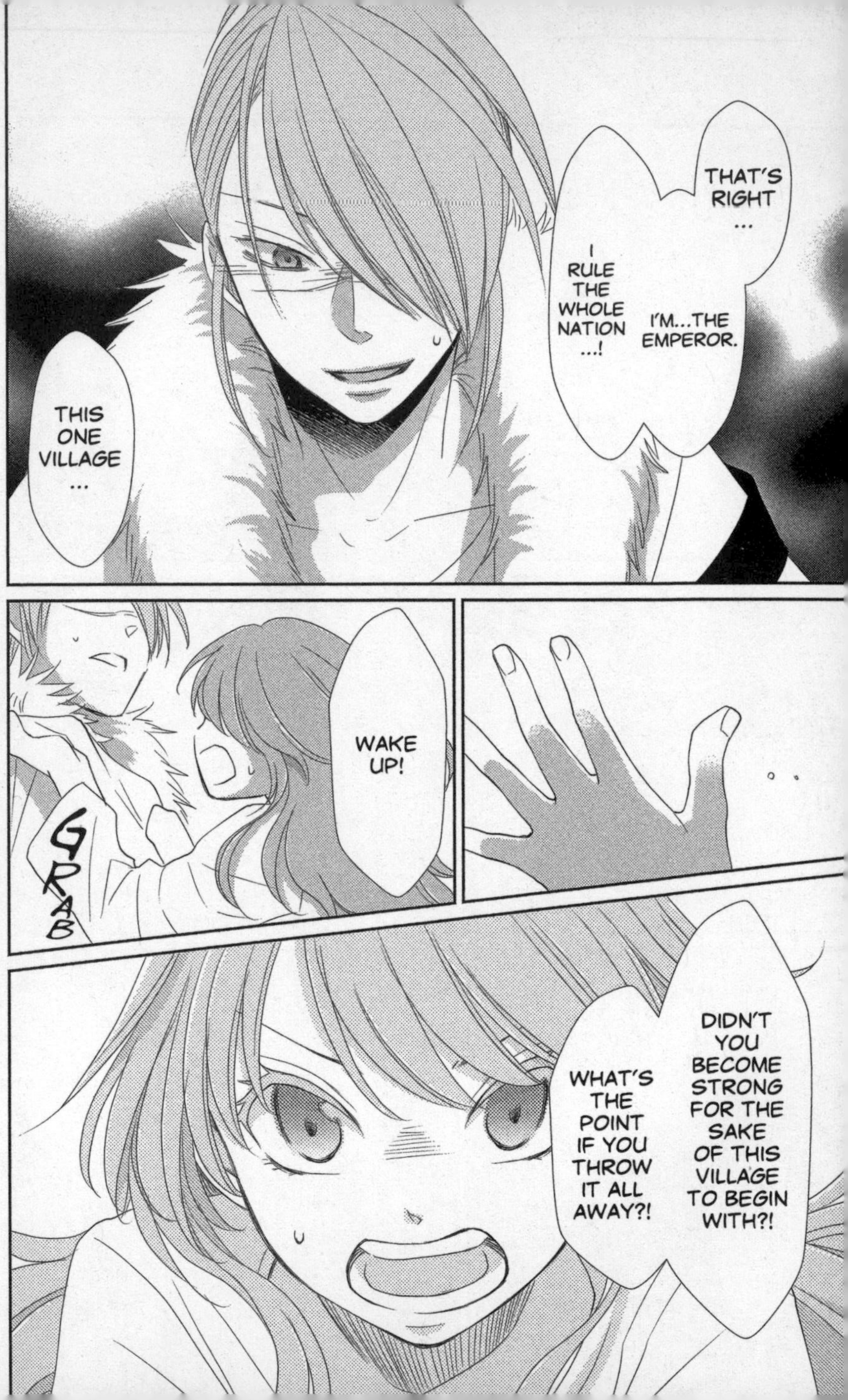
THAT'S RIGHT ...
I'M...THE EMPEROR.
I RULE THE WHOLE NATION ...!
THIS ONE VILLAGE ...
WAKE UP!
GRAB
DIDN'T YOU BECOME STRONG FOR THE SAKE OF THIS VILLAGE TO BEGIN WITH?!
WHAT'S THE POINT IF YOU THROW IT ALL AWAY?!

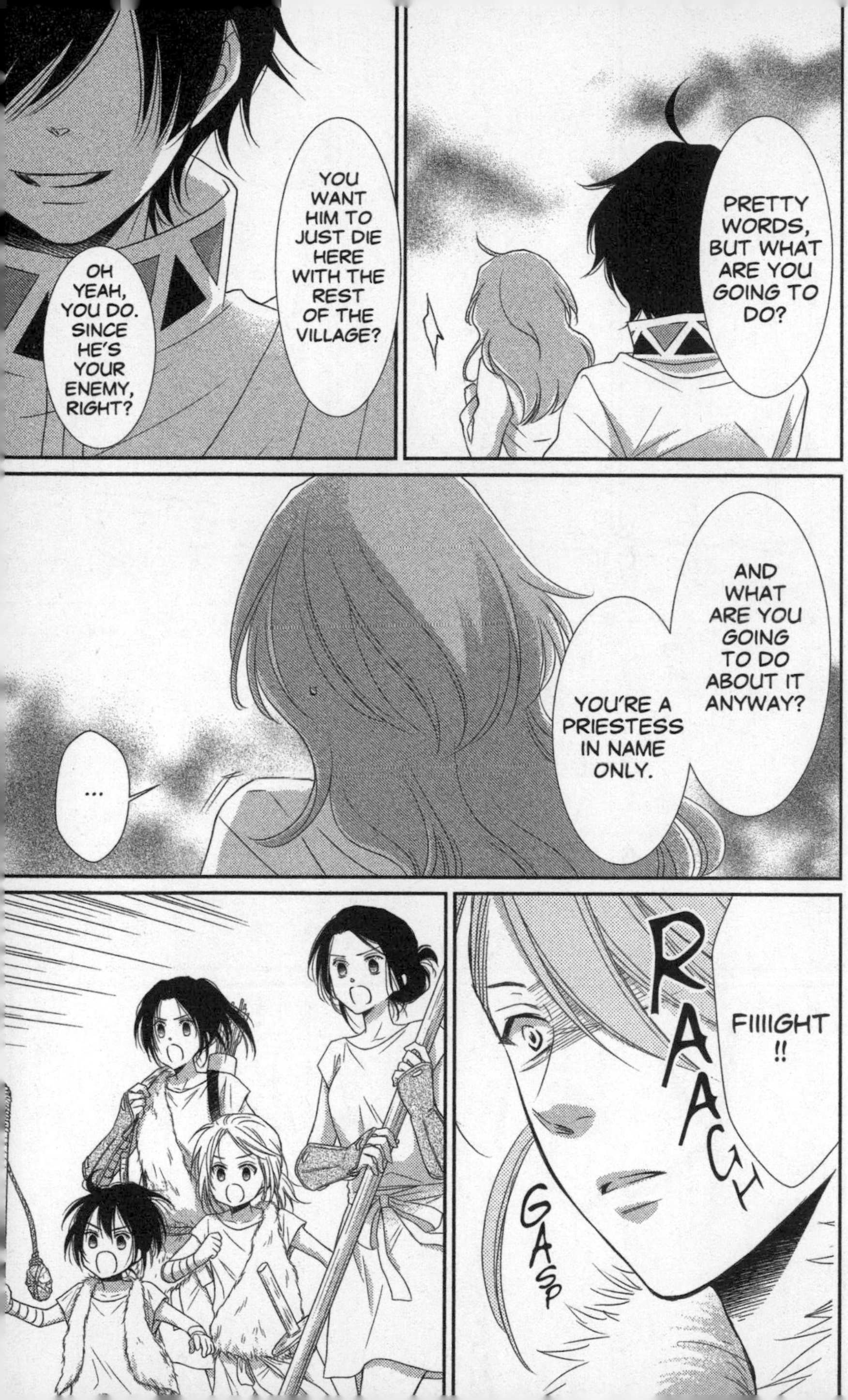
PRETTY WORDS, BUT WHAT ARE YOU GOING TO DO?
YOU WANT HIM TO JUST DIE HERE WITH THE REST OF THE VILLAGE?
OH YEAH, YOU DO. SINCE HE'S YOUR ENEMY, RIGHT?
AND WHAT ARE YOU GOING TO DO ABOUT IT ANYWAY?
YOU'RE A PRIESTESS IN NAME ONLY.
...
RAAGH
FIIIIGHT !!
GASP

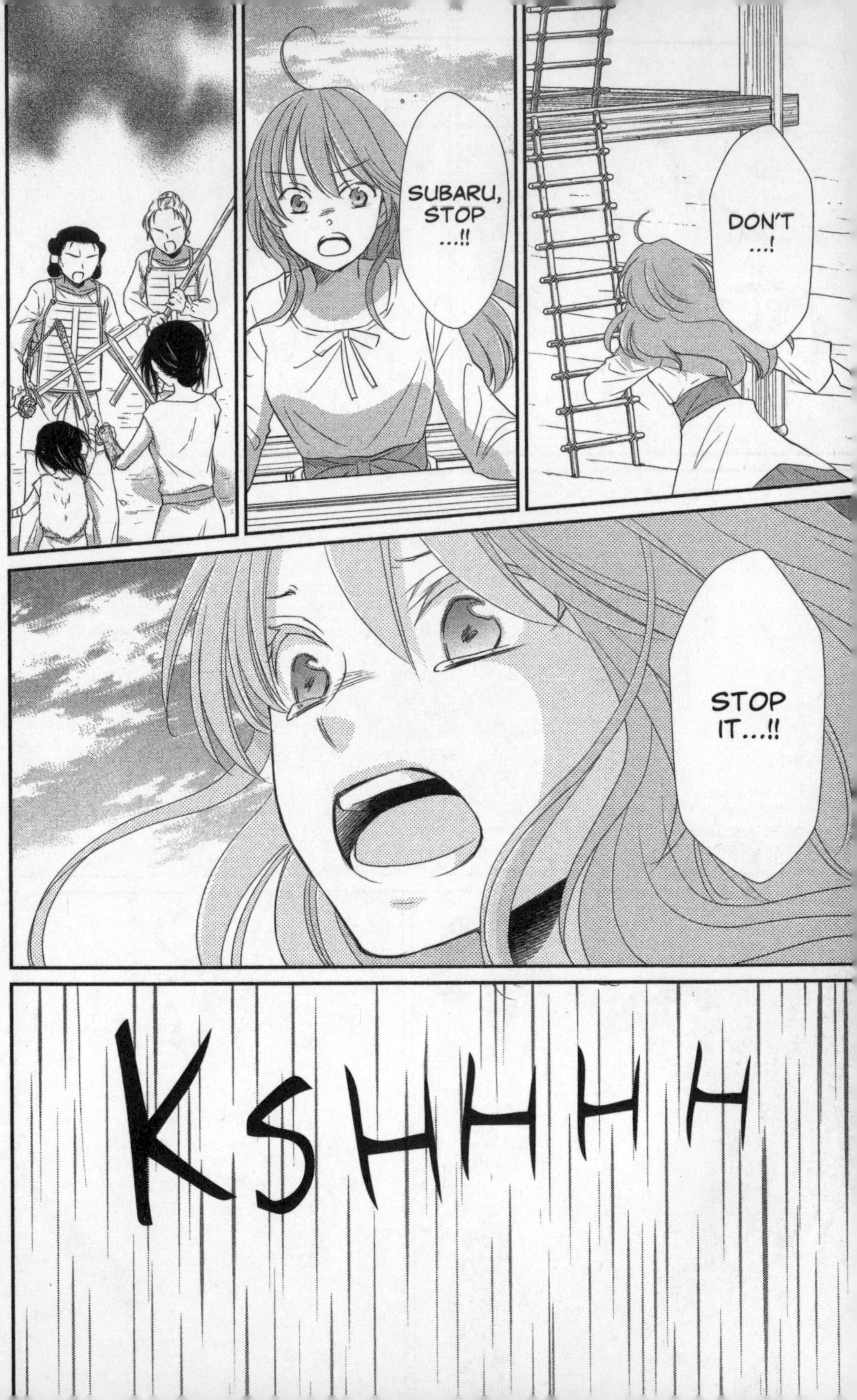
DON'T ...!
SUBARU, STOP ...!!
STOP IT...!!
KSHHHH

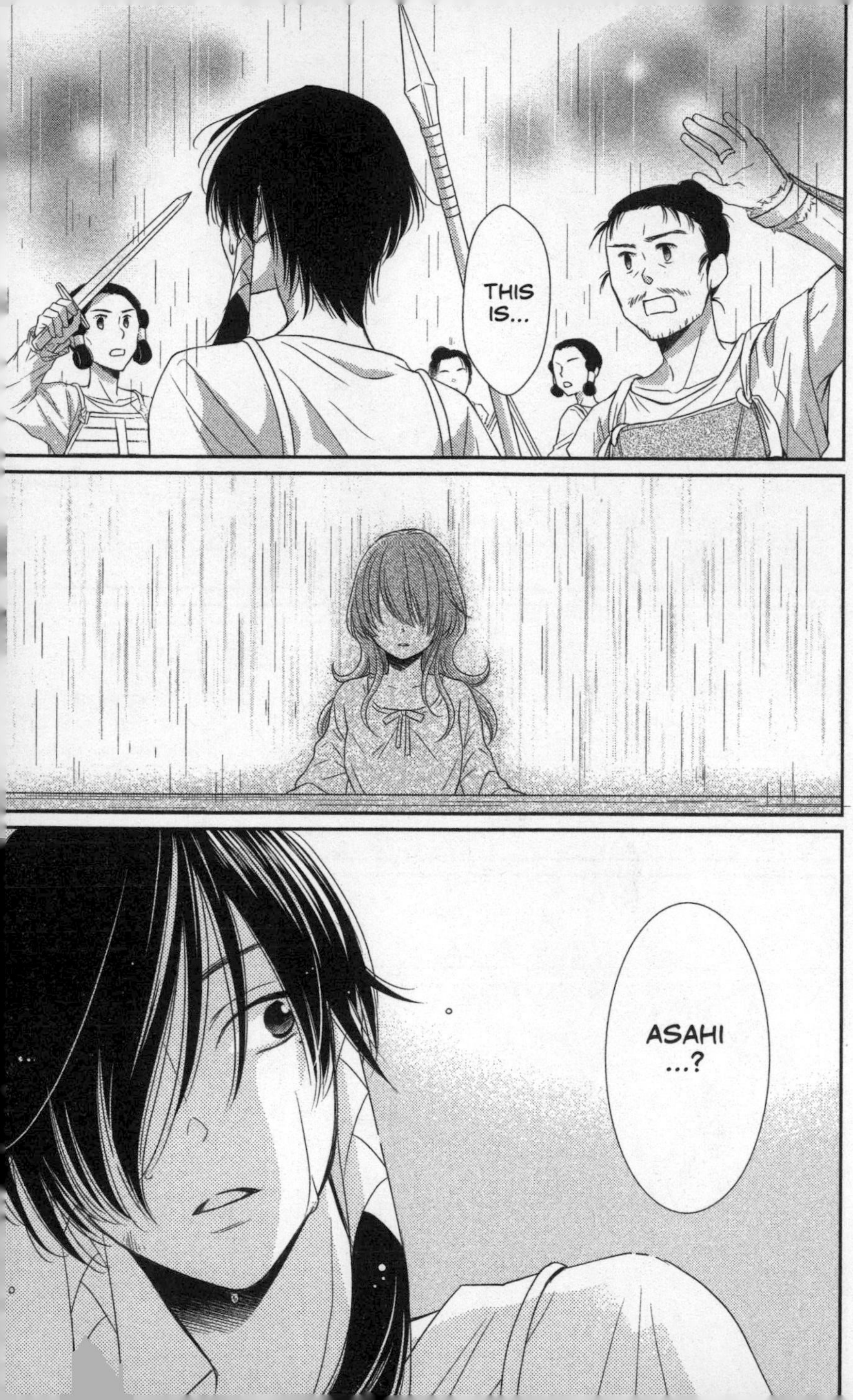
THIS IS...
ASAHI ...?

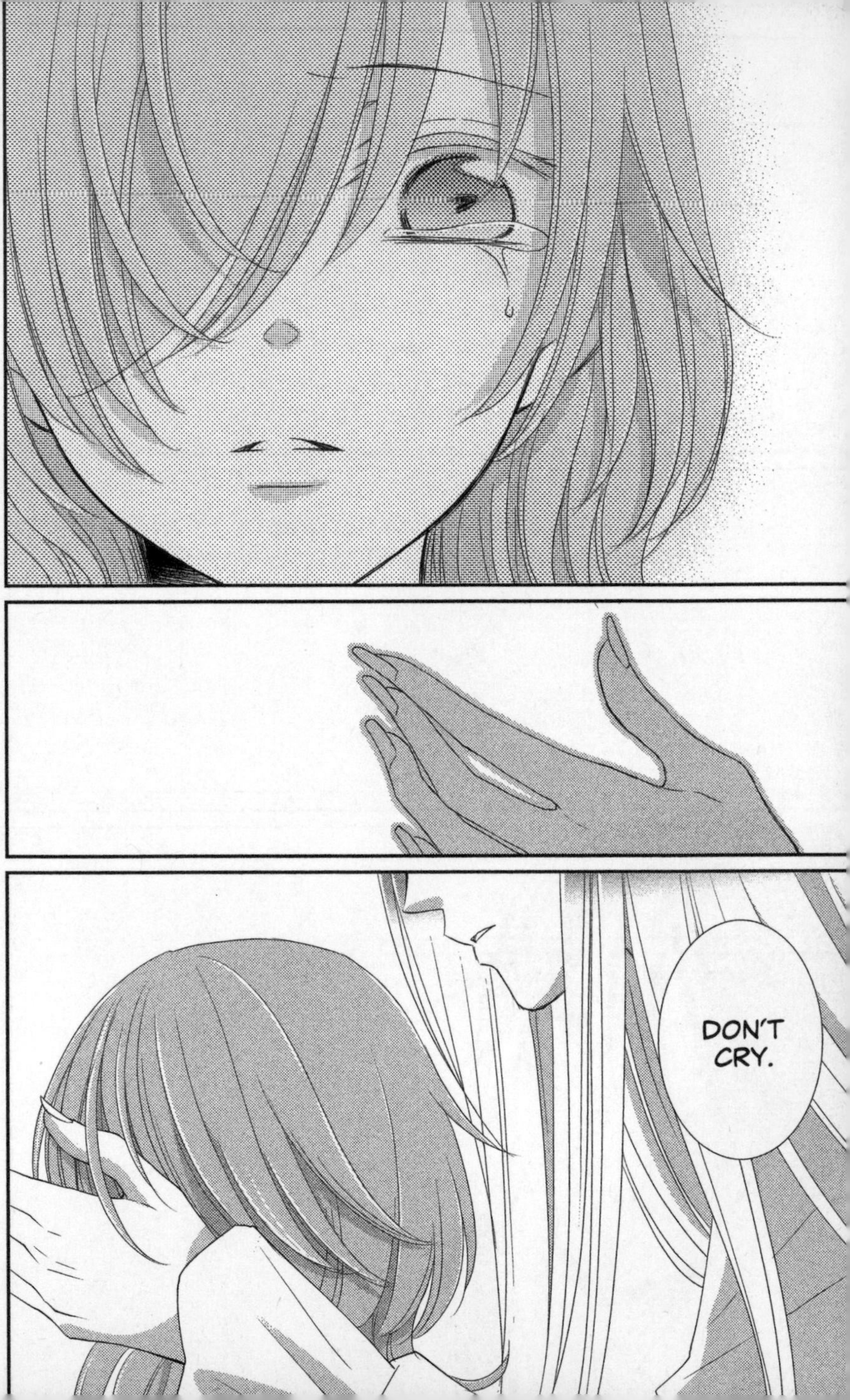
DON'T CRY.

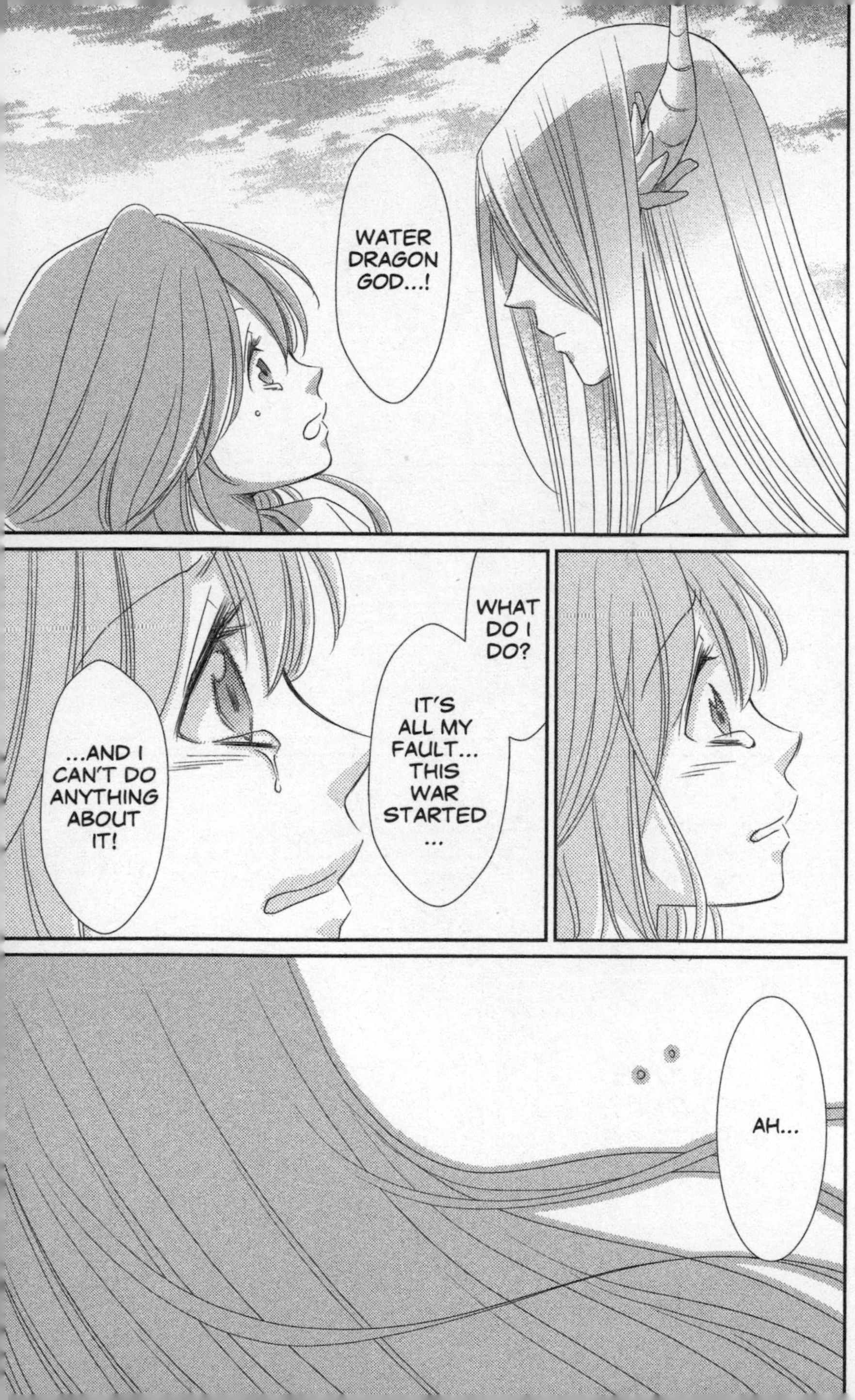
WATER DRAGON GOD...!
WHAT DO I DO?
IT'S ALL MY FAULT... THIS WAR STARTED ...
...AND I CAN'T DO ANYTHING ABOUT IT!
AH...

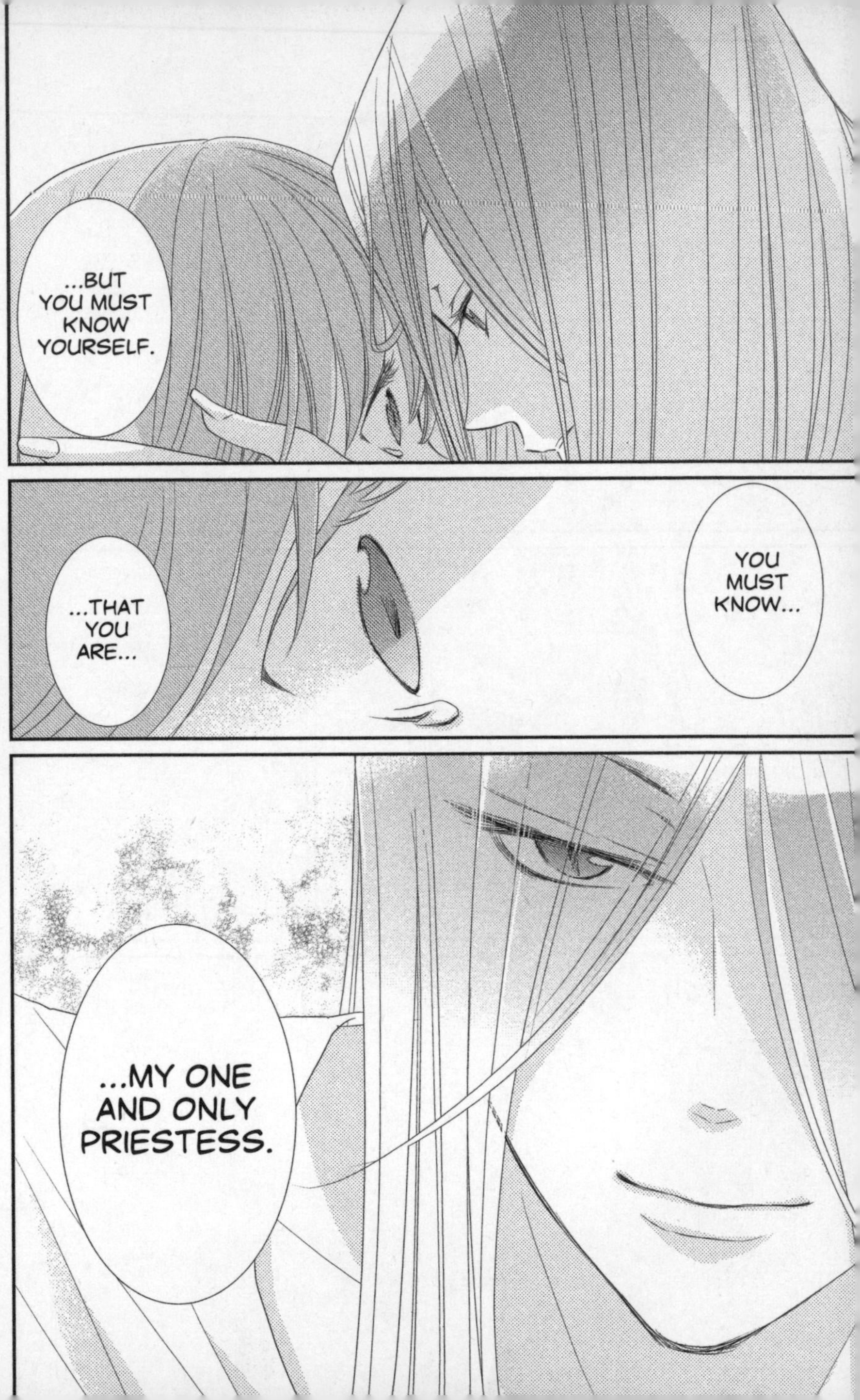
...BUT YOU MUST KNOW YOURSELF.
YOU MUST KNOW...
...THAT YOU ARE...
...MY ONE AND ONLY PRIESTESS.

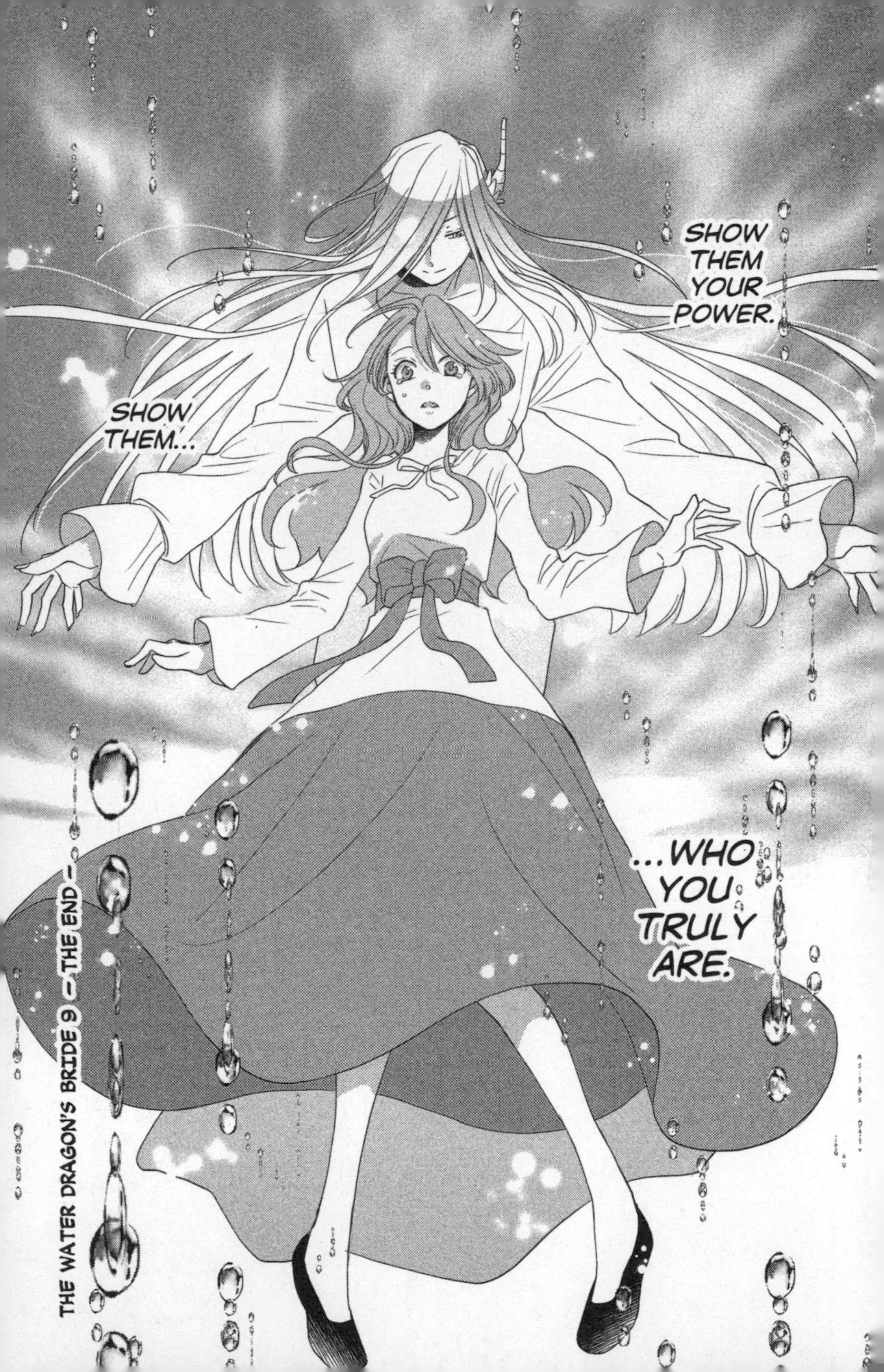
SHOW THEM YOUR POWER.
SHOW THEM...
...WHO YOU TRULY ARE.
THE WATER DRAGON'S BRIDE 9 – THE END –

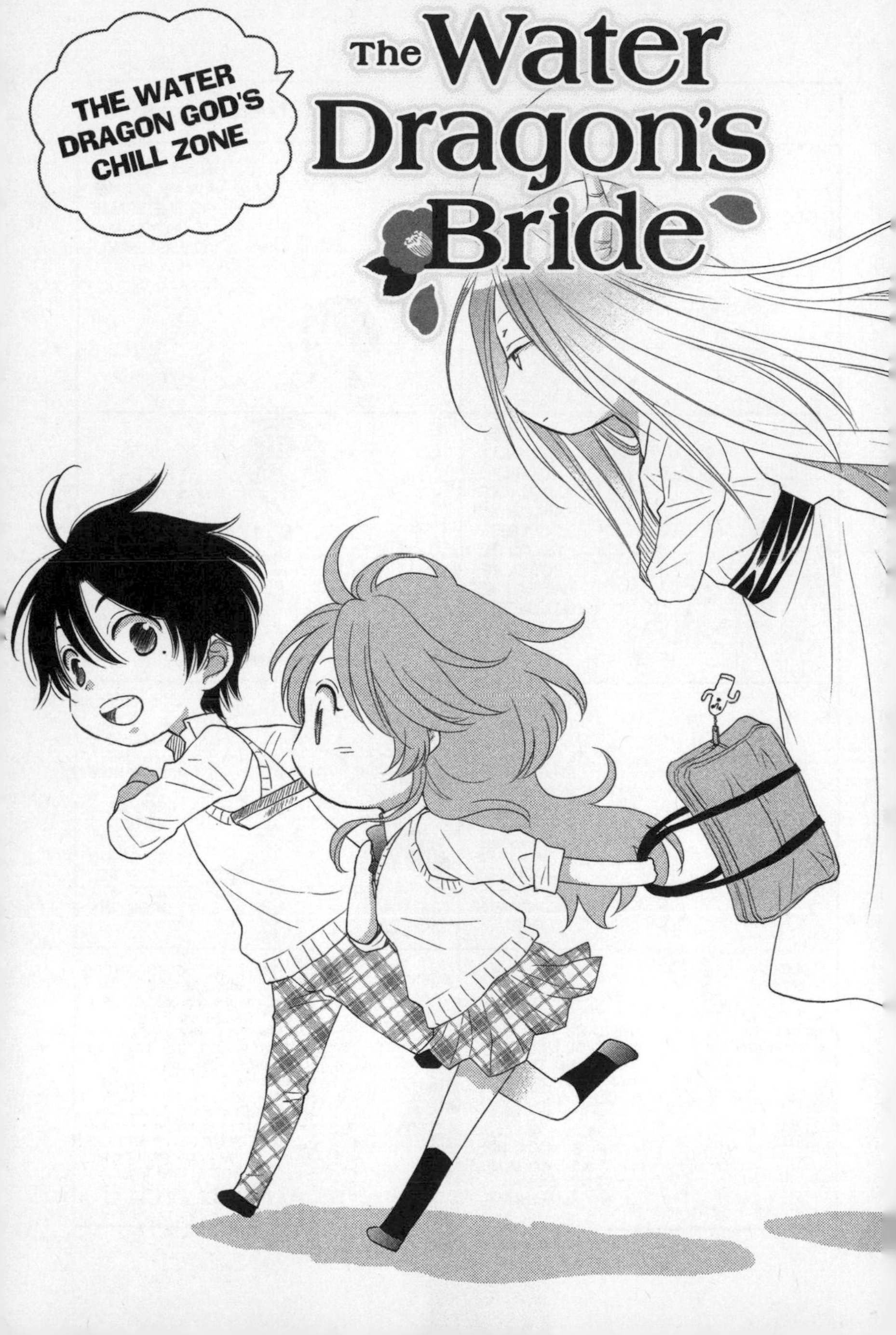
The Water Dragon's Bride
THE WATER DRAGON GOD'S CHILL ZONE

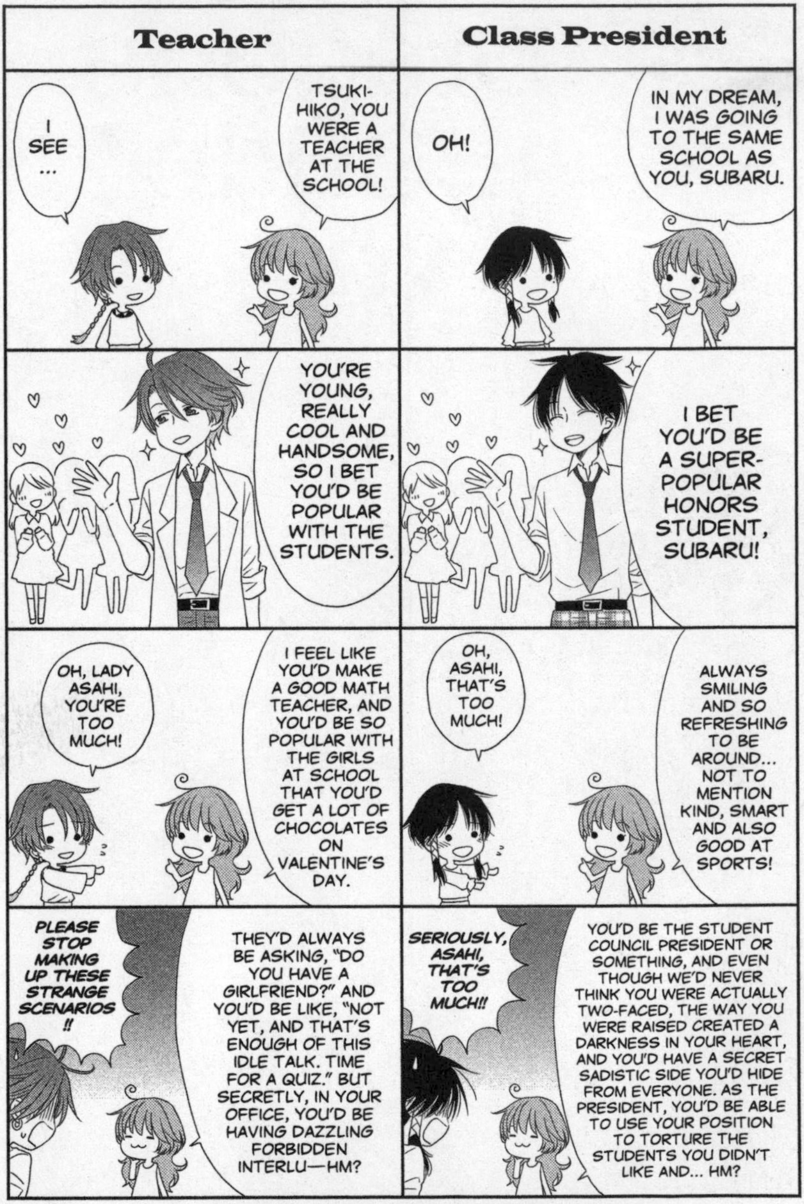
Class President
IN MY DREAM, I WAS GOING TO THE SAME SCHOOL AS YOU, SUBARU.
OH!
I BET YOU'D BE A SUPER-POPULAR HONORS STUDENT, SUBARU!
ALWAYS SMILING AND SO REFRESHING TO BE AROUND... NOT TO MENTION KIND, SMART AND ALSO GOOD AT SPORTS!
OH, ASAHI, THAT'S TOO MUCH!
YOU'D BE THE STUDENT COUNCIL PRESIDENT OR SOMETHING, AND EVEN THOUGH WE'D NEVER THINK YOU WERE ACTUALLY TWO-FACED, THE WAY YOU WERE RAISED CREATED A DARKNESS IN YOUR HEART, AND YOU'D HAVE A SECRET SADISTIC SIDE YOU'D HIDE FROM EVERYONE. AS THE PRESIDENT, YOU'D BE ABLE TO USE YOUR POSITION TO TORTURE THE STUDENTS YOU DIDN'T LIKE AND... HM?
SERIOUSLY, ASAHI, THAT'S TOO MUCH!!
Teacher
TSUKIHIKO, YOU WERE A TEACHER AT THE SCHOOL!
I SEE...
YOU'RE YOUNG, REALLY COOL AND HANDSOME, SO I BET YOU'D BE POPULAR WITH THE STUDENTS.
I FEEL LIKE YOU'D MAKE A GOOD MATH TEACHER, AND YOU'D BE SO POPULAR WITH THE GIRLS AT SCHOOL THAT YOU'D GET A LOT OF CHOCOLATES ON VALENTINE'S DAY.
OH, LADY ASAHI, YOU'RE TOO MUCH!
THEY'D ALWAYS BE ASKING, "DO YOU HAVE A GIRLFRIEND?" AND YOU'D BE LIKE, "NOT YET, AND THAT'S ENOUGH OF THIS IDLE TALK. TIME FOR A QUIZ." BUT SECRETLY, IN YOUR OFFICE, YOU'D BE HAVING DAZZLING FORBIDDEN INTERLU—HM?
PLEASE STOP MAKING UP THESE STRANGE SCENARIOS!!

*THIS COMIC HAS NOTHING TO DO WITH THE ACTUAL STORY.

Oh, Totally

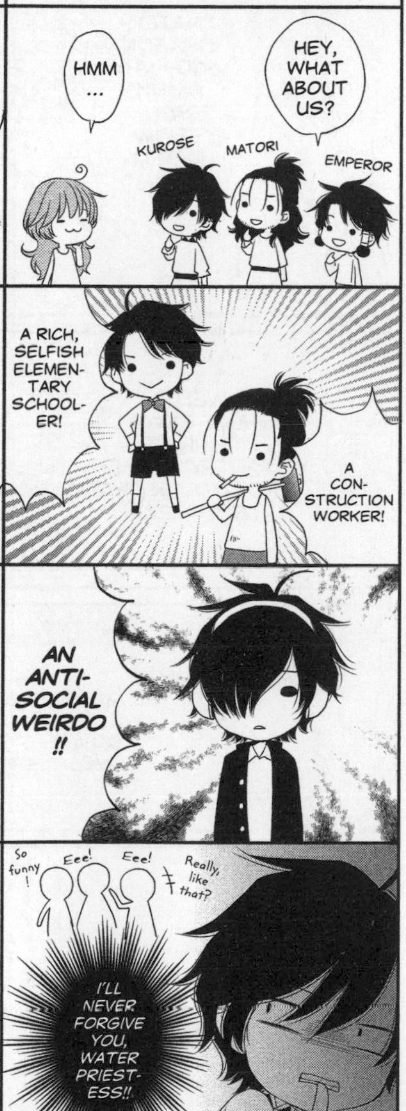
HEY, WHAT ABOUT US?
EMPEROR
MATORI
HMM...
KUROSE
A CONSTRUCTION WORKER!
A RICH, SELFISH ELEMENTARY SCHOOLER!
AN ANTI-SOCIAL WEIRDO!!
Really, like that?
Eee!
Eee!
So funny!
I'LL NEVER FORGIVE YOU, WATER PRIESTESS!!

Class President 2

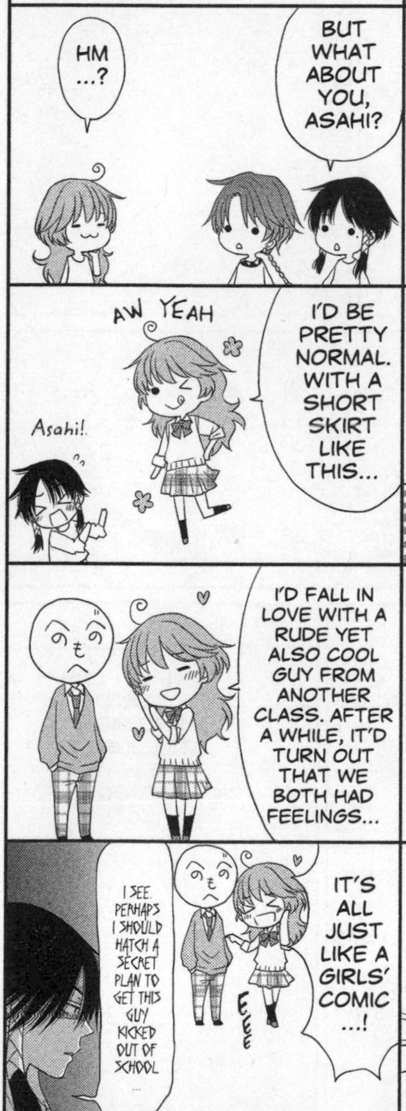
BUT WHAT ABOUT YOU, ASAHI?
HM...?
I'D BE PRETTY NORMAL. WITH A SHORT SKIRT LIKE THIS...
AW YEAH
Asahi!
I'D FALL IN LOVE WITH A RUDE YET ALSO COOL GUY FROM ANOTHER CLASS. AFTER A WHILE, IT'D TURN OUT THAT WE BOTH HAD FEELINGS...
IT'S ALL JUST LIKE A GIRLS' COMIC...!
EEE
I SEE. PERHAPS I SHOULD HATCH A SECRET PLAN TO GET THIS GUY KICKED OUT OF SCHOOL...

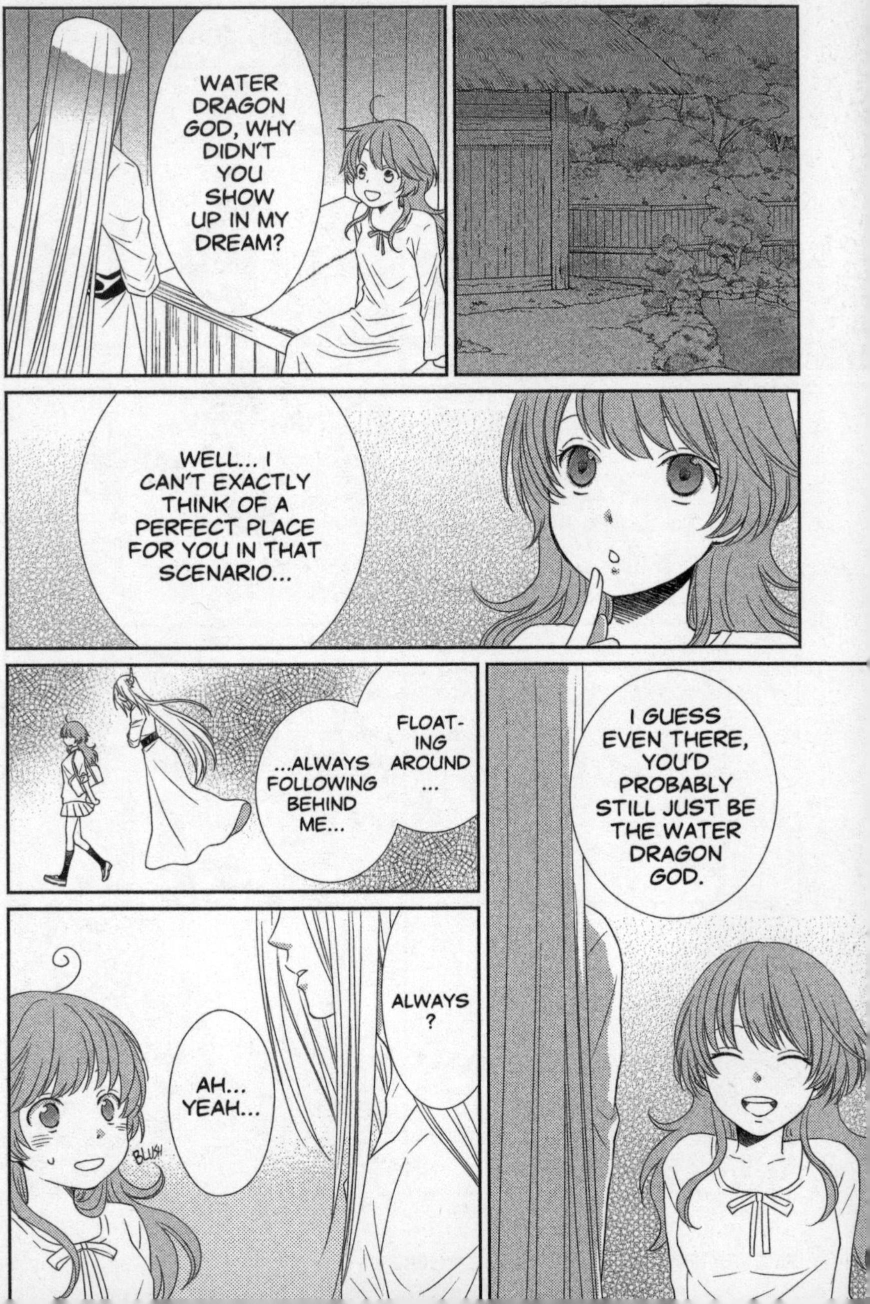
WATER DRAGON GOD, WHY DIDN'T YOU SHOW UP IN MY DREAM?
WELL... I CAN'T EXACTLY THINK OF A PERFECT PLACE FOR YOU IN THAT SCENARIO...
I GUESS EVEN THERE, YOU'D PROBABLY STILL JUST BE THE WATER DRAGON GOD.
FLOAT-ING AROUND ...
...ALWAYS FOLLOWING BEHIND ME...
ALWAYS ?
AH... YEAH...
BLUSH

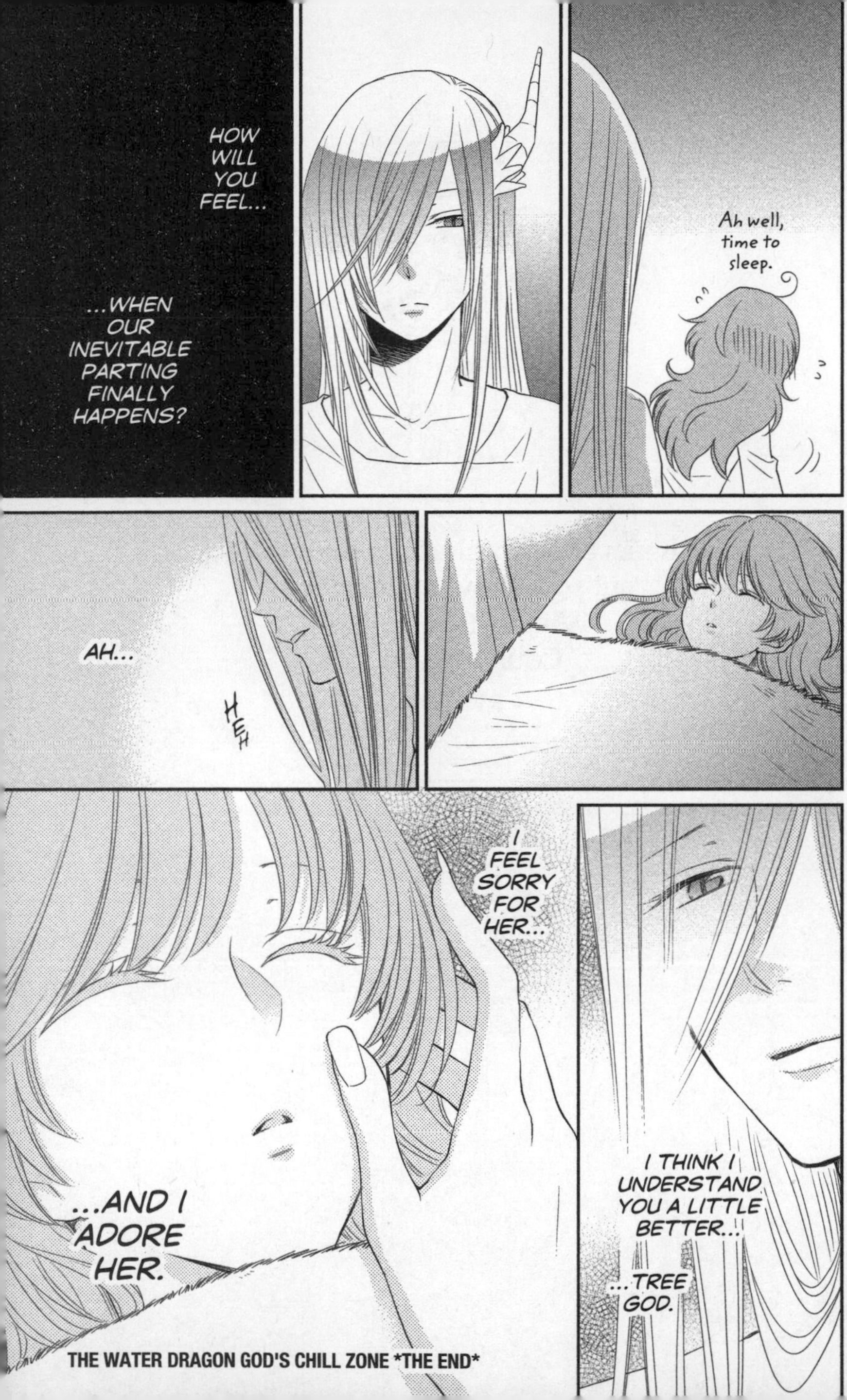
Ah well, time to sleep.
HOW WILL YOU FEEL...
...WHEN OUR INEVITABLE PARTING FINALLY HAPPENS?
AH...
HEH
I THINK I UNDERSTAND YOU A LITTLE BETTER...
...TREE GOD.
I FEEL SORRY FOR HER...
...AND I ADORE HER.
THE WATER DRAGON GOD'S CHILL ZONE *THE END*

Sharks and piranhas are both scary,
but somehow enticing too.
What is this feeling?
Could this be...?

– REI TOMA

Rei Toma has been drawing since childhood, and she created her first complete manga for a graduation project in design school. When she drew the short story manga "Help Me, Dentist," it attracted a publisher's attention and she made her debut right away. After she found success as a manga artist, acclaim in other art fields started to follow as she did illustrations for novels and video game character designs. She is also the creator of *Dawn of the Arcana*, available in North America from VIZ Media.

The Water Dragon's Bride
VOL. 9
Shojo Beat Edition

Story and Art by
Rei Toma

SUIJIN NO HANAYOME Vol.9
by Rei TOMA
© 2015 Rei TOMA
All rights reserved.
Original Japanese edition published by SHOGAKUKAN.
English translation rights in the United States of America,
Canada, the United Kingdom, Ireland, Australia and New
Zealand arranged with SHOGAKUKAN.

ORIGINAL COVER DESIGN/Hibiki CHIKADA (fireworks.vc)

English Translation & Adaptation **Abby Lehrke**
Touch-Up Art & Lettering **Monaliza de Asis**
Design **Alice Lewis**
Editor **Amy Yu**

Printed in the U.S.A.

Published by VIZ Media, LLC
P.O. Box 77010
San Francisco, CA 94107

10 9 8 7 6 5 4 3 2 1
First printing, April 2019

viz.com

shojobeat.com

You may be reading the wrong way!

In keeping with the original Japanese comic format, this book reads from right to left—so action, sound effects and word balloons are completely reversed. This preserves the orientation of the original artwork—plus, it's fun!

Check out the diagram shown here to get the hang of things, and then turn to the other side of the book to get started!

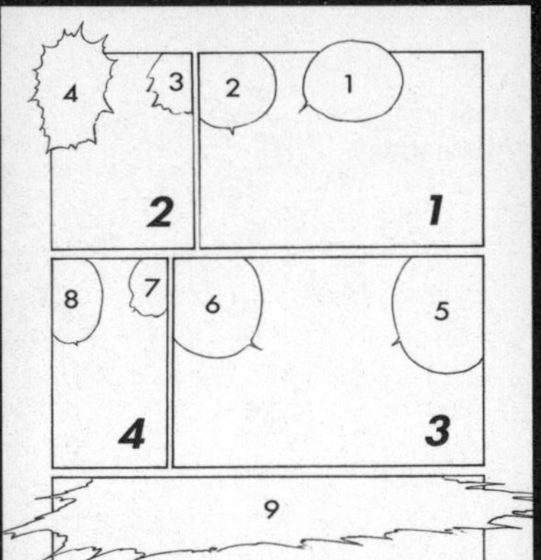
1
2
3
4
1
2
5
6
7
8
3
4
9
5
142

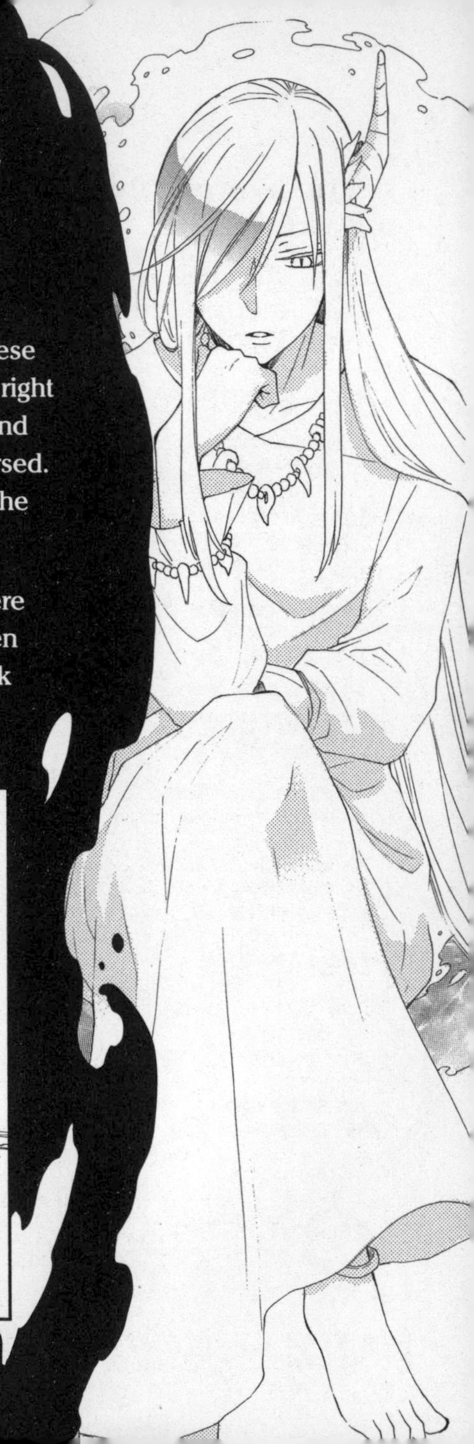

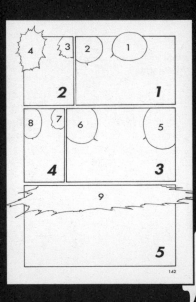